HINDU GOD, CHRISTIAN GOD

Hindu God, Christian God

How Reason Helps Break Down the Boundaries between Religions

FRANCIS X. CLOONEY, S.J.

OXFORD
UNIVERSITY PRESS

2001

OXFORD
UNIVERSITY PRESS

Oxford New York
Athens Auckland Bangkok Bogotá Buenos Aires Cape Town
Chennai Dar es Salaam Delhi Florence Hong Kong Istanbul Karachi
Kolkata Kuala Lumpur Madrid Melbourne Mexico City Mumbai Nairobi
Paris São Paulo Shanghai Singapore Taipei Tokyo Toronto Warsaw

and associated companies in
Berlin Ibadan

Published by Oxford University Press, Inc.
198 Madison Avenue, New York, New York 10016

Oxford is a registered trademark of Oxford University Press

Library of Congress Cataloging-in-Publication Data
Clooney, Francis Xavier, 1950–
Hindu God, Christian God : how reason helps break down the boundaries between religions / Francis X. Clooney.
p. cm.
Includes bibliographical references and index.
ISBN 0-19-513854-6
1. Christianity and other religions—Hinduism. 2. Hinduism—Relations—Christianity. I. Title.
BR128.H5 C57 2001
261.2'45—dc21 00-046528

9 8 7 6 5 4 3 2 1

Printed in the United States of America
on acid-free paper

Preface

It seems that I began work on this book before I knew it. In 1993 I spent a week in Āḻvār Tiru Nagarī, the home of Śaṭakōpaṉ, a great Hindu saint from eighth-century South India who wrote beautiful and powerful poetry in honor of Lord Nārāyaṇa. It was the time of the winter festival in honor of Śaṭakōpaṉ, and I joined in the daytime and nighttime events celebrated in the great temple there. Perhaps because I had been studying his great *Tiruvāymoḻi* for several years and because I had been so graciously received in Āḻvār Tiru Nagarī by Annaviar Srinivasan, a priest in the temple, I felt as much at home as I ever had in India. To be in the temple, with the saint's people and before Nārāyaṇa, who he had praised, was a holy moment. But I also saw clearly that I was not a Hindu and could not be one. It had to do with the color of my skin, my ever-faltering Tamil, my Irish Catholic upbringing in New York City, and my longer years of study of Christian philosophy and theology. It also had to do with the deeper commitments of my heart, since I had always tried to be one of those who simply "left everything and followed Him" (Luke 5). One does not lightly trade such commitments for new ones.

I had reached a boundary, faced with a powerful, beautiful, and compelling religious encounter with a Hindu God in the living context of a Hindu tradition, and this offered me great consolation. I did not see a way to go forward, yet neither did I wish simply to walk away from it. In retrospect, I can see that part of my concern was professional too. Some comparative work really gives theologians something to think about. I knew that some of my theological colleagues back in America had no use for comparative study and felt comfortably at home within the walls of their own Christian theology. I also wanted to find a way to say why it is good—and compelling—for believing theologians to persist in thinking at that edge where faiths encounter one another.

That South Indian experience found its way more or less directly into *Seeing through Texts: Doing Theology among the Śrīvaiṣṇavas of South India* (1996), where I attempted as best I could to enter the world of *Tiruvāymoḻi*, dwell there, and then find my way back to Christian insight. But over time I realized that I still needed to find a more convincing and arguable way to make sense of spiritual and intellectual connections and commitments that cross religious boundaries, convincing even for those unable to travel to Āḻvār Tiru Nagarī. Improbably at first, I decided that thinking—logic, reasoning, and argument—offers us a sturdy bridge for making our way forward in our encounters with faiths and religious ways other than our own. The mind may sometimes hold us back, but quite often it travels ahead of us, where the heart has not yet reached, where words are still worrying themselves into existence. I could not be Hindu and could not cease to be Roman Catholic, but my mind, and with it my inquiring faith, regularly probed the religious traditions of India, posing questions and improvising answers. This process produced some new and enduring connections and changed how I think through my Christian faith; it also gave me an insight into how all of us who think and can continue to call ourselves Christian or Hindu—or Śaiva or Vaiṣṇava, Catholic or Methodist, Buddhist, Muslim, or Jew—in a world where we cannot credibly dismiss the beliefs of others. *Hindu God, Christian God* strives mightily to articulate some of the more vexing problems confronting those who believe and yet also think. I have deliberately convened an odd and uncomfortable conversation among theologians normally not read together. I have introduced Hans Urs von Balthasar, for instance, to Vedānta Deśika and Aruḷ Nandi; Kumārila Bhaṭṭa and Sudarśana Sūri to Karl Barth—they all think and believe deeply enough that they have much in common and much about which they disagree. My goal has been to show how even the more difficult and stubborn points of religious and theological difference remain places where the mind can willingly visit, think, speak, and thus infuse new vitality and insight into believing lives.

One perceptive student who read through an early version of the manuscript commented that (as had not been the case in several of my other books) I seemed to disappear from the chapters of *Hindu God, Christian God*. My hope is that the thoughts that follow may upon reflection show themselves to be the insights of a theologian who traveled to the edge, pondered unchanging commitments and new invitations, and decided, reasonably enough, that the only way forward was to think. May this book be an occasion for thinking and moving forward for my readers as well.

At this point in my life I am more aware than ever of how the deeply solitary work of writing thrives only in a richly communal atmosphere, and I have many people to thank as I write these words. I am grateful to Boston College for a sabbatical year during 1998–1999 and particularly to J. Robert Barth, then dean of the college, for his "more than administrative" encouragement of my scholarly ventures. I am very grateful to the Center of Theological Inquiry in Princeton, New Jersey, for a year's fellowship during that same sabbatical, for splendid living and working facilities, gracious hospitality, and fine conversations which made my work speed along. The director, Wallace Alston; the associate director and theologian in residence, Robert Jenson; the administrator, Kathi Morley; and Maureen Montgomery, Mary Beth Lewis, Mary Rae Rogers, and Cecilio Orantes were most generous and helpful in every way. I am also grateful to Professor George Migliore of the seminary faculty for reading chapter 5 of my manuscript and to the staff of the Princeton Theological Seminary Library for their efficient assistance in procuring books needed for my research.

My Jesuit brothers have enriched my thinking in many ways, most basically in our community life together each day in the Barat Jesuit Community at Boston College. I am particularly grateful to the Jesuit professors with whom I worked most closely in our long-term project, Jesuit Scholarship in a Postmodern Age. Arthur Madigan and James Bernauer have offered stimulating insights into philosophical wisdom as old as the Greeks and as new as the most recent postmodern thinkers, and they prompted me to keep on deepening and widening the framework for my project. Ronald Anderson's research in the encounter of theoretical physics, philosophy of science, and postmodern spirituality has helped me to see in a new light the crossing of boundaries.

In various small and large ways, colleagues have aided me in clarifying the tasks and goals of what I will repeatedly call an interreligious, comparative, dialogical, and (yet again) confessional theology. In the Boston area, Mark Heim, Kurt Richardson, Roger Johnson, and Wesley Wildman were helpful in thinking through my ideas at various stages of their development. At Boston College, Louis Roy, O.P., whose writings bring together the wisdom of Thomas Aquinas and Bernard Lonergan with that of Asia, has exemplified for me the virtues of the committed and faithful scholar who crosses theological boundaries for the sake of honest theological and spiritual inquiry. John Makransky's work in Buddhist studies and now in Buddhist theology has been encouraging and complementary on multiple levels. My younger colleagues Ruth Langer and Qamar-ul Huda have brought new life, new questions, and new energy to the project of comparative theology at Boston College. I am also grateful to current and former students who have taken the time to read and comment on portions of this book, including Joseph Molleur, Hugh Nicholson, Reid Locklin, Dominic Longo, and Joan LaFrance Maselli. Charlotte Hilmer meticulously proofread the galleys.

Further afield, I am grateful to other faithful comparativists as well. John Keenan, Middlebury College, continues to instruct us in how to do comparative theology well by his creative engagement of the Christian and Mahayana Buddhist traditions. Daniel Sheridan, dean at St. Joseph's College of Maine, and Paul Griffiths, University of Illinois, remind me of the deeper truths and values at stake in comparative work. James Fredericks, Loyola-Marymount University, keeps showing me just how very Catholic—and enjoyable—the comparative project can be. Tamal Krishna Goswami, currently at Cambridge University, and Vasudha Narayanan, University of Florida, regularly rejuvenate my work by so compellingly exemplifying the intelligence and integral nature of Hindu theology in the modern world. Parimal Patil, a Hindu theologian currently on the faculty at Emory University, has generously helped me to actualize the dialogical nature of this project by agreeing to contribute his "Prolegomenon to 'Christian God, Hindu God,'" which appears at the end of this volume. In it he brilliantly reviews my project, its possibilities and limitations, from a Hindu theological perspective. I dearly hope that his exemplary response will encourage other readers to respond in similar ways.

Finally, I am particularly grateful to three more senior scholars whose ongoing lifelong projects of theological inquiry demonstrate the power of minds that are both faithful and open. Robert Neville, dean of the School of Theology at Boston University, has exemplified the nearly unlimited reach across religious boundaries of the faithful, open theological mind; he also exercises the powers and virtues of the good administrator by creating situations where comparative study can be shared and deepened in collaboration. I benefited very much from participation in the three-year Comparative Religious Ideas Project, which Bob initiated in the late 1990s and invited me to join. Franz Josef van Beeck, S.J., Loyola University of Chicago, has always managed to combine a deep love of the Christian tradition with an enthusiasm for what is new, including generous encouragement of my own work. John Carman, Harvard University, has pursued scholarly interests, both Christian and Hindu, that exemplify how one can study India deeply and keep on probing the mysteries of the Christian faith at the same time. I would like to think that *Hindu God, Christian God* will enrich that ongoing conversation across religious boundaries that they were already carrying on before I even got started.

Contents

HINDU GOD, CHRISTIAN GOD

I

Widening the Theological Conversation in Today's Pluralistic Context

Theological Conversations across Religious Boundaries

A Seventeenth-Century Missionary Talks to Learned Hindus

"Who could ever doubt that there is a Sovereign Lord of all things who is at the same time their ultimate cause?" asked Roberto de Nobili, a Roman Catholic priest and Jesuit missionary who traveled to South India in the early seventeenth century and spent most of the next forty years in the city of Madurai. De Nobili continues:

> Looking at this house in which we are, we are compelled to admit that some workman must have built it; a fortiori, when we look at the heavens which are the abode of many living beings, it becomes evident that someone has made all those things although we do not see them. To say, as you do, that this world is self-existent, and that its grandeur and beauty prove that there is no power capable of making it, is a great error. On the contrary, that grandeur and beauty prove that they have been created by someone and not by themselves.[1]

De Nobili lived the lifestyle of a renunciant, yet strove also to be a scholar. He wrote treatises in Latin, in the vernacular Tamil language, and, according to tradition, in classical Sanskrit. His writings on God, religion, and various

1. To N. Mascarenhas (Archivum Romanum Societatis Jesu, document no. 12 in the Shembaganur Archives, 378), November 12, 1627.

controversial themes reflect deeply instilled principles drawn from the medieval Catholic theology of Thomas Aquinas and likewise give evidence of his commitment to conversation with learned Hindus. In his treatises and letters we glimpse one of the earliest moments when this book's theme, "Hindu God, Christian God," might have been engaged in a focused manner. As the letter cited at the beginning of this chapter indicates, a kind of Hindu-Christian theological conversation was already under way 400 years ago. It had become possible and opportune for a Christian theologian to discuss the nature of God with Hindu theologians.[2]

To make his version of a cross-cultural and interreligious conversation possible, de Nobili thought that if these were properly understood both sets would be recognized as the same and used toward similar, agreeable conclusions. Clear reasoning about the world and its cause, for instance, could be shared most widely, regardless of cultural and religious differences.

Although de Nobili never dismissed the importance of revelation, he allowed reason to do as much of the work as possible. While correct reasoning could not cause faith, it could dispel contrary ideas, which impede recognition of just how sensible the Christian faith is. Not only did he refrain from explicit appeals to biblical authority, since these would obviously hold little weight with Hindus, but he also pushed back as far as possible the limit beyond which revelation alone could be the necessary guide. Even there, at reason's limit, its yielding to revelation would be a reasonable activity, since God's revelation is in accord with reason even if not entirely comprehended by it. Conversation leads to rational agreement, which in turn opens a way to conversion; reason paves the way for faith, reason reasonably gives way to faith.

His approach was in part pragmatic too, since he was wagering that honest reasoning was the most immediate point of contact for people with different languages, cultures, and religions. Even de Nobili's intention to change India and Indians depended on respect for the Indian intellect, his belief that already and without European interference Hindus were quite capable of reasoning and of appreciating sound arguments as well as any European. Indian philosophical terminology was a substantially sound vehicle for the expression of correct ideas; properly understood, they would be conducive to the formulation of a Christian world view.

If de Nobili believed that right norms of religious behavior and morality could be made clear in a way acceptable to all reasonable people, he also believed, even more contentiously, that the categories of the Thomistic tradition were particularly clear and insightful regarding the basic structures of the world, the human person, human knowing, and God—insofar as humans could apprehend something of who God is. He was confident that these categories enabled him to understand the strengths and weaknesses of Indian

2. On de Nobili, see Saulière. See also Clooney, 1999a; Amaladass and Clooney, 2000. On later instances of Hindu-Christian argument, see Young.

culture better than could Hindus themselves. He believed that he could explain his viewpoint in such a way that they too could see just how plausible were his theological positions and religious beliefs.

In the end, he expected that by God's grace but also in conformity with reason the most sensible Hindus would come forward to seek catechetical instruction and baptism. He vigorously defended his methods in argument with other missionaries, who preferred direct evangelization and a radical break between the old religions and the new. His slow, reasoned approach, and not their more explicit and active evangelical provocations, would lead to enduring conversions.[3]

Thus, for example, de Nobili was happy to argue simply about the nature of the world and its cause, since he believed that he and his Hindu counterparts could do this successfully, other differences notwithstanding, and that there was considerable value in debating topics such as the cosmological proof of God's existence. That is, when reasonable humans examine the world and sift through possible explanations for why the world is the way it is, there will eventually emerge a rational consensus that there must be a God who is the maker of everything. The order, beauty, and grandeur of the world indicate that their maker is great, and one only:

3. In another letter de Nobili justifies his gradual approach more explicitly, and with reference to a tradition about the methods of Thomas the Apostle, he writes:

> I take this opportunity to remark on the opinion of certain zealous men who disapprove of our manner of preaching the Gospel to the pagans and who accuse us of being too indulgent, too reserved, not preaching *in the manner of the apostles*, that instead we are taking recourse to political ruses and a worldly prudence. It seems that they mean that we should, right from the start, attack the temples and the superstitious beliefs of these people. I respect their zeal, but I believe that they fool themselves and experience fully convinces me of this.

De Nobili then traces his own view back to biblical and apostolic precedents:

> To attack [pagan] prejudices frontally would uselessly arouse hatred and persecution, close their spirits to the truth, arouse their passions, and confirm them in their own opinions. Baronius speaks very well to this subject: "Do not be surprised if the apostles, at the beginning of their preaching, did not declaim with vehemence against the divinities of the pagans. The recommendation of *Exodus* is, '*Do not speak against the gods*.' This applies in the same way to the deities of the gentiles. It is not that these false divinities are not worthy of all opprobrium, but rather that this method, far from producing any fruit, impedes the conversion of souls. Metaphrastes, speaking about St. Thomas, the apostle of the Indies, wrote these remarkable words, 'Seeing that the cult of demons exercised its empire over these people and that it was deeply rooted in their spirits, the holy apostle did not press his attack and refute these errors, he did not have recourse to severe reprimands, he did not seek in rigor a remedy for this evil; he knew that it is difficult to destroy impressions and ideas that habit has at length strengthened and so to speak even identified with our souls; gentle persuasion is more able than violence to change them.'"

De Nobili concludes with a comparison: one does not need loud noises and violent blows to drive shadows from a room, only a single candle (my translation from Bertrand, 2:264–265; emphases are Bertrand's).

> Just as from the grandeur and beauty of the world we infer that it has been created, in the same way from the connection between the various parts of this world and the order which reigns in it, we can clearly see that there is but one supreme creator and governor. . . . I shall show this to you more clearly by proving to you that there is only one supreme creator and not several; they are either self-existent or dependent on another for their existence, and then we come to our Self-existent.[4]

It is reasonable, moreover, that this same divine maker should also be the trustworthy teacher of the moral order by which humans should live and so too the revealer of the sure path to salvation.

De Nobili's writings and conversations offer the tantalizing prospect of a real meeting of minds, a conversation in which people of different religious traditions reason together and manage to discuss matters of great religious weight and importance in a way that could alter what the participants believed and how they live. But de Nobili was also willing to argue specifically for the Christian God and against Hindu gods. A vigorous critique, honestly reasoned, could be an appropriate tool for gaining the attention of thoughtful people. He thought that it could be demonstrated that an explicitly Christian understanding of God's involvement in the world is more reasonable and morally constructive than competing mythologies about other gods. He eagerly pointed out deficiencies in Hindu beliefs and practices, which he thought any honest and reasonable person could recognize. In *The Dialogue on Eternal Life*, for instance, the teacher (a figure much like de Nobili himself) critiques Hindu beliefs as erroneous and the activities of the gods as immoral. He attacks the divine descents of Nārāyaṇa (known also as Viṣṇu, Rāma, or Kṛṣṇa) as distorted images of appropriate divine activity. Rāma, the hero of the epic *Rāmāyaṇa* and one of the most important and beloved of Hindu gods, is singled out for particular criticism. Rāma's weaknesses and sins are numerous, and they show us that he cannot measure up to the standard to which people should adhere when they use the word "God" intelligently. The Incarnation of the Son of God can be recognized by intelligent and fair-minded people as harmonious with the kind of noble action God would appropriately undertake. But no such case could possibly be made for the supposed activities of Hindu gods.[5]

The polemical and sectarian tone of some of de Nobili's writings is surely distasteful today to those of us who do not expect conversations to become so religiously pointed or who have little hope that religious arguments can be profitable. Nevertheless, even if we find ourselves grappling with a more complex interaction among reasoning, culture, and religion, it would also be a mistake to go to the other extreme and dismiss the possibility that religious people might profitably engage in a theological conversation where faith is susceptible to reasonable examination and articulation. Intelligent argument is a sign of communication.

4. Ibid.
5. *The Dialogue on Eternal Life*, in Amaladass and Clooney.

This work is dedicated to retrieving the promise inherent in this early conversation and to finding bridges of learning and reason to cross otherwise broad gaps between religious people possessed of their own dearly held beliefs. We cannot and do not wish to replicate either his approach or his attitude entirely. We know more than he did, and we understand differently how religious and theological traditions enter into conversations with one another. But like him, today's theologians do well to allow careful reasoning to guide them in conversations that cross religious boundaries. Once believers hold that their positions are intelligible and plausible, they commit themselves to the possibility of such a conversation, in which both questions and answers may diverge from what is familiar in one's own tradition. Even the views held most dearly and sacredly within traditions can be discussed theologically from differing angles in a conversation in which theological insights come from all sides. If my beliefs are intelligible, an unexpected audience may begin to listen in, offering opinions, suggestions, and improvements.

In the next pages I point out four aspects of theological discourse that preserve the best insights of de Nobili and his ideal of an interreligious theological conversation in the context of what is viable today.

Theology as an Interreligious, Comparative, Dialogical, and Confessional Enterprise

Theology is often and usefully described as "faith seeking understanding." In a theistic tradition, the goals of theology may in the end also be reduced to the simpler aim of knowing a loving God more completely and intelligently. As an intellectual discipline, though, theology occurs when religious people scrutinize their own faith traditions with an eye toward understanding (and then living) that faith more adequately. By theological scrutiny, the faith becomes clearer to the community's insiders and, often enough, to outsiders too.

This broadening of theological inquiry into an interreligious conversation occurs for a number of reasons, mostly small, which add up to a larger shift. Traditions stand in growing proximity to one another, and today believers know a great deal more about other people's religions, regardless of how they may be disposed to react to this new knowledge. Religious people are moving about, ideas are shifting back and forth, and religions with their diverse claims are encountering, complementing, and correcting one another.

The phenomenon of interreligious encounters has sharpened, complicated, and consequently changed how believers understand themselves, even when they continue to insist on their uniqueness and incomparability. The fact of a plurality of living religious traditions now impinges on believers of all traditions and powerfully affects how those believers think about themselves, their theologies, and their most basic beliefs. A community may intend simply to speak to itself, but once it ventures to think and speak its theology out loud, it will find itself in conversation with others who are listening, including people of other faith and theological traditions. They will join the community's internal conversation, sometimes to agree and sometimes to disagree, and will offer competing claims about what is reasonable and worth believing. Hoping to avoid this result, traditions' often stylized images of other religions have usefully served to reinforce their own self-images and their own hopes about themselves. As we shall see, intelligent and open conversations with people of other religions lead to important changes in theology as well.

Hindu God, Christian God takes to heart this more complex and intense situation of religious and theological proximity by initiating an extended conversation between the Hindu and Christian theological traditions on four topics: God's existence, the true God, divine embodiment, and the measuring of religions by revelation. By focused comparisons, I intend to bring the Hindu and Christian views on these topics into dialogue and even argument and thus promote a new, more integral theological conversation wherein traditions can remain distinct although their theologies are no longer separable. A religion may be unique, but its theology is not. Yet, even as I suggest reimagining theology in this way, I also hope to preserve what is best in confessional theology: well-articulated beliefs; intelligent reasoning on matters of faith; the maintenance of a close interconnection among religion, revelation, and reason; and the willingness to treat religious claims as compelling for all and not just for insiders. This rejuvenated theology is distinguished by interreligious, comparative, dialogical, and confessional (or apologetic) dimensions.

First, *theology* is now interreligious; in fact, it has always been so, because when humans theologize they continue to think like humans. Faith may be a gift that neither originates in nor is improved by theology, comparative or not. At first theology may be a personal and communal reaffirmation of beliefs in terms that easily make sense to fellow believers and require nothing more by way of elaborate explanation. Theology occurs when believers begin to think through, probe, and explain what they believe. This more extended and complex intellectual project is not unique to any particular religious tradition. Rather, it is composed of intellectual practices, which will be widely familiar to intelligent believers in all traditions. Very little of importance in content or method belongs solely to any one theological tradition or even one religion, even if such concepts and themes, as one conceives them in actual circumstances, remain deeply rooted in the particularities of specific faith traditions. But while theologizing is a fundamental human interreligious activity, for the most part it can and should still be undertaken in accord with particular traditions' beliefs, statements, and practices. There is Christian (or Roman Catholic or even Thomistic) theology and Hindu (Vaiṣṇava or, let us say, South Indian Śrīvaiṣṇava) theology, but they are all examples of theology.

The common features of human reasoning make it possible for believers in many different traditions at least to understand one another and possibly to agree on topics such as the nature of the world as a dependent reality, the existence of God, the qualities and activities of God, the possibility that God might become embodied, and the idea that God speaks to humans in particular words. Such points remain liable to argument, but arguability indicates some common ground. If faith is articulated in reasonable terms and defended reasonably, then that reasoning provides a shared theological ground, and intelligent disagreements become possible in an interreligious context. *Hindu God, Christian God* highlights this shared ground by demonstrating how much Christian and Hindu theologians share on several important theological issues.

Second, since traditions and their key components are neither identical nor entirely dissimilar, an intelligent interreligious theology is already a comparative theology where similarities and differences are taken into account; ideally, it becomes explicitly comparative. Theologians do their work better if they are comparativists who notice similarities and differences between their own theologies and those of other theologians even in other faith traditions. They can learn to be professionally aware that the details of their own theological traditions are more often than not shared with the theologies of other religious traditions, and they can also interpret that shared ground with theological sensitivity. Opportunities for clarification and distinction abound once theologians engage the details of traditions, specific texts, ideas, images, and practices with an eye to continuities and discontinuities and the meaning of these. If they become self-consciously comparative and notice shared and differing features, they can discern what is shared and what is (or isn't) distinctive to their particular theological traditions, and they can likewise learn from questions, methods, and conclusions seemingly unique to some other traditions.

The fact that there are features common to many theologies does not mean that all "religion" is the same. Differences will persist and may emerge in a sharper and more interesting way once one has recognized that theology is interreligious. But whether differences or similarities predominate, the comparative process reaches fruition in the transformation of theologians' consciousness and theological practice. Intelligent and attentive scholars become able to theologize within their own traditions in a way that neither blocks thinking across religious boundaries nor interprets reductively the similarities that become obvious.

To contribute to the large project of making clear theology's interreligious nature and responsibilities, this volume explores the Hindu and Christian traditions and illustrates how theology, in its details, is interreligious and therefore intelligently comparative. By a few good examples from the two traditions, we will reflect on important and specific similarities and differences. The examples are meant to be used intelligently by scholars who are interested in theological similarities and differences and willing to take them seriously. To read this book is to engage at least incipiently in the practice of this richer and more complex theology.[6]

Third, if theology is an intellectual religious activity practiced in various cultural settings, and if theologians can profitably notice similarities and differences across religious boundaries, this comparative and interreligious

6. I have developed the notion of comparative theology in Clooney, 1995.

theology ideally becomes dialogical. Neither the interreligious situation in general nor the particular similarities and differences that are discovered in comparison prove something merely on their own. Rather, what is learned from interreligious and comparative perspectives must be actualized in a richer interactive encounter among the traditions involved, as learning becomes more complex and as believers learn to speak to one another across religious boundaries. Theologians cognizant of theology's interreligious and comparative dimensions learn to stop judging other religions from afar based simply on their understandings of their own traditions; instead they learn to write in a way that speaks and responds to people in other traditions as well. They also become accustomed to conversing with their peers in those other traditions about theological issues of shared concern. Theologians are thereafter doubly accountable. They explain what they believe in a way that others, even believers in other religious traditions, can understand. They become accountable to those others for the accuracy and theological relevance of what they write, and likewise they become receptive to what those believers in other traditions have to say about basic theological claims. While "comparative" and "dialogical" mark off the same terrain, the two activities can usefully be conceived as sequential: comparative attentiveness leads to dialogical accountability and mutual learning.

This book is not filled with accounts of firsthand theological conversations, although I have engaged in more than a few over the years. Rather, it reflects the interior dialogue, more common in theological circles, that occurs when theologians read and ponder what they read. While dialogical accountability may be primarily actualized in shared experience, social interaction, and actual theological conversation, it also proceeds fruitfully as a textual dialogue in which one reads and ponders the great ideas of other traditions. Dialogue does not end with texts and ideas, but it can begin and flourish by reliance on the written word. As opportunities allow, one can also engage in a living dialogue with believers who belong to those traditions, but for most of us, most of the time, our theological dialogue will be primarily textual.

As this dialogue occurs, informed accountability—giving an account of myself and being accountable to the other who may respond—becomes a signal feature of good theology. The full meaning of a theology, then, is no longer contained entirely within its own religious tradition. Significance is established across the boundaries of traditions, and conclusions are decided only in the back-and-forth dynamic of a theological conversation across religious boundaries. This is a practical matter.

In the end, though, the dialogical nature of an interreligious theology does not mean that there should only be agreements across religious boundaries. Rather, the fourth feature of an interreligious, comparative, and dialogical theology is that it remains confessional. The dialogue essential to an interreligious theology must be vital enough that it can become an argument in which differences are highlighted, accentuated, and debated. Even after initial comparisons and during dialogue, theologians should be able to affirm the content of their faith as true, render it intelligible to those who believe it already, and venture to put persuasive arguments before outsiders in order to demonstrate the truth of the faith, which might even lead some outsiders to believe and convert. A proper theology is always the work of believers who may be expected to adhere to the truth of their faith positions as expressed theologically, even if those claims of truth need to be tested and purified through interreligious, comparative, and dialogical practices.

The purposes of a comparative and dialogical theology can be furthered and accomplished in part by these good arguments, which may sometimes result in agreement and consensus and sometimes not. Even stubbornly held contrary claims can be profitably understood, assessed, and negotiated if we notice how theologians go about arguing, criticizing, and giving explanations across traditional boundaries. Indeed, a theologian who sees that theology is interreligious, comparative, and dialogical is more able to speak and write convincingly and fruitfully confessional again, since that scholar is more accurately aware of what is common to multiple traditions and what really needs to be said to make a convincing case before a complex theological audience. In an interreligious context, one can (and should) still be a confessional theologian, but the cost of a confessional theology is now higher.

The deeper, more difficult, and more acute differences become, the more slender the distinction between a "confessional" theology, where one pronounces and explains the truth of one's positions, and an "apologetic" theology, where one also asserts the error of others' positions.[7] For this reason I speak of an interreligious theology's "confessional and even apologetic" dimension. Strong arguments in favor of one's own tradition often go along with critiques of others' theological positions, and theologies are often confessional and apologetic at the same time, testifying and criticizing, explaining and arguing, persuading and disproving. But even criticism need not be a problem if it is offered respectfully and professionally. That is, the theologian must actually know something about the theological tradition being criticized, become engaged in a receptive dialogue with theologians of that other tradition, admit that areas of disagreement are probably far fewer than areas of consensus, and concede that one's own theology is not beyond criticism. Such is the high price for a useful apologetics today.

By exploring specific examples of theological reasoning in two traditions, I will highlight vividly the particular difficulties that arise when competing claims are recognized and thought through together. Although I do not attempt to decide here the truth of particular claims about the nature of reality, God, and the interaction of God with humans, this volume aims to restore a proper context in which professions of truth can become intellectually credible, and a well-informed apologetics can be plausible and useful.[8]

7. I make this distinction between "confessional" and "apologetic" theology without intending it as an invariable norm.

8. On apologetics in a comparative context, see Griffiths; Stackhouse. On the related issue of orthodoxy, heresy, and heterodoxy, see Henderson, 1998.

Moreover, although *Hindu God, Christian God* is not primarily a work of apologetics, it does stake out particular preferred theological positions that make sense and can be supported by some Hindu and some Christian theologians, even if disputed by others. I favor certain theistic theological positions that have long been argued and explored in different ways in both the Hindu and Christian traditions regarding God's existence, identity, embodiment, and revealed word. I leave my judgments—that there is a God, that one can know something of who God is, that God can become embodied, and that God does speak to us and instruct us—open to further comparative and dialogical testing and do so contentedly, since there is no urgency to finalize such judgments before one has actually conversed and even argued in an interreligious context. Theologians not engaged in comparative work are quite often willing to be tentative in their conclusions, which remain open to revision and correction, and there is no reason to demand speedier progress of comparative theologians.

The Themes and Methods behind This Book

It is important to narrow down the still rather large topic outlined in the preceding section by specifying how *Hindu God, Christian God* aims to contribute to this new understanding of interreligious theology. In the following pages I therefore describe the four themes central to this book's four major chapters; the book's focus on religious reasoning; the value of theologizing by way of examples; and the actual Hindu and Christian examples that form the book's substance.

Four Central Themes: God's Existence, Identity, Embodiment, and Word

In chapters 2–5 of this volume, I introduce four major themes: (1) the existence of God (chapter 2); (2) the one true God (chapter 3); (3) divine embodiment (chapter 4); and (4) revelation and religion (chapter 5). These themes may also be posed in the form of questions; it is reasonable, plausible, and useful to ask:

Is there a God who is maker of the world? (chapter 2)
Can God's true identity be to some extent known? (chapter 3)
Can God become embodied? (chapter 4)
Is revelation the norm by which to judge religions? (chapter 5)

I have chosen the four themes because they also point up positions that are arguable and arguably true. As I will explain in chapter 6, I favor conclusions such as these:

The world is a coherent combination of finite parts, a composition that can best be explained by accepting that there is a God who is the world's maker.

This maker God can be further identified through additional reasonable conclusions about who God is and how God is likely to act.

God can choose to become involved in human affairs, even to the point of embodiment in a particular form.

Revelation, God's word, both confirms and surpasses human reasoning, is articulated in particular texts, and guides humans in assessing the religious significance of the many religions.

Chapters 2–5 take up these increasingly difficult themes, questions, and claims one by one, as we move from claims more widely accessible to reason ("there is a God," "there is one God") to deeper and core religious beliefs ("*this* is God's name," "God is embodied in *this* way but not in *that* way," "God's special word gives us particular guidance regarding other people's religions"). But I am not proposing that there is a necessary, unfolding logic to this ordering of chapters, as if one should first assert the existence of God in a general sense and believe in that God and only thereafter begin to fill in details about who God is. One might conceivably proceed that way, but believers do not ordinarily begin with an idea of God and add details one by one; everything is there from the start. Nevertheless, this sequence of chapters is useful in an interreligious context, since questions about whether there is a God and what God is like are more general than questions about divine embodiment and divine speech. But all four chapters are meant to be read together. In chapter 6 I will return to the issue of the possible importance of this sequence of chapters.

More broadly, *Hindu God, Christian God* is meant to support the possibility that positions such as these four can be normative, provided they are tested and reconceived in an interreligious, comparative, and dialogical context. This book is therefore more than simply a comparative study or set of theories about how a Christian might go about learning from non-Christians. As I will show in the following chapters, these themes are acceptable to most (though not all) Christian theologians and to many Hindu theologians as well. As arguable claims, though, they are likely to remain controversial. Even within a single tradition, and certainly in a broader interreligious theology, believers will disagree about what can be known and stated about God. There is much here for theologians in all religions to investigate, discuss, and argue. Yet the argument is worthwhile, since this volume presumes that theology is a faithful inquiry into the truths of faith and that theology's goal is a deeper, more direct knowledge of God.

Focus on Religious Reasoning

Instead of examining exegesis, ritual practice, community structures, social adaptations, and so on, *Hindu God, Christian God* focuses rather narrowly on how Christian and Hindu theologians reason theologically, discern, assert, and defend the truth, and aim to persuade both insiders and outsiders of that truth. We begin each chapter by observing a Christian theologian's position regarding one of the four themes, and we will investigate the kind of theological reasoning involved, the steps in argument, and the logical conclusions, limits, and compromises made regarding the demands of intelligibility and faith. Similarly, in the center of each chapter we will be asking whether some Hindu theologians think in more or less the same way on these topics as do their Christian counterparts. If, as I suggest, we do think alike in significant ways, this tells us something important about the human mind, religion, theological reasoning, and even God, insofar as God can be known by faith in cooperation with reason.

Restoring cogency to religious reasoning in a comparative context is key to this book. I wish to revive, in a way that is plausible today, the project undertaken by Roberto de Nobili and others in fashioning an interreligious discourse that is both religious and reasonable, as faith and reason richly shape one another. If we understand better how the theological mind operates in two traditions and in an interreligious theological context, we will understand better our own theologies, and it will become all the harder simply to walk away from conversation with people in other traditions. Reasoning is not everything, but it is indispensable in making possible a theology that is interreligious, comparative, dialogical, and yet again confessional.

Of course, the comparative features of religious reasoning must be differentiated and assessed in appropriate ways. On some topics, for instance, the induction of God's existence, Hindu and Christian theologians do think very much alike; on others, for instance, the role of revelation in defining the community of believers and the status of those who are not believers, the common ground will be more limited and the opposition more intense as one tries to decide which embodiment or which revelation is significant. But we shall see that the commonality of theological reasoning is sufficiently broad and deep that we can still conclude that there is a common reasoning in the Hindu and Christian traditions. This reasoning enables the most fervent believers to share a productive theological conversation that crosses religious boundaries, a reasoning that also makes it illogical not to.

Theologizing by Way of Particular Examples

I do not attempt to survey the rich complexity of the Hindu and Christian religious traditions undergirding the theologies that grew up in those traditions. Neither do I attempt to discuss every presupposition or feature implied by interreligious reasoning, nor do I attempt to develop a typology by which one might discover those features and tenets, nor do I account in advance for all the particular problems that will arise when particular religious traditions are considered.

It is reasonable to be selective instead of trying to cover the entirety of traditions. Working by examples also has the advantage of making it clear that I am not attempting a general theory about theology and religion nor about Christianity and Hinduism in order to explain everything, all at once. So too, this preference for particularity plunges us rather immediately into the substance of the various theologies rather than postponing particulars until we have in place a refined theory about religions and what their theologies are supposed to mean.

In the following chapters I aim simply at some incremental progress in understanding the concerns of Hindu and Christian theologians together, by way of a careful consideration of some details of a few particular cases. My claims are not meant to float above the materials presented in the several chapters, as if merely illustrating theological claims that are already known abstractly or in all their major features. The examples I have chosen show us what the respective Hindu and Christian theologies are actually like as theologians reason about what they believe, and they should correct habitually inaccurate images about these theologies, particularly the misconception that Christian theology and Hindu theology are radically different enterprises situated on either side of the chasm dividing "West" and "East." This presentation of the Hindu and Christian traditions is meant to have force only within the confines of several key examples, whose meanings are probed and reflected on, both separately and together. Those who wish to make grander statements are welcome to do so, provided they too offer us Hindu and Christian examples that compellingly support their positions.

Thinking about important theological themes by way of examples also makes it impossible to stay neatly within traditional boundaries. Attentive readers who take these Hindu and Christian examples seriously will find it difficult to think about the two traditions in isolation from one another or to back up to a single-tradition theologizing. New ideas and words begin to flow back and forth across established boundaries in a creative (and untidy) way, which is both unsettling and enticing. Theology becomes interreligious when we actually take examples seriously. Of course, I have attempted to choose illuminating examples and to reflect on them in a fruitful fashion. *Hindu God, Christian God* itself is meant to be a good example, a useful resource that enables readers who have not read widely in the two traditions to begin moving back and forth between them in order to form theological positions cognizant of and indebted to both.

It should be clear then that I do not present the materials in this book as the complete and exclusive set of best examples. They are meant to further a comparative and dialogical reflection, not to conclude it, and so they may remind readers of other examples, which also may bring other better, or more pertinent complexities to the fore. I welcome improvements upon what I have done. I hope too that readers who disagree with my approach will do so not merely in theory but by way of good examples and will bring forward both Christian and Hindu texts to problematize my positions in specific ways.

Particular Christian and Hindu Examples

FOUR CHRISTIAN THEOLOGIANS: RICHARD SWINBURNE, HANS URS VON BALTHASAR, KARL RAHNER, AND KARL BARTH

The range of Christian theological materials is admittedly very selective, even merely suggestive. Each chapter begins with the example of a twentieth-century Christian theologian who forcefully engages the key issues considered in the chapter.[9] In chapter 2 I give special attention to the contemporary philosopher of religion and Orthodox Christian theologian Richard Swinburne. In a series of volumes published during the 1980s and 1990s, he developed the case for a strong rational approach to what can be known of God, God's existence, and the divine relationship to human beings. Unlike many theologians Swinburne argues that theistic and Christian positions make sense and have cogency for whoever is willing to think them through, even if they are not already believers. I also look briefly at critiques of Swinburne's positions by those more skeptical about the substantive role of reasoning in religious matters. As we shall see, arguments in favor of or against this role are crucial to this book.

Chapter 3 explores how theologians have argued for an identification of a particular representation of God's name and deeds as *the* necessary and proper identification of the divine identity. Here I introduce the Roman Catholic Swiss theologian Hans Urs von Balthasar (1905–1988), a formidable and prolific author whose abundant writings are only now becoming appreciated in the English-speaking world. He focuses unreservedly on Jesus Christ as the complete presence of God in the world, the privileged and sole adequate form in which God encounters humans. Christ is accordingly also the standard by which to assess and pass judgment on paler and lesser representations of God and the divine such as have been devised in other religious traditions naturally and by limited human reasoning. Von Balthasar poses his positions argumentatively and in opposition to Hindu and other faith positions and rarely is his theology drawn upon for a constructive comparative theology.[10] Nevertheless, he unwittingly reflects a theological sensibility evident in the writings of the Hindu theologians we shall meet in a moment, as if to say, "It does not make sense to evoke God in terms other than those which make sense to me."

Divine embodiment is the topic of chapter 4, and here I introduce Karl Rahner (1904–1984), probably the most influential Roman Catholic theologian of the twentieth century. Rahner retrieves and rethinks the dominant Thomistic theological synthesis for the Roman Catholic community in the post–World War II era of incipient globalization. He attends to a wide range of issues confronting modern Roman Catholics and draws on twentieth-century European philosophy in order to restate traditional beliefs in terms that make sense in the twentieth century. The resultant theology is intellectually highly sophisticated and also intensely affective and devotional. To know Jesus is a matter of truth and of love. Rahner's approach captures both the intellectual depth and the religious intensity behind devotion to God incarnate and

9. For background on the Christian theologians introduced here, see Ford; Fiorenza and Galvin.

10. For an assessment of von Balthasar's possible contribution to an interreligious theology, see Gawronski.

embodied in Jesus Christ. He is a Christian theologian who has many soulmates among the theologians of traditional Hinduism.

Chapter 5 takes up the difficult issue of the role afforded to revelation in the evaluation of religions. Here I turn to Karl Barth (1886–1968), a Protestant Christian theologian in the Reformed tradition. In his *Church Dogmatics* I.2 he proposes a powerful Christian perspective on revelation and religions. He sets revelation over against religions and argues for a strict judgment against religions as human constructions that most often obscure and obstruct the powerful communication of revelation. He sharply rejects Hindu, Buddhist, and other theological traditions, since their beliefs and theologies—unlike his own—do not derive entirely from God's Word uttered in the revelation of Christ. But even in this somewhat unfavorable environment we find unexpected parallels, since Barth thinks like a Hindu. We will read Hindu theologians who make similar points in light of Barth's theology, and we will encounter several "Hindu Barthians."

That I have chosen to introduce rather traditional twentieth-century theologians rather than their classical predecessors is another among the many shortcuts taken in this book. While classical figures such as Augustine, Aquinas, Luther, and Calvin could certainly be aptly compared with Hindu counterparts, I have chosen Swinburne, von Balthasar, Rahner, and Barth in order to engage the traditions they represent while at the same time recognizing how they have helped reshape those traditions in the contemporary world. Even among twentieth-century theologians, of course, I might easily have chosen other figures, who would be more obviously interreligious. Swinburne's writing may seem too confidently rational, even rationalistic, for readers favoring a more experiential approach to the religions of India. But I wish to appreciate, right from the start, how rational Hindu thought can be and how fruitful attention to reasoning can be in creating a common ground for Hindu-Christian theological conversations. Some readers may balk at the rather stern Germanic image of Christian theology presented by Barth and von Balthasar—who stand very near the conservative end of the spectrum and are not known for their openness to other religious traditions—and even Rahner, who inevitably thought more in terms of options appropriate to mid–twentieth century Europe than to the twenty-first-century global scene. I readily admit that these theologians do not fit smoothly into a predictably congenial comparative exercise; instead, they draw our attention to particularly difficult aspects of a conversation that crosses religious boundaries. They are worthy counterparts to the Hindu theologians we shall consider, challenging figures who are all the more interesting because they are so committed to the truths about which they write. If we can draw Swinburne, von Balthasar, Rahner, and Barth into a theological conversation with interreligious, comparative, dialogical, and confessional dimensions, we will have made real progress. By reading them together we too will be compelled to reason religiously and in an interreligious context. In any case, *Hindu God, Christian God* is not the final word, and readers are welcome to reconstruct the arguments of this book by drawing other Christian theologians into the dialogue.

HINDU THEOLOGIES IN THE NYĀYA, MĪMĀṂSĀ, VEDĀNTA, TAMIL VAIṢṆAVA, AND TAMIL ŚAIVA TRADITIONS

Our Hindu examples are drawn primarily from three bodies of classical Sanskrit-language source materials, Nyāya, Mīmāṃsā, and Vedānta,[11] plus a few South Indian Tamil-language texts. Whereas the Christian theologians are each introduced in an individual chapter, the Hindu theologians will appear in all the chapters.

Nyāya is the traditional school of Hindu logic. In the early centuries BCE the Nyāya logicians undertook the project of describing the world in a coherent rational fashion and without reliance on revelation or a commitment to any particular deity. Nyāya's primary text, the *Nyāya Sūtras* of Gautama, can be read as a neutral analysis neither favoring nor opposing the idea of God. As we shall see in chapter 2, the Nyāya commentarial tradition brings the topic of God to the fore as one way of explaining the world's existence and order and only thereafter as *the* preferred way of doing this. In the Nyāya tradition we find increasingly detailed and complicated arguments for God's existence, but in chapter 2 we draw on just two relatively easy expositions, the *Nyāya Mañjarī* of Jayanta Bhaṭṭa (ninth century) and the *Tarkasaṃgraha* of Annaṃbhaṭṭa (seventeenth century).[12]

Mīmāṃsā is the school of brahmanical ritual analysis that developed in the early centuries BCE in response to problems in the exegesis of Vedic ritual texts and the performance of Vedic rituals. The *Mīmāṃsā Sūtras* of Jaimini (c. second century BCE) organized the principles and practices of right interpretation into 2,700 short statements (*sūtras*). Śabaraswāmin (first–second centuries CE) wrote an elaborate commentary on the *Sūtras*, and in turn Kumārila Bhaṭṭa (eighth century CE) wrote extensive commentaries on Śabara, the *Ślokavārtika*, *Tantravārtika*, and *Tupṭīkā*, which constitute the foundation for the premier Mīmāṃsā school. In chapter 5 we shall have occasion to turn to the *Prakaraṇa Pañcikā* of Śālika Nātha Miśra, a theologian in the other major Mīmāṃsā tradition, which traces itself back to Prabhākara Miśra, a near-contemporary of Kumārila.

Theologically, Mīmāṃsā holds several distinctive positions relevant to this book. The Veda, a body of oral scripture providing the content and structure of ritual performance, is a primordial revelation older than creation. It is flawless and not dependent on any divine or human author. Since the Veda focuses on ritual performance, it does not give information about worldly or even higher realities, such as gods or immortality. It tells us not what to think but what to do. Only what can be extrapolated from issues related to ritual performance should be taken as authoritatively communicated by the Veda.

11. Throughout this book, "Hindu" is used as a convenient shorthand for multiple traditions that can be grouped under that name; it also refers to a coherent system of religious and theological systems, which justly deserve a common appellation.

12. Since those defending the induction of God's existence are deeply engaged in debate with exponents of the Buddhist view that God's existence cannot be demonstrated, in chapter 2 we refer also to an important Buddhist text, the *Pramāṇavārtika* of Dharmakīrti (sixth century).

The Mīmāṃsā theologians worked with a simple, realistic world view and were even willing to acknowledge the gods as legitimate recipients of worship and invocation. But since it suffices for ritual purposes to assert that the gods can be invoked, they also felt that there was no need to speculate further about the nature of these gods. While Mīmāṃsā is not antitheistic, it has no need for the postulate of a Supreme Being, Lord, or Creator. On the whole, ordinary reasoning about any religious topic must defer to the logic of ritual obligation and the world it implies.[13]

The Vedānta schools are devoted primarily to the interpretation, defense, and practice of the teachings of the Upaniṣads. These are influential texts generally placed at the end of the Vedic corpus and in the eighth–third centuries BCE. They are informative about the self and ultimate reality, and aimed at the realization of liberation. The fifth-century CE *Uttara Mīmāṃsā Sūtras* (or, more commonly, the *Brahma Sūtras*) of Bādarāyaṇa organized the teachings of the Upaniṣads and clarified important passages that were difficult to understand theoretically or implement practically. The *Sūtras*' ultimate aim was to provide a framework for clear teachings on self, reality, and liberation. Like the Mīmāṃsā theologians, the Vedānta theologians privileged revelation over reason and ordinary modes of learning, such as perception. Although Brahman is recognized as a reality that exists outside the Upaniṣads, it nevertheless is known first of all only from the Upaniṣads. Thereafter, however, Brahman can be reflected on and reasoned about, and wrong ideas can be criticized and discarded.[14]

The Vedānta schools have much in common with one another, but there are some important differences, particularly regarding the role afforded to God. The Nondualist (Advaita) school of Śaṃkara (eighth century) resolved the difficulty by holding for the ultimate unity of all reality as Brahman. The Qualified Nondualist (Viśiṣṭādvaita) school of Rāmānuja (eleventh century) argued for distinction within Brahman, the highest and uncompromised reality within which material and conscious beings existed. Even in Śaṃkara's Nondualist system one finds what is tantamount to a theology of God, despite the fact that in this tradition Brahman cannot be qualified by any enduring positive expressions indicative of personhood. By contrast, Rāmānuja's Qualified Nondualist tradition defends a refined and safeguarded equation of Brahman with God, the Lord, and Nārāyaṇa.[15]

13. On Mīmāṃsā, see Clooney, 1990.

14. Vedānta is also known as the Later (*Uttara*) Mīmāṃsā, because its first text, the *Uttara Mīmāṃsā Sūtras* (or *Brahma Sūtras*) of Bādarāyaṇa (c. fifth century CE), is dedicated to the same project of the defense of sacred texts and performance that we find in the earlier *Mīmāṃsā Sūtras* of Jaimini, even if Vedānta focuses on the Upaniṣads and not the ritual texts. Like the commentators on Jaimini's *sūtras*, the commentators on the *Brahma Sūtras* were obliged to elaborate cryptic teachings expressed in extremely brief statements (*sūtras*). In Vedānta, philosophical issues came quickly to the fore, particularly regarding how to reconcile Brahman, to whom all perfections are attributed, with a world (including conscious beings) that has Brahman as its spiritual and material source.

15. There are numerous other schools of Vedānta, but our analysis is limited to these two.

We will also have occasion to look at later Vedānta theologians. Nṛsiṃhāśramin was a sixteenth-century Nondualist whose *Advaita Dīpikā* further systematized Nondualist epistemology and language theory, and he also made explicit the view that Brahman is necessarily beyond sectarian beliefs. Sudarśana Sūri (twelfth century) wrote a commentary on Rāmānuja's *Śrībhāṣya* interpretation of the *Uttara Mīmāṃsā Sūtras*. As we shall see, Sudarśana Sūri developed the sectarian, Vaiṣṇava (devoted to Nārāyaṇa, Viṣṇu) side of Rāmānuja's tradition. Vedānta Deśika (fourteenth century) also belonged to the tradition of Rāmānuja, and he elaborated the teachings of this theistic Vedānta tradition in Sanskrit, in Tamil, and in mixed Tamil-Sanskrit writings.

Regarding the religious traditions of Śaivism (which are devoted to Śiva), we will look into the *Śrīkara Bhàṣya* of Śrīpati Paṇḍita Ācārya (thirteenth century), who reads the Upaniṣads and *Sūtras* as professing Śiva and not Nārāyaṇa to be the lord of the universe and ultimate Brahman. We will draw regularly upon the *Śiva Jñāna Siddhiyār* of Aruḷ Nandi (fourteenth century), a full-length exposition in Tamil of the religion of Śiva and a refutation of other religious and philosophical views. This work is particularly interesting because its complete theological exposition of Śiva as Lord presumes the truth of the older Sanskrit theological texts but also reformulates that theological system with attention to the vernacular Tamil traditions.

Readers familiar with a broader range of Indian materials will notice what these examples share and also what they exclude. They are largely brahmanical, male-authored prose compositions, God- and not Goddess-oriented, highly conceptual, and only occasionally indicative of the rich narrative and dramatic traditions of Hindu India. Some readers may worry about the suspiciously rational and systematic Hinduism that is being put before other, unsuspecting readers. But one must begin somewhere, and these examples introduce us to important Hindu theologians whose works present topics fundamental to Hindu theology. But here too I welcome the proposal of other examples, by Hindu or Christian thinkers, that will challenge the patterns I am suggesting and broaden still further what counts as Hindu theology.

Each chapter begins with attention to a particular Christian theologian; each chapter's second part explores the chapter's theme in the Hindu traditions; and in each chapter's final section I reflect on both sets of materials together. Since I assume that most of my readers will know more about the Christian tradition than about the Hindu tradition, more of *Hindu God, Christian God* is given to an exposition of Hindu theologies than to Christian theologies.

Hindu God, Christian God in the Context of Christian Theology

The Project of This Book Compared with Some Theologies of Religions

As a theological work, *Hindu God, Christian God* seeks to inform readers about the two traditions in a manageable way; it invites Christian theologians to enter into conversation with great theologians of the Hindu traditions and likewise invites contemporary Hindu theologians to the study of Christian theology. This process will make all of us better theologians. *Hindu God, Christian God* is not a theology of religions and its project does not rise or fall in relation to any particular theology of religions, but it has a great deal to say that is relevant to Christian thinking about religions and to understanding what is required if that thinking is to be plausible in today's interreligious context. Since I write from within the Christian tradition and from a Christian perspective, it is necessary to say something about this book's relationship to the work of some Christian theologians who are studying the relationships among religions. In this section I briefly compare and contrast my work with the works of three distinguished theologians of religions: Jacques Dupuis, S. Mark Heim, and Keith Ward.

Jacques Dupuis, a Belgian theologian who spent many years in India earlier in his career, wrote *Toward a Christian Theology of Religious Pluralism* (1998) in order to state and defend a Christian theological position that is open to what is good in other religious traditions, while yet remaining explicitly and firmly Roman Catholic. One of his key goals is to show how a Christian understanding of God as Trinity enables a richer and more comprehensive openness to other religions. To make his case, Dupuis meticulously explores the ancient Christian tradition, Vatican documents, papal statements, and recent writings by other theologians of religions. He says that his theology of religions is confessional in the sense that it arises from "the faith-commitment of the person or religious community which is the subject of theologizing."[16] He goes on to state:

> The model that needs to be developed then is not that of mutual assimilation through a reduction of faith-content but that of interpenetration and cross-fertilization of the various traditions in their diversities; not a leveling of religious identities but a dialogical openness and mutual enrichment through conversation. Personal commitment to one's own faith and openness to the faith of others need not be mutually exclusive; rather they ought to grow in direct proportion.[17]

This confessional but open theology allows room for interreligious sensitivities: "While a Christian theology of religions cannot but be Christian, it must leave room and indeed create space for other 'confessional' theologies of religions, be they Muslim, Hindu, or otherwise."[18] Christian theology preserves an opportunity for a real exploration of "the reality—no matter how mysterious—of the religious experience actually lived by people in the context of their respective religious traditions . . . in the light of the Christian faith and the mystery of Jesus Christ."[19]

16. P. 6.
17. P. 7.
18. Ibid.
19. P. 8.

What kind of "space" and "exploration"? In his introduction Dupuis asks whether a theology that treats religions in general terms can be of theological value. He responds that while specifics may be important, "there still remains room for a general theology of religions which embraces them all and asks how the other religious traditions—and their component parts—relate to the Christian mystery." This general theology of all religions must come first "*before* the particular theologies dealing with the distinct relationship of one religious tradition to the Christian mystery." It "asks general questions which apply to all cases and need to be studied before specific questions can be considered which concern Christian conversation with one specific tradition."[20] But Dupuis still wants to combine the deductive and inductive approaches, attending both to "the concrete religious experiences of others"[21] and to Christian sources:

> Thus, while being with general questions regarding the relationship between the Christian mystery and other religious traditions, we shall, nonetheless, keep in touch with particular situations which form part of the global reality. To this end, and in order not to fall into abstraction, we shall frequently appeal to concrete elements of particular religious traditions with a view to verify and substantiate the theological views proposed. Moreover, wherever it seems important and necessary, we shall branch off from general considerations and make particular applications to distinct religious traditions.[22]

Dupuis's intention to "keep in touch," "verify," and "substantiate" his interreligious inquiry by appeals to concrete elements and "particular applications" indicates that he is working out a Christian theological position that should hold up when tested by select examples from the other traditions. But his actual attention to those other traditions is minimal, well short of the verification or substantiation he desires.

In one of the few instances where Dupuis actually considers another religion in particular he takes up the Hindu teaching on divine descent into the world (*avatāra*) and reflects on its tantalizing similarity to the Christian doctrine of incarnation. He notes Kṛṣṇa's explanation of *avatāra* in chapter 4 of the *Bhagavad Gītā*, touches on several terms used by the Vedānta theologians Śaṃkara and Rāmānuja, and mentions the view of Sri Aurobindo, a well-known twentieth-century Hindu thinker. Dupuis then states that although Hindus do not have a proper sense of history, the teaching on *avatāra* can nevertheless be seen as a kind of stepping-stone toward the Christian teaching on incarnation—the "universal human aspiration to enter into contact with the Ultimate Reality of the Divine on a human plane," a desire fulfilled only at the incarnation.[23] We shall return to the concept of *avatāra* in chap-

20. P. 9.
21. P. 18.
22. P. 20. Dupuis's examples are primarily from Hindu scriptures. He does not engage the theologians of the Hindu traditions in any significant way.
23. Pp. 302–303.

ter 4; but here it suffices to observe that Dupuis's treatment and conclusions are so sketchy as to preclude any fruitful theological conversation with Hindu theologians.

However generous Dupuis's Christian theological judgments may be, in practice he extends the usual dynamic that has characterized Christian reflection on religions: a priori reflection, which treats numerous religions in the same way and attends to details only in a fragmentary fashion. By contrast, *Hindu God, Christian God* aims more resolutely at systematic fidelity to particular details in resistance to the tendency to generalize about religions, a tendency that is detrimental even to Christian theology.

In *Salvations: Truth and Difference in Religion* (1995), American Protestant theologian S. Mark Heim seeks to identify a viable theological context in which religious pluralism can be addressed without intentionally or inadvertently enthroning relativism as the sole immutable religious truth. Heim recounts the virtues of his key notion, "orientational pluralism," in this way:

> For orientational pluralism the diversity of views about religious diversity is, like religious diversity itself, rationally justified and therefore reasonably enduring. . . . Orientational pluralism combines a more thoroughgoing commitment to the warranted justifiability of pluralism in religion with a more positive view toward the actual practice of witness on the part of believers commending their visions to others. It is highly skeptical of readiness to attribute others' differing religious attitudes to pure irrationality, immorality, or bad faith. It also encourages serious attention to the evaluative viewpoints from which neighbors' faiths cohere, since the development of our own truth can only proceed by incorporating more of what we may come to view as valuable in theirs. This is part and parcel of our commitment to the universal import of the truth we believe we partially grasp (otherwise we could rest content in ours and leave others to theirs) and of our commitment to learn from as well as differ with those who construe the world differently.[24]

Later Heim summarizes his view of salvation(s) in this way:

> I insist salvation can be understood in the plural. Religions may be seen as both true and as alternative rather than necessarily either true or false, and thus two "true" religions need not be assumed to represent the same thing. All religions that are true do not have to be true "in the very same sense." And it does not necessarily follow that the adherents of two true religions must each regard the other as anonymous members of its own tradition.[25]

Heim aims to provide a solid intellectual foundation for taking other traditions' theologies seriously, "a way to recognize much more extensively and concretely within the traditions, truths, and valid practices that are integral to religious fulfillments." One must learn to think through faiths' truth claims

24. Heim (1995), p. 143.
25. Ibid., pp. 225–226.

with respect for the theological terms that frame the discussion in those particular traditions and likewise realize that we who interpret are also interpreted: "The capacity to at least recognize that these are other, alternative views which have the means to 'read' and subsume us in their categories is an important one, not least because it allows more room for critical judgments that may be brought against us and the assumptions of our current context."[26]

This practical openness nicely previews the position I develop in this volume. The claims of various traditions are to be taken seriously, and to do this one must recognize the reality and force of the theologizing that occurs in those traditions. Alternate theological claims are respected as viable and must be brought into dialogue with one's own theology, even if one may still wish to assess critically whether any particular position is sufficient or desirable. One can criticize theological positions developed in other traditions, but first one has to engage them seriously in an interreligious, comparative, and dialogical context. For this to happen, a theologian's encounter with other religious traditions has to be theological right from the start and at every stage, as one learns how to study those traditions theologically and to interpret what one learns from them. It does not make sense to borrow data from philosophers and historians of religion who worked without theological interests and then to assess that data theologically, only to find it theologically lacking. Heim's approach enables us to keep a much closer connection between learning from religions and Christian theologizing. One test of *Hindu God, Christian God* will be whether it exemplifies Heim's theological perspective by showing a genuine and nonreductive theological interest in both the Hindu and Christian traditions and a genuine commitment to think through the traditions together, so that ensuing Christian and Hindu theologies are both seriously infused with each other's perspectives.[27]

Keith Ward is a respected Oxford theologian, who has recently completed a series of four important volumes in comparative theology: *Religion and Revelation* (1994), *Religion and Creation* (1996), *Religion and Human Nature* (1998), and *Religion and Community* (2000). The volumes reconsider major themes in the Christian theological tradition, both as traditionally stated and as restated in the contemporary context, in light of related materials from four non-Christian traditions: Judaism, Islam, Hinduism, and Buddhism. Ward's estimable project advances the work of a seriously interreligious theology because he engages in considerable reflection on the various religious

26. P. 125.

27. Were the idea that there are multiple mediations of salvation taken as Heim's final position, which I do not believe to be Heim's intention, I would have reason to question it further. I see his recognition of multiple paths as a necessary antidote to the tendency to dismiss other traditions' claims about salvation by rejecting them or reducing them to one's own. The theologian may wish to argue for some positions and against others, but listening and learning must come first. See also Heim's more recent *The Depth of the Riches: A Trinitarian Theology of Religious Ends* (2000), in which he extends his thinking by exploring a trinitarian basis for the plurality of religious ends.

traditions and their theological positions before presenting a contemporary Christian position cognizant of those other religious positions and of other religious issues of concern to modern Western theologians.

In explaining his method, Ward stresses the necessary interreligious nature of theologizing as it is reconceived today:

> I am suggesting that it is wrong to limit theology proper to one's own group and make it simply an exploration of what is officially believed by that group or even of what is contained in the Scripture and tradition of that group. I would go further and suggest that to advocate a "Catholic theology" or an "Anglican theology" or even a "Christian theology" is unduly restrictive. For it suggests that there is a specific intellectual discipline which can only be undertaken by Catholics or Anglicans or Christians. It seems preferable to say that theology is the discipline of reflection upon ideas of the ultimate reality and goal of human life, of God, and of revelation. It can be undertaken by people of many diverse beliefs. It is better undertaken in knowledge of and in conversation with those of beliefs other than one's own.[28]

People who theologize according to this awareness will explore any given theological topic—such as creation or revelation—in several traditions and then articulate their positions in light of common features that have been discovered. The scholars who do this are those who deserve to be recognized as "full and proper theologians."[29]

What kind of theology is actually at stake? In his first volume, *Religion and Revelation*, Ward makes a fundamental methodological distinction between confessional theology and comparative theology, the former focused on revelation, the latter on God's wider work in the world:

> One can therefore distinguish two types of theology. One is confessional theology; the exploration of a given revelation by one who wholly accepts the revelation and lives by it. The other may be termed "comparative theology"—theology not as a form of apologetics for a particular faith but as an intellectual discipline which enquires into ideas of the ultimate value and goal of human life, as they have been perceived and expressed in a variety of religious traditions. . . . Comparative theology differs from what is often called "religious studies," in being primarily concerned with the meaning, truth, and rationality of religious beliefs, rather than with the psychological, sociological, or historical elements of religious life and institutions.[30]

Ward locates his four volumes in the latter category, comparative and not confessional.[31]

I concede the merit of distinguishing between comparative and confessional theologies, but I do not wish to separate them, as Ward appears to do, nor to distinguish "the exploration of a given revelation" (in confessional theology)

28. Ward (1994), p. 46.

29. Ibid.

30. P. 40.

31. Perhaps because he understands comparative theology as a kind of "inquiry into ideas," Ward does not seem to go far in integrating his own confessional theology with what he learns

from a broader survey of traditions (in comparative theology). Rather, I suggest that theology can still be specified as confessional provided we first realize that "theology" is not unique to any particular confession. Comparison retains a confessional dimension, while confession is disciplined by comparative practice. My model of theology as interreligious, comparative, dialogical, and confessional reintegrates Ward's confessional and comparative theologies into a single though complex theological practice, which might be described more dynamically as moving from a confessional base through intervening intellectual inquiries to a renewed and transformed reappropriation of confessional views. Neither theological comparison nor confession can flourish in separation from the other, and each constantly transforms the other.

In the summation of his project that concludes the last volume, *Religion and Community*, Ward places more stress on the necessarily cooperative and dialogical nature of a comparative theology and previews more nearly the integral project exemplified in *Hindu God, Christian God*. He readily identifies his books as the work of a Christian theologian working in a Christian context,[32] but he also stresses the importance of conversations that cross religious boundaries and entail real cooperation among theologians of different traditions. At the end of four volumes he seems willing to blur his earlier distinction between confessional and comparative theology. Now it is Christian theology, the believer's confessional project, which is transformed through the work of comparison:

> The religious situation of our world requires an attempt, at least on the part of those committed to reflection, to interpret traditional beliefs in the light of our ever-growing knowledge of the material cosmos, and in awareness of the many differing traditions of belief that exist about the nature of human existence in the world.[33]

Ward balances his commitment to a fundamental disclosure of God in Jesus with a sense that comparative study changes our understanding of that disclosure:

---

by his comparative theological venture. In *Religion and Creation* and *Religion and Human Nature*, for instance, the information about the various traditions serves mainly as a cautionary preface to Ward's articulation of his own positions in light of contemporary Western thought. Comparative study roots out some errors that might otherwise be made. Thus, after describing Hindu and Buddhist positions on the human self in the first 100 pages of *Religion and Human Nature*, Ward barely refers to that material in the remaining 200 pages of the book. While perhaps there is a more subtle process of integration under way, it is puzzling to see so little use, in the second part of each volume, of the materials from other traditions that have been so diligently described in the volumes' first parts. In *Religion and Revelation* and *Religion and Creation*, Ward continues to use materials from the various traditions, although here too his primary conversation partners are proponents of contemporary Western views on religions. By contrast, in *Hindu God, Christian God* I seek to engage and incorporate materials from the Hindu and Christian traditions throughout the entirety of my investigations and to root conclusions in my reflection on the materials of both traditions.

32. Ward (2000), p. 339.

33. Ibid.

> There is such a thing as divine revelation, which is the basis for Christian reflection. It is primarily found in the apostolic witness to the life, death, and resurrection of Jesus. But those paradigm events can only be understood by the use of imagination and reflection, and may only adequately be understood when they are placed within a context of global history, informed by a growing scientific understanding of the nature of the cosmos, and illuminated by other strands of religious insight and disclosure.[34]

What Ward suggests on a large scale, I wish to illustrate and nuance by a few more detailed examples. *Hindu God, Christian God* explores in depth some traditional Hindu theologies, but it does not attend (as does Ward's work) to contemporary reformulations of that theology. Each chapter includes the work of just one Christian theologian, read and reread in light of the Hindu primary materials. Buddhist perspectives are mentioned rarely, while Jewish and Muslim concerns are not mentioned at all. It is written on a smaller scale, just one volume focused simply on certain theological ideas in the Hindu and Christian traditions, and may be taken as complementary to Ward's larger and more ambitious project. The overall aim of the work is less magisterial than Ward's project, though in its own way *Hindu God, Christian God* is perhaps more ambitious. My goal is to unsettle the religious and theological boundaries that have neatly divided theologians according to their religions. I argue that whether theologians are Hindu or Christian they are still colleagues at least intellectually accountable to one another. There is no Christian nor Hindu theologian whose project merits an exemption from the tensions and challenges of comparative study.[35]

Is Hindu God, Christian God *a Work of Christian Theology?*

This book seeks to exemplify a theology that is interreligious, comparative, dialogical, and yet still confessional. Such a theology could be Hindu, but this one is Christian for several reasons. It seeks to present four recognizable themes with reference to the works of respected Christian thinkers (Swinburne, von Balthasar, Rahner, and Barth), and it seeks to develop plausible views on God's existence, character, embodiment, and revelation in a way that is recognizable to Christians and able to be affirmed by Christians. It is written by a Christian theologian who has been educated as a Christian and wishes to remain Christian. In a way, *Hindu God, Christian God* is a kind of Christian witness.

34. Ibid., p. 347.

35. My comments on Dupuis, Heim, and Ward by no means exhaust the list of important works that contribute to our understanding of theology as an interreligious endeavor. Other authors deserve mention. In particular, John Keenan (1989, 1995) has reflected deeply on Christian doctrines and sources in light of his study of Mahayana Buddhism. John Carman (1974, 1994) has likewise ensured that his study of the theology of Rāmānuja influences his appropriation of the Protestant Christian theological tradition, particularly the daunting challenge articulated in the works of Karl Barth.

Yet "Christian" ought not be taken as indicating a desire to move quickly to a confessional mode nor to back away from the interreligious, comparative, and dialogical aspects of theology by invoking privileges or duties peculiar to Christian faith. I do not presuppose that the Christian versions of positions considered here are superior to the Hindu alternatives. Other theologians may wish to make the case for a judgment of that sort, but they will first have to join an interreligious, comparative, dialogical, and confessional conversation in which some of their peers, to whom they are answerable, are Hindu. Only when an interreligious theological conversation is actually taking place can there be progress in drawing conclusions from it and about it, either to reaffirm or revise established theological positions.

There is no problem then in calling *Hindu God, Christian God* a work of Christian theology, provided one understands that the confessional overtones of such a claim must at every stage be properly specified within the frame of an interreligious, comparative, and dialogical theological conversation.

2

Arguing the Existence of God: From the World to Its Maker

Most religious people believe that there are values and truths beyond the competence of reasoning, but many of these same people assert that their faith is reasonable and are willing to defend that faith in argument with people holding contrary views. Even believers who are reluctant to judge faith by the standards of reasoning and who assert instead that revelation must be the ultimate criterion for truth may still concede that reasoning serves an important subsidiary role in defending the faith, exposing the errors of other ways, and (in some settings) clearing a shared space in which reasonable persons can explore the truth and uncover error. We saw in chapter 1, for example, how the Christian missionary Roberto de Nobili prized reason as a valuable resource in dialogue with Hindus.

Among Hindu and Christian theologians we have a wide range of views regarding how faith and reason fit together. As we shall see, important theologians in both traditions have insisted on giving prominence to the reasonable dimension of religion. Quite a few have for a long time explored and debated various arguments intended to demonstrate God's existence. When we examine reasoning about God's existence as a comparative topic with respect to traditions as diverse as the Hindu and Christian, interesting and difficult differences emerge. Nevertheless, the strong similarities we discover suggest what amounts to an interreligious project of reasoning about God. Many Hindus and Christians are thinking in similar ways when they say, "God exists," and indeed they frequently make similar arguments in support of that assertion. Even those Hindu and Christian (and Buddhist and other) theologians who thought that the existence of a God who is a world-maker could not be demonstrated still insisted that the point could be debated intelligently and profitably. Religious differences notwithstanding, boundaries can be crossed in the course of intelligent agreements or disagreements. There is a common ground for theological reasoning and conversation on topics of this sort. Good theologians from many traditions should be able to converse intelligently about God's nature and existence.

To elucidate the wider theological and comparative issues, in this chapter I consider Christian and Hindu perspectives on the cosmological argument in favor of God's existence: there is a world that requires explanation, and "God made the world" is the simplest adequate explanation. Although the broader set of arguments related to God's existence are also interesting, I focus on this single argument as a good example that shows us how religious reasoning functions in an interreligious context. Adhering to the principle of economy explained in chapter 1, I will avoid surveys and rely on just a few examples, which make clear what is at stake in debates over the cosmological argument. I begin by considering the position of Richard Swinburne, a contemporary Christian philosopher of religion and theologian who energetically undertakes the project of demonstrating that it is probable that God exists. In light of Swinburne's position and objections to it, I will then consider how the cosmological argument has been developed and argued in several important Hindu traditions. In the final part of the chapter we can then assess the common features of the Christian and Hindu versions of the argument for and against the induction of God's existence and also see whether this shared religious reasoning supports the claim that theology is an interreligious practice.

Richard Swinburne's Contemporary Christian Argument for God's Existence

According to one enduring strand of Christian and Western theological reflection, careful reasoning can tell us, with certainty or at least strong probability, that there is a God who is a supreme personal being possessed of maximal perfections such as omnipotence, omniscience, and benevolence. This view is traceable in part to Greek philosophical sources and in part to the Bible, for instance, the Book of Wisdom 11–13 and St. Paul: "For what can be known about God is plain to them because God has shown it to them. Ever since the creation of the world his invisible nature, namely his eternal power and deity, has been clearly perceived in the things that have been made" (Letter to the Romans 1.19–20).

Over the centuries, the project of making a reasonable case for God's existence has been pursued in different ways by many important theologians. It can be argued, though short of proof, that all reasoning persons who think clearly should admit that there is a God. Depending on any particular theologian's overall theological views, this reasoning about God has been more or less complementary to and dependent on a knowledge of God communicated through revelation, tradition, communal religious practice, and mystical experience.

Swinburne is an influential modern proponent of the cogency and usefulness of reasoning about God's existence. He defends the viability of the arguments for God's existence in numerous writings, especially in his trilogy—*The Existence of God*, *The Coherence of Theism*, and *Faith and Reason*—and in the subsequent *The Christian God*. Throughout, Swinburne draws on contemporary scientific and philosophical analyses and reaches back into the Western theological and philosophical traditions in order to present forcefully the case for persuasive reasoning in favor of God's existence. His work therefore offers a useful vantage point from which to view contemporary Western and Christian thinking about God's existence.

In *The Existence of God* Swinburne defends the probability of God's existence by examining various traditional proofs, including arguments from consciousness, morality, and providence as well as ontological, teleological, and cosmological arguments. The last of these is our focus here. His conclusion, previewed even in the book's preface, is that by reasoning we can justly draw conclusions about realities we do not perceive directly, such as God, and so can justly affirm that God exists. Since such affirmations are probable and not indubitable, they still leave room for faith.[1]

Swinburne locates his version of the cosmological argument in continuity with important eighteenth-century versions, particularly those of G. W. Leibniz and Samuel Clarke, who stressed the inductive and a posteriori nature of this reasoning about God. Swinburne rejects the view, argued by David Hume also in the eighteenth century, that the individual states that make up the world can be adequately explained in terms of prior states and that this adequate explanation is complete, thus rendering superfluous any reference to God as prime cause. Swinburne denies the adequacy and completeness of such accounts. It is more plausible, he says, to assert that the various states of the universe require a cause—"G"—which can ultimately be called the comprehensive cause, God:

> Like Leibniz, I conclude that the existence of the universe over infinite time would be, if only scientific explanation is allowed, a brute, inexplicable fact. Just the same would apply if the universe does have a first state. That state S_1 would be a brute, inexplicable fact. The existence of the universe over time comes into my category of things too big for science to explain. If the existence of the universe is to be explained, personal explanation must be brought in, and an explanation given in terms of a person who is not part of the universe acting from without. This can be done if we suppose that such a person G brings it about at each instant of time.[2]

From this it follows:

> whether the universe is of finite or infinite age, that G is a full cause of the existence of the universe throughout its history (with its permanent character-

1. P. 2.
2. Swinburne (1991), p. 126.

> istics). For he is a full cause of each state of the universe, by his making it the case (through some intention of his) that the prior state brought it about, and yet his states are not states of the universe. G would be the cause of the existence of the universe (with its permanent characteristics) over all the time that it exists, by a series of intentions, or rather a continuing intention to keep it in being. If we are to postulate G we should postulate the simplest kind of G for the purpose, and that means a G of infinite power, knowledge, and freedom, i.e., God. . . . The choice is between the universe as stopping-point and God as stopping-point. Can we rest with the universe as a brute, inexplicable fact?[3]

Therefore,

> the supposition that there is a God is an extremely simple supposition; the postulation of a God of infinite power, knowledge, and freedom is the postulation of the simplest kind of person which there could be. . . . If something has to occur unexplained, a complex physical universe is less to be expected than other things (e.g., God).[4]

Simpler arguments are to be preferred over those that are more complex, and positing God as the maker of the world is simpler than other possible explanations.

At the end of the chapter on the cosmological argument,[5] Swinburne assesses the probabilities in this way:

> There is quite a chance that if there is a God he will make something of the finitude and complexity of a universe. It is very unlikely that a universe would exist uncaused, but rather more likely that God would exist uncaused. The existence of the universe is strange and puzzling. It can be made comprehensible if we suppose that it is brought about by God. This supposition postulates a simpler beginning of explanation than does the supposition of the existence of an uncaused universe, and that is grounds for believing the former supposition to be true.[6]

As mentioned, *The Existence of God* is not devoted exclusively to the cosmological argument. Swinburne does not hold that any particular argument is by itself sufficient to demonstrate that God exists. But he does suggest that the cosmological argument, together with other arguments in favor of God's existence, forms a convincing case: it is more reasonable than not to affirm God's existence.

Although Swinburne does not portray his arguments as necessarily supportive of God as known and honored in the Christian tradition, he refines his positions in specifically Christian ways. In *The Christian God* (1994), his rehearsal of the probabilities regarding the nature and existence of God as a personal ultimate reality is followed by two chapters exploring the probabili-

3. Ibid., pp. 126–127.
4. Ibid., p. 130.
5. Ibid., chap. 7.
6. Ibid., pp. 131–132.

ties of Christian beliefs regarding the Trinity and Incarnation. He does not attempt to prove that God is Trinitarian and Incarnate, but he does assert that these Christian claims are probable once the existence of God has been accepted as probable.

His reflection on the Trinity is typical of his disposition to portray Christian beliefs as eminently reasonable. After discussing the place of love within the ultimate reality and the need for love to be relational, he draws this conclusion:

> Only fairly strong inductive arguments can be given for the existence of God. Given that, arguments for there being a God and God being "three persons in one substance" will be of the same kind. Our claim is that the data which suggest that there is a God suggest that the most probable kind of God is such that inevitably he becomes tripersonal. It is for this reason that the doctrine of the Trinity is not a more complicated hypothesis than the hypothesis of a sole divine individual.[7]

While the hypothesis that it is probable that God is tripersonal may not persuade all the readers who had followed Swinburne to that point, there is consistency to his argument: as we learn more about God, our knowledge of God remains consonant with reason.

Swinburne can be taken as representative of a wider group of theologians and philosophers who are willing to reason about God and defend the persuasiveness of arguments in favor of God's existence and who also think that this reasoning about God is most smoothly compatible with specifically Christian conclusions. Even those who disagree with Swinburne should feel able and challenged to engage him in arguments where reasoning is a key norm for the determination of religious truth.

Of course, those who disagree with Swinburne are many. His approach has been criticized by numerous philosophers of religion and theologians, including those who believe in God but do not accept the force of the arguments proposed in favor of God's existence. Some ask whether Swinburne's arguments themselves are convincingly argued; whether preliminary complications regarding religion, language, and logic have been properly taken into account; and what exactly it is that is supposed to be learned about God by this reasoning process. Many of these objections do not directly reject the entire project of demonstrating God's existence but rather simply ask whether the demonstration has been argued plausibly.

In *The Existence of God* and in the subsequent *Faith and Reason* Swinburne acknowledges a variety of stances from which one can criticize his position, and to each he offers a vigorous albeit brief response. Thus, he rejects the Kantian proposition that the existence of God as cause postulates something beyond empirical observation and therefore beyond our knowledge. He notes that a great deal of current scientific knowledge postulates "un-

7. Swinburne (1994), p. 191.

seen" sources for what is seen and that this postulation should not cease when more comprehensve and final explanations, such as those that pertain to God, are at stake:

> Science has been able to explain observable phenomena (e.g., lines in photographs of cloud chambers) in terms of unobservable causes (the movements of such fundamental particles as electrons, protons, and positrons). The science of the last two centuries has told us of fields and forces and strange entities such as quarks and gluons underlying and causing observable phenomena. The grounds for believing the claims of science here are that science postulates entities in some respects simple, whose interactions lead us to expect the observable phenomena.

Consequently,

> granted that the scientist has given good reason for believing in the existence of the entities which he postulates, there is no reason in principle to suppose that knowledge cannot advance so far as to explain the whole physical world, observable and unobservable, e.g., in terms of the act of a Creator God.[8]

Swinburne also disputes the position, which he attributes to John Hick, that belief in God is so fundamental that it must remain simply inarguable. On the contrary, Swinburne points to the long tradition of argument about God, which includes successful arguments that have been persuasive in changing people's minds. It is useful and meaningful to assert that God exists. He concludes, "There is no a priori reason to suppose that with common beliefs about the world and common inductive standards, men cannot advance to a rational belief about the existence of God."[9]

Most heated perhaps are the objections that suggest that Swinburne's arguments can never provide believers with useful knowledge about God and instead may actually do a disservice to faith. Even within one coherent culture or within a particular religious tradition, one cannot really argue about God in a useful way, since God is known by faith, through tradition, in worship, and in religious experience and not by a rational inquiry that purports to operate independently of those religious apprehensions. Whatever might be achieved by reasoning never suffices to justify conclusions about God's existence.[10] Swinburne rejects a Barthian version of this concern, which would hold that the Christian God is so different from the world that there can be no successful argument from the fact of the world to the existence of God. In Swinburne's view, so total a disjunction would reduce religious language to nonsense. We would either be using human words inappropriately or using them in so contorted a fashion that we would no longer know what they mean.[11]

8. Swinburne (1983), p. 83. Swinburne also discusses his disagreement with Kant in *The Existence of God* (1991), pp. 11–12.

9. Swinburne (1983), p. 85.

10. Ibid., p. 84.

11. Ibid.

Even if those who disagree with Swinburne are raising issues that demand consideration, Swinburne's reasoning about God's existence adds up to a quite plausible case, and I favor Swinburne's confidence in religious reasoning as a logical position that is also very helpful in comparative study. But *Hindu God, Christian God* is not the place for the resolution of the difficult issues touched upon in the preceding paragraphs. Rather, I aim to shed new light on the positive and negative aspects of thinking about God's existence by introducing materials from a very different religious and cultural setting, that is, the philosophical and (largely) Hindu theological sources of India, to which we now turn. As we shall see, to reason about God is an interreligious and cross-cultural project, which is confirmed and strengthened by comparative study.

The Traditional Indian Rational Inquiry into the Existence of God

The Emergence of Discourse about God in the Hindu Traditions of Empiricism and Logic

Both Swinburne's views and those of his critics are mirrored in the Indian context. By examining Indian positions that favor the cosmological argument and positions opposed to that argument, we will indicate a common ground for conversation and argument across the boundary between Christian and Hindu positions among theologians of either religion who highlight reasoning about God's existence or are suspicious of it. Because this broader comparative framework is not confined by any one set of religious, philosophical, or historical debates, we have to reflect on it without easy recourse to previously settled conclusions based in readings of the history of Western thought. The interreligious theological context makes it necessary for us to think anew and all the more intently about God's existence in a way that unsettles traditional boundaries.

Since many readers of *Hindu God, Christian God* will be less familiar with the traditional Indian debate about the existence of God, I begin with some background on its origins.[12] Thereafter I will consider two standard and well-formulated versions of the cosmological argument for God's existence—Annaṃbhaṭṭa's concise *Tarkasaṃgraha* and Jayanta Bhaṭṭa's lengthier *Nyāya Mañjarī*—and then I will turn to some important critiques of the theistic induction.

The discussion of truth—and accordingly of religious truth—as right knowing developed rather technically in the orthodox Hindu traditions. Hindu philosophers and theologians analyzed human knowing with great sophistication, arguing subtle relations and distinctions among the *pramāṇas* (means

12. On the Hindu tradition of rational theology, see also Chemparathy; Clooney 1999b, 1999c, 2000b, 2000c.

of right knowing), *prameyas* (objects of right knowing), and *pramā* (right knowledge).[13]

In part, the Hindu—brahmanical—search for a grounding for truth that can be empirically known and convincingly reasoned was motivated by the desire to refute Buddhist and Jaina skepticism about whether reality can be adequately known and described and whether the imperceptible supernatural realities to which the brahmins appealed (e.g., ritual, self, or God) can be verified or indeed are necessary at all.

Perception is honored as the simplest and most persuasive means of right knowing. But since the straightforward quest to know everything is never completed adequately just on the basis of perception, other means of right knowledge, such as induction and knowledge gained by verbal testimony, are eventually acknowledged, although these are always kept as close as possible to the truth of perception. By defending perception as the reliable means of knowledge, while yet conceding other means of knowledge, albeit stubbornly, to fill in gaps left by perception, one could be assured of a reliable apparatus for right knowing. On that basis one can map out a complete list of the proper objects of knowledge.

At one end of the Hindu spectrum is Vaiśeṣika naturalism, an old Indian scientific and philosophical system with strong empirical and scientific leanings. Its goal is the achievement of a coherent empirical account of all that can be known. In the beginning, at least, Vaiśeṣika thinkers had no need for God as an intellectual principle. Nearer the other end of this spectrum is Nondualist Vedānta, which subordinates perception to revelation, the authoritative word of the Veda. Perception may ultimately confirm what revelation tells us, but in the short term both perception and reason must defer to revelation. We will return to Vedānta below and in subsequent chapters, so let us focus for a moment on the Vaiśeṣika system and how it oriented early Indian thinking about God's existence.

The Vaiśeṣika thinkers did not ask questions about God because they thought of God as a potential object to be known but rather because they sought to determine foundations for right knowing. What more do we need to know in order to affirm the reliability of what we already know from ordinary experience? God is considered among other possible sources that might be called on to validate ordinary correct knowing, since the facts of ordinary reality raise questions that cannot be answered by appeals to particular aspects of ordinary empirical reality; most important, the world as such is knowable as a whole only if there is some plausible cause for its wholeness.

A standard example in Vaiśeṣika and the Nyāya logical discourse is an ordinary clay pot made of upper and lower parts shaped from clay and then joined together. Unless there is a maker who forms a complex object in that shape and join its two parts, then even pots cannot be explained. Even if the potmaker is not seen, he must be posited as the cause for the synthesis that

13. On the complexities of brahmanical Hindu epistemology, see Biardeau; Bilimoria.

constitutes the visible pot. Analogously, one may also presume that the world, which is a kind of composite, has a maker, who is God.[14] Complex things require an explanation for their complexity, yet the preferred explanation is simpler, and "God" marks the simplest such explanation.

In the Nyāya school of logic, early on allied with Vaiśeṣika naturalism, the earliest discussions of religious topics did not include the question of God as a central one. The question of God was raised as part of a longer consideration, in books 3 and 4 of the *Nyāya Sūtras* (the oldest Nyāya text), of the "twelve realities," six primal and six dependent, listed in *sūtra* I.1.9.[15] *Sūtras* 11–43 in IV.1 discuss the six dependent realities—activity, defect, rebirth, fruition, pain, and release—and speculate on their origins.[16] A discussion of God appears at *Nyāya Sūtras* IV.1.19–21,[17] but even this passage seems only gradually to have become an actual location for a discussion of God's existence.

IV.1.19–21 contain a terse argument about whether the postulation of God is required to ensure that human actions achieve their results:

> IV.1.19 The Lord is the cause, since we see that human action lacks results.
> IV.1.20 This is not so since, as a matter of fact, no result is accomplished without human action.
> IV.1.21 Since that is efficacious, the reason lacks force.[18]

Since the obscure *sūtra* 21 is part of a series of proposed explanations for the origins of complex material things—explanations that are all rejected—it is most probably also a rejection of the need for a God intended to guarantee the efficacy of human activity. Since human action can be explained without positing God, it is wise to avoid this superfluous postulate. One can postulate that the contingent simply arises from the contingent and take this as sufficient to account for reality as we observe it. By this reckoning, *sūtra* 21 reads as a criticism of the postulation of theism:

> IV.1.21 Since that action is efficacious only due to human effort, the reason put forth in IV.1.19, that it is necessary to posit a Lord, lacks force.

14. See Bronkhorst, pp. 281–394.

15. See G. Jha's introductory note to book 4 of *The Nyāya Sūtras of Gautama*, p. 1429. The six primary realities are soul, body, sense organs, prime objects of the senses, apprehension, and mind; these are treated in book 3.

16. In IV.1.11–13 it is determined that manifest things are generated out of other manifest things; then, in IV.1.14–43, eight alternative explanations are considered and, it seems, rejected: production from a void (*sūtras* 14–18), or by God (*sūtras* 19–21), or due to chance (*sūtras* 22–24); that all things are evanescent (*sūtras* 25–28), or eternal (*sūtras* 29–33), that there is only diversity (*sūtras* 34–36); or that nothing exists (*sūtras* 37–40); or that the exact number of things can actually be known (*sūtras* 41–43).

17. Perhaps first–second century BCE.

18. Since no specifications are made, we may appropriately read the context as pertaining to the results of action in general, but the concern may actually be narrower and focused only on the results of ritual action. In Mīmāṃsā ritual theory there is a similar debate about how ritual actions achieve the religious results—earthly and heavenly rewards—with which the Veda connects them.

But perhaps because of the need to provide a more definitive account of how the perceived world came about and, more important, also because of the rise of theism as a dominant characteristic of Hindu orthodoxy, the Nyāya commentators opted for a theistic focus and read the sūtra as a defense of God's existence. The third and final version of *sūtra* 21 therefore reads as follows:

> IV.1.21 Since that human effort is efficacious only with divine help, the reason put forth in IV.1.20, that a Lord is superfluous, lacks force.

Human effort is too frail and fragmentary to bring about the results of actions, so it is obvious that effort would have to rely on God if actions are to be fruitful. Since human efforts are fruitful, it is therefore reasonable to assume that there is a God who makes them so.

Once the logicians entered this debate and decided to link an intelligible explanation of the world with the postulate of God, they pursued this line of reasoning with great vigor. Many of the Nyāya accounts are exceedingly technical and lengthy, and here we will look at just two of the more manageable ones, Annaṃbhaṭṭa's seventeenth-century *Tarkasaṃgraha* and Jayanta Bhaṭṭa's ninth-century *Nyāya Mañjarī*.

Early in the *Tarkasaṃgraha*, at 2.1.8, Annaṃbhaṭṭa lists various kinds of things that can be objects of knowledge, and among these he includes two kinds of self, "the lord" and the finite (human) self. He does so without comment, but in his own *Dīpikā* commentary elaborates a bit by admitting three objections and then offering a proof for God's existence. The first objection is that the proposed God cannot be perceived nor can he be intuited even in the way that one intuits a human consciousness "inside" a perceptible human body. Annaṃbhaṭṭa deals quickly with this objection, agreeing that God can be neither perceived nor intuited in that way. To another objection (placed third), that there is no scriptural text indicating that there is a Lord, Annaṃbhaṭṭa responds simply by supplying one: "He is the knower of all, he knows all" (*Muṇḍaka Upaniṣad* I.1.9).

The intervening objection is that God's existence cannot be inferred since there is no similar instance in support of such an induction. An inference of God's existence would be like no other known inference, and therefore it must be considered dubious. For example, when we see smoke on a distant hill we know that there must be fire there too, since experience tells us that smoke is produced from fire. But the world with all its component parts is not an instance like any other, and one cannot merely posit that the world is composed of parts in order to justify the assertion that there must be a God who integrates the parts. In his brief rejoinder to this objection Annaṃbhaṭṭa steadfastly defends the idea that God can be inferred in just this way. This is because in relevant respects the world can justly be compared to other familiar instances: "Sprouts, etc., are caused by some agent since they are products, like pots. Thus, the existence of the Lord is proved by inference." That is, neither living things (such as humans and sprouts) nor inanimate things (such as rocks and pots) are eternal, so they must have a maker who has fashioned them into their current condition.

In the *Nṛsiṃha Prakāśikā* commentary on the *Dīpikā*, Rāya Narasiṃha elaborates Annaṃbhaṭṭa's proof.[19] He argues that we can deduce from the fact of an effect not just a cause (*kāraṇa*), but also an activity (*kṛti*), which implies an agent (*kartṛ*). It can be shown that making the world is an activity, and it can also be shown that will and knowledge are involved in this activity. It is this combination of activity, will, and knowledge that defines an agent and here a world-making agent. In the required maximal measure descriptive of a world-maker—infinite knowledge, perfect will, and ever-successful activity—such attributes together define an original maker, and it is this maximal figure who is meant when we speak of God. Rāya Narasiṃha defends the reference to a sprout as an appropriate example, although sprouts are not artificial in the way pots are and although we do not actually observe anyone making the sprouts that we observe. Sprouts are natural and do not seem to have a maker, yet clearly they are neither eternal nor self-made. Like pots, they begin to exist, are complex, and require a cause—and therefore an agent—to synthesize them out of simpler elements. Sprouts are an ordinary example with which to compare the much broader example of the world and in accord with which to affirm the claim that the world has a maker, even if this maker is nowhere to be seen.

The Existence of God According to Jayanta Bhaṭṭa's Nyāya Mañjarī

The preceding discussion of God is presented more amply in the *Nyāya Mañjarī* (The Bouquet of Reasoning) of the ninth-century theologian Jayanta Bhaṭṭa. Though in some ways clearly shaped by the old tradition of commentary on the *Sūtras*, the *Nyāya Mañjarī* is perhaps the first noncommentarial treatment of the nature of God in Nyāya, preceding at least by a century Udayana's more famous *Nyāya Kusumañjali*. But Jayanta did not write in a vacuum. Like earlier logicians, he worked out his theology in a context where the doctrine of God was under fire from those who did not accept the existence of God at all and (although he does not engage them in argument) from believers who refused to concede that an induction of God's existence was necessary.

The discussion of God's existence is found in part 1 of the *Nyāya Mañjarī*,[20] in the course of a discussion of the authority undergirding verbal—and scriptural—testimony. Jayanta adheres to a realist religious viewpoint of God and the world and defends the possibility of reasoned arguments in favor of God

19. The *Nṛsiṃha Prakāśikā* of Rāya Narasiṃha is a commentary on the *Dīpikā* that is included in the edition of the *Tarkasaṃgraha* edited by Satkari Sarma Vangiya.

20. Part 1 of the *Nyāya Mañjarī* considers the means of right knowledge (*pramāṇa*), with an emphasis on the nature, kinds, and epistemological value of perception, induction, and verbal communication. In this context a range of epistemological and theological issues are treated. Part 2 analyzes the objects of right knowledge (*prameya*), the rhetorical strategies useful in valid argumentation, and the flaws in argumentation, which are to be avoided.

as a realistic and adequate cause of the world. The world is finite, so it requires an explanation, and "God" marks that adequate explanation. God is therefore knowable at least insofar as he is the world-cause. Upon further consideration, additional attributes can also be included in the definition of a God capable of making the world: power, knowledge, will, agency, and so on.

Jayanta begins his discussion of God's existence by listing objections to the theistic position, which can be summarized as ten:

i. God cannot be perceived.
ii. Therefore, God cannot be known based on a specific or general inference drawn with respect to something perceived.[21]
iii. "The world" is not "something made," an effect.
iv. There is no need to postulate a maker beyond the various evident causes.
v. A maker must have a body and therefore would suffer the various limitations that bodies entail.
vi. It cannot be shown that there is just one maker.
vii. It is not possible to imagine a purpose for God's making the world; if God made this unhappy world simply because he wanted to, beings would be suffering subject to divine whims, and God would be cruel.
viii. If there is a determining divine will that is not subordinate to rules, the merits and demerits of beings will not necessarily matter (as they would if reward and punishment were a matter only of cause and effect); even liberation might not be permanent, since God could simply reverse it.
ix. Perception and induction therefore do not offer convincing grounds for postulating a God—and so too other possible sources of authoritative knowledge (e.g., verbal testimony and comparison) do not succeed in demonstrating the existence of God.
x. Popular beliefs cannot be taken seriously as increasing certainty regarding God's existence.[22]

Excepting the first (regarding perception) and the last (regarding popular opinion), these objections all aim at problematizing induction and undercutting the likelihood of determining by inductive reasoning that God exists. The seventh and eighth mark special problems that arise as one thinks further about a God known by induction, but most of the criticism, and Jayanta's response, has to do with showing that the induction itself works.

After listing the objections, Jayanta names three adversaries: materialists (Cārvākas), Mīmāṃsā ritual theologians, and Buddhists (Śākyas). Like others who mention the materialists, Jayanta deals with them cursorily, charging them with inconsistency. They are accused of wanting to undercut the Veda by asserting that it must be finite and must have a human author—while at the same time arguing that no maker need be posited for the world, which is also

21. A "specific induction" would be, for example, the induction that there must be rain clouds, because it is raining, or that it must have been raining upstream because the water is higher than usual here. A "general induction" would be, for example, the induction that a pot requires someone to have made it.

22. These objections can be found on pp. 401–406 of the *Nyāya Mañjarī*.

finite. But if a finite Veda needs an author, then a finite world similarly needs a maker. If the world has no maker, why must the Veda have an author?

The Mīmāṃsā theologians are adversaries of a quite different sort. Vehement opponents of both the Cārvākas and Buddhists, they are orthodox Hindu ritual theorists who staunchly defend the Vedic scriptures and rituals. But since they do not adhere to belief in a supreme God—their system requires no God or world-maker and works better without one—they are key opponents of the logicians too. As Jayanta presents their position, the Mīmāṃsā theologians object to the idea of portraying the world as an effect that requires a particular cause. Jayanta rejects this view, arguing that if one admits that the world is perishable, as one must, then it is also necessary to admit that it is an "effect," which requires a cause and, more specifically, a maker.

Third, Jayanta presents the Buddhists as similarly denying that effect ("something made") properly names anything we observe around us. "World" itself is just a label superimposed on the flux of reality and does not tell us anything important about that flux. So it is misleading to see the world as an entity that requires an explanation or a cause. Against this view Jayanta defends the possibility of real reference for terms like "world" and accordingly the possibility of intelligently arguing that world as a particular effect has a particular cause.

Below we will investigate Buddhist and Mīmāṃsā skepticism about the induction of God's existence, and here we focus just on the general thrust of Jayanta's argument. In response to the ten objections listed earlier and against the materialist, Mīmāṃsā, and Buddhist perspectives, Jayanta wants to assert that it is possible to affirm a God who is maker of the world and guarantor of the Veda. Since God is not actually perceived, neither perception nor an induction that draws directly on some particular perception can prove God's existence. Since the Veda is not a universally accepted source of knowledge, citations from it are not likely to persuade skeptics. God's existence must therefore be established by a general induction, which notices patterns among impermanent, effected things and draws conclusions that can be expressed by a general rule.

According to Jayanta, the reasoning is actually rather simple. Things that are temporal are things that are made, and we necessarily assume that such things have makers. The world itself is no exception to this rule, so it must have a maker. Since the world is ever-changing and is clearly impermanent, it requires a maker possessed of adequate characteristics, such as sufficient knowledge and power. We name this maker "God." The major part of Jayanta's presentation on God is devoted to getting this general induction straight and establishing that it does give us certain knowledge about God's existence. Much of his argument has to do with the relative weaknesses and strengths of examples of induction and the relative weight that is to be accorded to exceptions.[23] Jayanta rejects counterexamples that would undercut his induc-

23. This section of the *Nyāya Mañjarī* is very complex, and in lieu of what would have to be a lengthy exegesis I have summarized and generalized Jayanta's arguments.

tion by suggesting that "making the world" or "being maker of the world" are not at all like "making a pot" or "being a pot-maker." He argues that analogies are never exact but are valid even if there are exceptions to them.[24] The fundamental plausibility of an induction is undercut only if it can be shown that the differences between cases—for example, between making a pot and making the world—are so great as to deprive the new induction of plausibility. In the case of the world and with respect to its maker, the similarities to pots, sprouts, and other artifacts outweigh the differences, so the analogy of pot and world, pot-maker and God holds. Things like pots require makers. The world is like a pot and has a maker. This maker is what we mean when we say there is a God.

Jayanta responds to all ten of the criticisms listed above, but it suffices to summarize just his responses to those related to the induction of God as maker:

iii. *Criticism*: the earth is not "something made." *Response*: materialists, Mīmāṃsā theologians, and Buddhists agree, in other contexts, that things are impermanent; but things that are impermanent are made, by some maker; the world is one of these things that has a maker.
iv. *Criticism*: there is no need to postulate a maker beyond the various causes. *Response*: however many various causes are involved, there must still be an intelligent maker.
v. *Criticism*: a maker must have a body and would suffer the various limitations that bodies impose. *Response*: there is no rule that makers must have bodies, and we assert that God can be a maker although he is not embodied—just as the self guides the body although it is not embodied.
vi. *Criticism*: it cannot be shown that there is just one maker. *Response*: if there was more than one God it would be confusing, since these multiple "Gods" could compete or work at cross-purposes. It suffices to assume there is just one God.[25]

In determining that it makes sense to say that the things observed in the world and the world itself are all artifacts dependent on causes and on agents, the logicians were also staking out a rational ground for religious arguments. They continually indicated their readiness to argue religiously with Jainas, Buddhists, and other skeptics who were still willing to discuss questions related to God reasonably. Since this public discourse could not rely on a consensus about the meaning of what was perceived, and since scripture as verbal testimony remained sectarian, inferential reasoning provided the only common ground between the extremes of empiricism and faith. As a form of

24. Exceptions are common. Occasionally there may be a fire that does not give off smoke. A clay pot is obviously made by a pot-maker, but we cannot generalize and say that anything made of clay must have just one maker. An anthill is made of clay, but there is no single maker for the anthill, only the contributing actions of many ants. Some things, even if finite, have no obvious makers. No one argues that the generation of a sprout from a seed requires the intervention of a maker. So too, some very large things, such as mountains, ought not even be counted as "made" in the same sense that pots are made.

25. The responses summarized here can be found on pp. 406–426.

reasoning, induction became the bridge enabling conversation across sectarian boundaries.[26]

In part 4 of the *Nyāya Mañjarī* Jayanta disposes of competing rationales for the authority of the Veda. Since Jayanta's argument in favor of God's existence is part of his wider quest to incorporate the authority of the Veda into an account of the intelligibility of the world as such, the defense of God's existence easily leads to the conclusion that the same God is also the author of the Veda. The Lord who makes the world is also the author of the Veda, for similar reasons. Combinations of words are impermanent and require a maker to synthesize them into reliable instruments of coherent speech. The Veda, which is comprehensive and perfect, requires an appropriately wise and flawless maker. Since it does not make sense to postulate that the world has one maker while the Veda has another, it is reasonable to conclude that both the world and the Veda depend on one maker, the Lord.

Although it will be the task of expert logicians to sort out in more detail the specific differences between Indian and Western logic and to consider ways in which Jayanta's version compares and contrasts with Swinburne's, the general features of this reasoning about God's existence by the logicians will surely be recognizable to those familiar with the Western accounts and vice versa. It should also be evident that the large differences in culture and religion that separate Swinburne and Jayanta do not radically differentiate their thinking about God's existence. They share a discourse about God that can be integral to both Christian and Hindu, Indian and Western, accounts of the world.

Of course, this is not to jump to the conclusion that the differences in culture and religion do not matter at all nor that Jayanta and Swinburne are really discussing the same God. Reasoning about God is never entirely separable from religious motivations. At the beginning of this chapter we noted that

26. Once Jayanta has shown that it is plausible to infer that there is a God who is maker of the world, he must also show that it is plausible to claim that this divine maker is the maker of the world as it actually is, i.e., as temporal, contingent, imperfect, and mixing sadness and joy. Thus he answers the seventh objection—why would a good God make an unhappy world?—by saying that it is not necessary to claim that a perfect maker must make a perfect world untouched by change or decay. One must distinguish between God's perfection and God's guidance of finite objects in an imperfect, changing world. Then, in response to the eighth objection—how can divine freedom respect an established moral order?—he asserts that God is free and acts not out of need but out of compassion. God's action is analogous to the free activity one engages in when playing games. Though acting freely, God still acts reliably and builds a world that is naturally and morally predictable. Jayanta also addresses objections related to the expectation that the merits and demerits of conscious beings—karma—form the only reliable basis on which to account for the world morally, so that an appeal to a deity would interfere with the regularity of religious and moral probity. The same issue arises in Vedānta too, where the omnipotence of God has to be balanced with a respect for the invariable advance of the karmic process. In both Nyāya and Vedānta the solution is similar: the moral order is stipulated to function as in the older nontheistic tradition but now as dependent on God's will. This is a divine choice that indicates neither divine subordination to a higher law nor capricious disregard for karma. See also Clooney, 1989.

Swinburne thinks that his mode of reasoning about God is particularly favorable to the truths of the Christian faith. Jayanta too has a sectarian affiliation. At the beginning of the *Nyāya Mañjarī* he makes a customary obeisance to God and addresses God as Śiva (Śambhu, Bhava), along with his consort Parvatī, and their child Ganeśa:

> Salutations to Śambhu, the self composed of eternal bliss, consciousness and lordship, who by his simple intent creates everything from the inanimate to Brahmā [the Creator God] with their actions' results. I bow down to the wife of Bhava whose hair is adorned by the crescent of the moon and who is verily the river of nectar extinguishing the burning due to existence. I tender my salutation to the lord of hosts Ganeśa whose feet are illumined by the radiance of the jewels on the foreheads of gods and demons, and who is the sun removing the darkness of obstacles.[27]

At the end of his defense of theism in part 3 of the *Nyāya Mañjarī* Jayanta prays:

> Reverence to the one by whose will alone the worlds arise and endure and dissolve at the end of the age, who distributes the experience of all actions' results, who is eternally awake and joyful, Śiva.[28]

It is therefore reasonable to assume that Jayanta belongs to a Śaiva tradition, even if the *Nyāya Mañjarī* remains neutral and is potentially inclusive of a variety of sectarian positions. Like Swinburne, Jayanta is a religious person who strives to think in a way that is independent yet supportive of his faith. His logical analysis contributes to piety mainly by undergirding the plausibility of faith and by ruling out contrary theories about the world's origins. In his system faith and reason are independent but mutually supportive, and they reach complementary conclusions.

In the following sections we explore more closely ways in which a critique of the induction of God's existence draws on more basic religious instincts about whether there is a God and how God might be known. Since the arguments remain very real, in this way we will also be able to reaffirm the rational core underlying the consideration of God's existence.

A Devotional Reformulation and Defense of the Argument for God's Existence in Aruḷ Nandi's Śiva Jñāna Siddhiyār

In his defense of the induction of God's existence Jayanta argues that it is logical to affirm that there is a God. Since he is more interested in establish-

27. P. 1.

28. P. 426. So too, at the end of part 3 he says, "Enough of this overly learned talk. This theory of the eternity [of words] must be discarded. Those who understand reasoning must accept that words are made; since words are made, their maker is the ancient maker, in whose power is the fullness of poetic brilliance, and in whose hair is the moon" (p. 483). At the very end of the entire work, he says, "Reverence to the one whose splendid hairs are like ten million rays of the moon, who is the wish-fulfilling tree for those who surrender, Śambhu" (2:208).

ing that the Veda has a divine author and less interested in what God says in the Veda, the claims of scripture do not significantly complement the achievements of reasoning nor is such complement required. The truths of reason and scripture are presumed to sit side by side, independent but harmonious.

Some Hindu theologians were comfortable with the induction of God's existence. Here we introduce just one explicitly theistic and sectarian system that accepts the induction of God's existence. Within the South Indian religious tradition devoted to Śiva as Supreme Lord, there is a systematic school of thought known as Śaiva Siddhānta. This school does not want to end up merely with a God known only by reason, but it is not opposed to the kind of induction proposed by the logicians. Of this school's many writings, we look at just one key text, the fourteenth-century *Śiva Jñāna Siddhiyār* of Aruḷ Nandi.[29] The first verse of Śiva Jñāna Siddhiyār offers a simple, minimal representation of the need for a creator:

> As he, she, and it, altogether, the whole world comes, abides, then goes again, and therefore there must be one who gives it all. He is the cause in the beginning, he ends it, he creates it again. He is beginningless, free, in form pure consciousness, he alone remains and abides.[30]

This programmatic verse sets the agenda for the rest of book I of *Śiva Jñāna Siddhiyār*, which analyzes in great detail the nature of the world, the role of God, God's independence in his interactions with the world, and the limitations of lesser gods. Echoing the Nyāya position, Aruḷ Nandi says that the world is an effect, even if it may be a beginningless effect eternally caused by its maker:

> There is an intelligent cause, and the effect exists within it too, so the world may be said to be beginningless. But there is a God who gives it all, it can also be said to have a beginning.[31]

It requires an intelligent agent who is different from limited, conscious beings and material things:

> The elements are the effect of an intelligent source. But a person knows only through a connection with matter while Māyā, the source for the elements, has no consciousness. Therefore there must be someone who makes all this happen.[32]

29. This important Śaiva treatise is itself a commentarial expansion of the fundamental text of Śaiva Siddhānta, the *Śiva Jñāna Bodham*, a set of twelve statements (*sūtras*) setting forth both the theory and the practice of the religion of Śiva, the metaphysical framework, and the dynamics of the guru-disciple relationship. The *Śiva Jñāna Siddhiyār* elaborates the Śaiva religion in two parts. One part is the *Supakkam* (Section on Our Own Position), which is a positive exposition of Śaiva Siddhānta theology. The other part is the *Parapakkam* (Section on Other Positions), a critique of other philosophical and religious positions.

30. I.1, p. 117. All references to *Śiva Jñāna Siddhiyār* are to Nallaswami Pillai's English translation. Throughout, however, I make adjustments in the translation based on my reading of the Tamil original.

31. I.1.16. p. 120.

32. I.1.17, p. 129.

Māyā, the creative divine power, is enlisted to bridge the gaps that vexed the Nyāya logicians. Matter comes forth from the Lord's *māyā*, his eternal power, and not directly from the Lord. Through *māyā* the Lord is truly an efficient cause, who makes things just as a pot-maker makes pots:

> Causes are of three kinds: material, instrumental, and efficient. For example, clay, the pot-maker's wheel, and the pot-maker are respectively the material cause, instrumental cause, and efficient cause. Similarly, the noble one, like a pot-maker, makes the worlds from Māyā, the material cause, with the aid of his Power, the instrumental cause.[33]

And "pots come from clay, due to the pot-maker. The Lord himself creates all forms, and all these effects are from their material cause.[34]

Echoing the Nyāya attribution of certain defining characteristics—knowledge, will, and power—to the maker God, Aruḷ Nandi describes the Lord in similar terms:

> The form of this power is pure intelligence. If asked whether supreme will and power are also found in this supreme intelligence, yes: where there is intelligence, there is will and power. As such, the power and will will be manifested also by the supreme Power of consciousness.[35]

The powers are used salvifically:

> This one highest Power becomes three as Powers of will, knowledge, and activity. Will may be defined as gracious love for all living creatures. By his knowledge power, God knows all that is good. Then, his gracious action is to make everything by himself.[36]

Śiva acts in the world by his grace;[37] unlike lesser gods, he freely chooses whichever form is suitable when he involves himself in the world:

> You may object that if form is ascribed to God, then another maker like the one who made our bodies will be required; or, if God wills his own body, you object that many other selves too might similarly will their own bodies. But we cannot assume any body we like, while the great God assumes any form he thinks of, just as do those perfected in yoga.[38]

At the end of the chapter Aruḷ Nandi stresses once again that this Lord, though in a true sense knowable from the fact of the world, is never merely knowable:

> Just as crystal appears as gold, blue, etc., yet remains unchanged, so God remains pure, one, and himself, in all the divisions of his Power. Though he blossoms forth by his gracious Power, [otherwise] he remains closed.[39]

33. I.1.18, p. 129.
34. I.2.29, p. 133.
35. I.3.62, p. 158.
36. I.3.63, p. 159.
37. I.2.36, I.2.46.
38. I.2.39, p. 135. I consider the Śaiva view of divine embodiment at length in chapter 4.
39. I.3.68, p. 160.

The God whose existence is known by induction is also the God who graciously reveals himself and acts marvelously in the world. God, the maker, is Śiva, Lord of the universe. Aruḷ Nandi does not deny that God can be known by reason, and he wants the induction to work. But as a believer he also draws on faith perspectives to strengthen reasoned positions and to ensure that Śiva remains ever mysterious, beyond thought. The solution is to assert both the induction and God's mystery, without letting either suffer for the sake of the other.

Some Nontheistic and Theistic Critiques of the Induction of God's Existence

Although there was significant support for the reasoning about God's existence elaborated by Jayanta and the other logicians, the Nyāya position was also criticized on logical grounds and with respect to its religious implications. Some found the proof itself unconvincing, while others were not eager to adhere to a God knowable by induction. In this section I introduce four adversarial positions that, although quite different among themselves on important religious issues, share resistance to the induction. First, we will consider the critique proposed by the Buddhists, who are both skeptical about the force of the proof and also religiously nontheistic: not God but the Buddha is the sole and sufficient source of religious wisdom. Second, we will consider the conservative brahmanical viewpoint represented by the Mīmāṃsā theologians already introduced briefly in the context of Jayanta Bhaṭṭa's position. Thereafter we will turn our attention to two schools of Vedānta theology, the Nondualist school and the school devoted to Nārāyaṇa (Viṣṇu), connected respectively with Śaṃkara (eighth century) and Rāmānuja (eleventh century). By examining these four positions we will be able to see more clearly the problems attendant upon reasoning about God, the persistence of reasoning in religious matters, and a series of differing ways in which the boundaries between faith and reason are negotiated. Our goal throughout is to observe both the specifics of their critiques and the ways in which differing religious sentiments shape their positions regarding the induction.

THE BUDDHIST CRITIQUE

Dharmakīrti was a seventh-century Buddhist thinker whose *Pramāṇavārtika* (Verses on the Means of Right Knowledge) offers an important and influential critique of the idea of a Supreme God, in particular of the project of inferring the existence of God from the empirical world clearly perceived and properly explained.[40] In the first section, "Establishment of the Means of Right

40. On the development of the argument about God in the Buddhist context in and prior to the thought of Dharmakīrti, see Jackson. Dharmakīrti's critique of the argument from effects to the existence of God is also described briefly in Oberhammer.

knowing," Dharmakīrti elaborates the mode of omniscience appropriate to the Buddha while also refuting the notion of an omniscient agent, that is, a Lord and maker of the world.[41] Jackson summarizes Dharmakīrti's critique of theism as follows:

> After defining *pramāṇa* [right knowing] . . . in the first six verses as uncontradicted, fresh cognition, Dharmakīrti asserts in verse 7 that the Buddha fills this definition. Before demonstrating generally (as he will in verses 29–33) that the Buddha is authoritative because he knows what is to be rejected and what accepted (*heyopadeya*) by those intent on liberation, Dharmakīrti provides a "nonaccordant example" for his definition of authoritativeness. This, of course, is *Īśvara* [Lord], whose authoritativeness, creatorship, and existence are rejected in verses 8–28.[42]

Dharmakīrti denies that it is possible to infer from the world that it actually has an omniscient maker or even that a changing world could possibly have the kind of omniscient, substantial, and unchanging maker the logicians have in mind. In verses 10–20 of the chapter he divides the theistic position into three arguments: things are intermittent and require guidance by mind; things have particular shapes, which require explanation; the fact that things are useful for particular purposes indicates the work of intelligence in their making.[43] Dharmakīrti criticizes each argument by quarreling with its logic and arguing that it does not lead to the conclusion for which the logicians hope. The three arguments are too complex to analyze here, but we can gain a sense of Dharmakīrti's style by indicating his response to the first argument, the requirement that what is intermittent must be dependent on what is not intermittent. Jackson summarizes:

> The argument from intermittence states that the fact that entities sometimes arise and sometimes do not, that is, are occasional or intermittent in nature, requires the postulation of a conscious being that serves as their cause at those times when they arise, and that being is *Īśvara*. Dharmakīrti points out, how-

41. Dharmakīrti is commenting on the opening verse of the sixth-century *Pramāṇa Samuccaya* of Dinnāga, in which five defining qualities of the Buddha indicate the intellectual and devotional focus of the inquiry: "Having paid reverence to him who is the valid knowledge-instrument incarnate, who desires the good of the world, the teacher, the Blessed One, the savior, I shall here make a compendium of my views [which have been expressed] in sundry places, for the establishment of [a] valid knowledge-instrument" (*Pramāṇa Samuccaya* 1.1), as translated by Nagatomi, p. 264. Nagatomi also cites a passage from Dinnāga's own commentary on the verse, which focuses attention on the Buddha's good intent: "His intention is a desire for the good of the world, and his application is his teacherhood by teaching the world. . . . the effect is perfect benefit for himself and perfect benefit for others." Dinnāga also cites the Buddha's three excellences—praiseworthiness, lack of recurrence (of the ill), completeness—and then adds, "These three [excellences] are intended to distinguish the perfect benefit [of the Blessed One] for himself, from that of non-Buddhists who are detached from passion, from that of Buddhist initiates, and from that of Buddhist adepts" (Nagatomi, p. 265).

42. Jackson, p. 323.

43. Ibid., p. 326.

> ever, that a being that serves as the cause of intermittent entities must, by definition, be a noncause, too, since a. an intermittent entity has times of nonproduction, when its eventual cause is actually its noncause, and b. at the time when the cause is generating the intermittent entity, there still are other intermittent entities that it is not generating, so it serves as the noncause of some entities at the same time as it serves as the cause of others.

But Dharmakīrti finds both of these problematic:

> a. Successive causality and noncausality poses a problem because the causal entity posited by the theist, *Īśvara*, is permanent. He cannot, therefore, change from moment to moment, and if he is asserted to be causal, then he must always be causal, and can never become noncausal, for that would entail a change in nature, an impossibility for a permanent entity. b. Simultaneous causality and noncausality poses a problem, because *Īśvara* is a single entity, yet is being furnished with contradictory qualities at one and the same time. Contradictory properties cannot be predicated of a single, partless entity at one and the same time, and if these properties are reaffirmed, then *Īśvara* cannot be single, but must be multiple.[44]

Therefore, "*Īśvara* cannot, thus, be the creator of intermittent entities."[45]

As we have already seen, Jayanta's *Nyāya Mañjarī* and many other Nyāya texts are concerned about the Buddhist arguments, and much of the logicians' energy is devoted to refuting Dharmakīrti and his allies. On both sides of the Nyāya-Buddhist debate the reasoning is meticulous, but it is also deeply influenced by prior religious dispositions about whether "God" is a useful religious idea. Jayanta, a theist, argued to support the thesis that there is a God; Dharmakīrti, a Buddhist, had no reason to be sympathetic to reasoning in support of God's existence. After his refutation of the Nyāya induction, Dharmakīrti offers a still longer exposition of Lord Buddha as the one possessed of right knowing and thus of the authority to teach. His desire to promote the Buddha as the sole guarantor of liberation motivates his critique of the inference of God's existence. In both the Nyāya and Buddhist theologies, faith directs reason, and reason still does its work. Although the logicians and Buddhists differ greatly on logical and religious issues, neither side considers argument fruitless. Religious truth can be argued, since proper reasoning supports one's deepest beliefs and undermines others' false beliefs.

THE MĪMĀṂSĀ CRITIQUE

A second nontheistic strand of critique against the induction of God's existence comes from within the orthodox brahmanical world. The school of ritual analysis and interpretation known as Mīmāṃsā, which (as noted in chapter 1) dates back at least to the early centuries BCE, most notably represents this orthodox Hindu rejection of a God who is world-maker and author of the Veda.

44. Ibid., pp. 330–331.
45. Ibid., p. 331.

The induction of God's existence cannot work, say the Mīmāṃsā theologians, and in any case, all that we need to know religiously is found in revelation, the Veda. The earliest Mīmāṃsā position on God was simple disinterest. The *Pūrva Mīmāṃsā Sūtras* of Jaimini (second century BCE) and the first commentary on the *Sūtras*, the *Bhāṣya* of Śabara (first century CE), seem to have been largely uninterested in cosmology and metaphysical issues. Neither Jaimini nor Śabara attempts to explain how the world came to be, and neither addresses the issue of whether there is a supreme God.

The Mīmāṃsā theologians were pragmatists who explained the intelligibility of the ritual world view and explicated its presuppositions primarily in order to defend its implementation as coherent and worthwhile. They were therefore disinclined to debate cosmological and theological issues; the fewer unseen realities postulated, the better. If one theorizes about an author for the Veda, that author may become more important than the scriptures themselves, so it is better to dispense with the notion of author. Rather than postulate a God who brings about the results of sacrifices, it is better to find in ritual action itself the seeds of its own fruition. Indeed, it does not matter how the world began, although it is worthwhile to exclude wrong views about the beginning. Postulating a maker God leads to further problems, while there is no need for such a maker God. On all grounds "God" is an unnecessary postulate. In the Mīmāṃsā view, the coherence of the Vedic system is justified internally according to the dynamics of language learning and interpretation. Appeals to external sources of coherence are judged unnecessary. Since the Mīmāṃsā theologians offer seemingly complete explanations of the world, which do not require a Supreme God, they implicitly undercut the attribution of substantial reality to God.

On the basis of Śabara's views there developed two important schools of Mīmāṃsā, one traceable to the teachings of Prabhākara Miśra (seventh–eighth century) and the other to Kumārila Bhaṭṭa (eighth century). Thinkers in the less-influential (though perhaps more traditional) school of Prabhākara relied principally on linguistic arguments to defend the self-sufficiency of ritual performance and the nonnecessity of God. Language learning is simply a process of juniors learning from their seniors, and there is no need to posit a maker of the original relationship between words and meanings. The truth about proper ritual performance is simply passed down through the generations; likewise, the world simply continues as it has in the past, without a need to posit a beginning or maker.

In the more dominant school of Kumārila Bhaṭṭa, the nontheistic position is similarly developed according to a theory about language, but Kumārila also takes up cosmological issues. First, in elucidating Śabara's commentary on Jaimini's *sūtra* I.1.5 Kumārila devotes several sections of his *Ślokavārtika* to topics related to language, word, and referent. He challenges a series of positions, including Buddhist arguments, that threaten the Mīmāṃsā understanding of linguistic reference and the nature of real things as real referents. He defends Mīmāṃsā's realistic understanding of the world as a self-sufficient whole and denies that there is a need for discussions about God.

But the Mīmāṃsā theologians were faced with an array of competing candidates for ultimate religious meaning, and eventually they had to take up the topic of the world and its origins. So too they had to discuss ideas about God—including God as the author of the Vedic scriptures, creator of the world, and recipient of all worship—even if only to refute them. Consequently, they had to consider the question of God in a variety of intellectual settings, not only ritual and linguistic but also cosmological, in order to show that God was not a useful hypothesis from any of these perspectives.

In a key section of the *Ślokavārtika* known as the *Sambandha Ākṣepa Parihāra* (The Deflection of the Criticisms of the Innate Relationship [between Words and Meanings]), Kumārila attacks the view that the word–meaning relationship is conventional and therefore reliable only when the original context is remembered. He says that there is no convincing way to explain how humans could suddenly have started connecting words and meanings that had hitherto been unconnected. It is simpler to believe that the relationship is simply a given, always prior to the intervention of potential speakers. Kumārila devotes the middle section of his critique to an attack on the related idea that there is a primordial God who composed the connections between words and referents in the beginning. Were there a God, this God would also be the prime candidate for the role of guarantor of language in general and of the composer of the Vedic scriptures in particular and could easily become more important than the scriptures and rituals themselves.

But Kumārila rejects the idea of God also for philosophical reasons. First, the idea of a world-maker is not viable, since one cannot conceive how such a person would make a world, or why. Second, it is hard to reconcile the idea of a perfect, divine maker with the widespread belief that creations and dissolutions are temporary and periodic. Third, the maker of a material world would require a material body, would be susceptible to the problems suffered by material beings, and indeed would also require a maker for his body. Fourth, systems that posit a higher, controlling consciousness (such as Vedānta and Sāṃkhya) fail to explain how this divine consciousness could interact with a changing, finite world without itself changing. Kumārila concludes, as do all the Mīmāṃsā theologians who followed this line of argument, that the idea of a world-maker is overly complex, problematic, and unnecessary.

Athough reasoning is the primary tool of analysis, a disposition toward atheism is a key factor in Kumārila's theology. Given their distaste for the idea of a Lord and world-maker, the Mīmāṃsā theologians had no interest in defending the credibility of inductions and other arguments supportive of God's existence. They had no incentive for considering sympathetically the kind of induction put forward by the logicians, so at every point they highlighted the problems the logicians sought to finesse, while ignoring the advantages of induction, which are so obvious to the logicians.

THE NONDUALIST VEDĀNTA CRITIQUE

As mentioned in chapter 1, Vedānta draws primarily on philosophical and religious speculations about world, self, and ultimate reality, as described in the ancient Upaniṣads. These texts are quite different from the ritual texts favored by the Mīmāṃsā theologians, in particular as they are open to considerations of underlying spiritual realities, including a substantial reality that is the source of the world, and the idea of God. Most Vedānta systems are actually theistic; even Nondualist Vedānta, which keeps some distance from the idea of a personal God, proposes Brahman as a substantial ultimate reality with many of the attributes one normally assigns to God: fullness of being, pure consciousness, and perfect bliss.

Methodologically, though, Vedānta extends Mīmāṃsā thinking to the Upaniṣads. It shares the same deep respect for the scriptures and also the same distrust for metaphysical claims, which, even if intended to explain the empirical realm, may inevitably undercut scripture's authority and give preference to extrascriptural sources of knowledge. It comes as no surprise then that the Vedānta theologians echo the Mīmāṃsā critique of the induction of God's existence and similarly defend the priority of scripture over reasoning as the primary source of right knowing. Vedānta therefore resists the Nyāya view that by reasoning we can know at least that God exists.

Two Vedānta texts from Bādarāyaṇa's fifth-century *Uttara Mīmāṃsā Sūtras* are relevant. First, we look at the second *sūtra*, I.1.2, and explore the common Vedānta view that reasoning about God, including induction, can only be secondary, in support of revelation. Second, we examine II.2.37–41, where the Nyāya and Śaiva concept of God as world-maker is criticized as an inadequate and misleading understanding of the source of the world.

The Vedānta critique of induction is straightforwardly asserted in the commentaries on *sūtra* I.1.2. The *sūtra* simply defines Brahman as "that from which the world has birth, etc." and is probably alluding to a verse from the *Taittirīya Upaniṣad*, "That from which all these beings are born, that by which they live after being born, that toward which they proceed, that into which they merge—strive to know that, that is Brahman," (*Taittirīya Upaniṣad* 3.1). Bādarāyaṇa, the author of the *Sūtras*, is probably generalizing that Upaniṣadic citation and taking it as a basic initial induction of the world source. But the various Vedānta schools hold that despite appearances the *sūtra* is actually criticizing the induction.

We can see this view illustrated in the early and influential exposition of Śaṃkara, the great Nondualist theologian. A Nyāya adversary suggests that the *sūtra* supports a simple notion of induction: the need to explain the ordered arising, continuation, and dissolution of the world prompts the reasonable conclusion that there must be a world-maker who is defined by the phrase "that from which the world has birth, etc." In the Nyāya view, I.1.2 thus supports the induction about God.

Śaṃkara rejects the Nyāya view and asserts instead that "the realization of Brahman is achieved only by deliberation on the [Vedic and Upaniṣadic] texts and their meanings and not by other means of knowledge, such as induction."[46] Although Brahman is a substantial reality, which exists apart from

46. *Brahma-Sūtra Bhāṣya* (1983), p. 15.

the Vedic texts, it is known only from scripture. That is, although Brahman is not a "performative entity" like rituals, which exist only insofar as their enactment is instigated by the texts, Brahman is still a unique reality, which cannot be grasped by ordinary perception nor established by induction:

> *Objection*: If Brahman is an established entity then it can be the object of other means of knowledge and so the exegesis of the Vedānta [Upaniṣadic] statements is unnecessary.
>
> *Response*: No; Brahman's relation with anything else cannot be grasped. It is not an object of the senses, since the senses naturally comprehend objects, but not Brahman. Were Brahman an object of the senses, one could know, "This effect is related to Brahman [as its cause]." But when an effect is recognized, one cannot ascertain whether it is related [especially] to Brahman or to something else. So the *sūtra* does not intend to indicate an induction.[47]

When the *sūtra* says "that from which the world has birth, etc.," this is not an induction, but simply a reference to what is stated authoritatively in the *Taittirīya Upaniṣad*.[48]

Underlying the Vedānta objection to induction is concern about the kind of God who is to be inferred, that is, a world-maker who is like a pot-maker fashioning clay, distinct from the pot and not its material cause. Not only is the source of material reality unexplained but, the Vedānta theologians charge, other problems ensue as one attempts to explain how a spiritual agent changes material things. One ends up with a material God who cannot actually create anything. Only by learning from scripture that Brahman is the material as well as efficient cause can one explain how God causes the world. So too the Nyāya position threatens the Nondualist religious conviction that knowledge of Brah-

47. Ibid., p. 17. In a comment in the *Parimala*, Appaya Dīkṣita explains that perception unaided by revelation (*śruti*) cannot perceive Brahman, but that once perception is purified by revelation, Brahman can ultimately be perceived (p. 91). One can also find an extended critique of the Nyāya induction of God's existence in Rāmānuja's *Śrībhāṣya* I.1.3.

48. A more technical variant of this Nondualist critique can be found in the third part of the sixteenth-century *Advaita Dīpikā* by Nṛsiṃha Āśramin. This work ties together the themes of Vedānta theology and philosophy by exegeting the Upaniṣadic phrase probably most important for the Vedānta theologians, *tat tvam asi*: "you are that, your true self is the Ultimate Reality, Brahman" (*Chāndogya Upaniṣad* 6.9). The third part, an exposition of the ultimate, transcendent reality expressed by the *tat*, is subdivided into seven parts: a brief explanation of *tat* (that); a rejection of the induction that there is a God (pp. 218ff.); how Brahman is known from scripture (pp. 232ff.); how Brahman is the material cause (pp. 283ff.); how Brahman is efficient cause (pp. 329ff.); the nature of the error by which the world is seen as separate and diverse (pp. 349ff.); and what can be said positively about Brahman based on scripture yet without sectarian entanglement in one or another image of God (pp. 447ff.). Nṛsiṃha Āśramin says that the Nyāya induction of a world-maker is a misleading way to begin thinking about Brahman. Divine agency is not a kind of exertion, an activity undertaken by a maker, nor can one assert an invariable relation between the world and the exertion-expending maker who is supposed to be the world-cause (p. 223). However, there can be causality without agent-generated exertion, which would be a true, divine "making" purified of anthropomorphisms (p. 224). It is simpler then to admit knowledge, a desire to act, and causality without adding the idea of exertion and consequently admitting an embodied maker (pp. 228, 230).

man is the sole key to liberation. Thinking that there is a God who is (merely) the maker of the world leaves one with some knowledge about reality but not a knowledge that can radically transform one's relationship to that world.

Since the Nondualist Vedānta theologians are not opposed to the idea that knowledge of Brahman conforms to reason, they readily concede that induction is useful after one learns from the Upaniṣads that there is a single infinite cause, which is possessed of certain superlative features. Religious truth is not discovered by reason and then supplemented by scripture, as the Nyāya theologians are said to suggest. Rather, it is given in scripture and confirmed by reasoning: "When, however, there are Upaniṣadic texts which speak of the origin, etc., of the world, consequent inductions which do not run counter to the Upaniṣadic texts are not ruled out, insofar as they are adopted as a valid means of knowledge reinforcing these texts."[49] Vedānta therefore weaves a delicate balance: scripture alone is the source of knowledge of Brahman while reason, which cannot proceed on its own, is still usefully supportive of claims about Brahman.

The issue of God's existence as world-maker is discussed in *Uttara Mīmāṃsā Sūtras* II.2, a section entirely dedicated to criticism of deviant philosophical positions, Sāṃkhya, Yoga, Vaiśeṣika, three schools of Buddhism, and Jainism, arranged in order of diminishing error. At II.2.37–41 attention is turned to certain Śaiva and Vaiṣṇava religious traditions, respectively the Pāśupata and Pañcarātra sects. Śaṃkara says that the position limiting God to the role of efficient cause is championed by Sāṃkhya and Yoga, Vaiśeṣika natural philosophers and Nyāya logicians, and various schools of Śaiva devotees, groups that, though quite different from one another, all make the same mistake in reasoning about the cause of the world:

> The Lord cannot be a maker, because this position is incoherent; the relationship [of God and the world] would be implausible since it would also be implausible to hypothesize the governing [of a material world by an immaterial maker]. Should one say that [this governing] is like [the governing] of the sense organs [by one's inner self, we respond] no, since [then the Lord would be subject to] sense pleasures, etc., and would be finite, not omniscient.[50]

The *Uttara Mīmāṃsā Sūtras* are primarily intellectual and theoretical, so the critique in II.2.37–41 is primarily an intellectual debate, not a judgment on religious beliefs and practices. At issue primarily are theoretical positions connected with religious views, such as the nature of divine causality, but not the specific sectarian beliefs themselves.[51] Śaṃkara is reluctant, it appears, to shift from an intellectual critique—of Buddhists and other outsiders—to any comparably fierce criticism of Hindu positions, which are religious and practical as well as theoretical.

49. *Brahma-Sūtra Bhāṣya* (1983), p. 15.

50. Thus *sūtras* II.2.37–41, pp. 434–438.

51. In chapter 3, however, we will see how the Śaivas and Vaiṣṇavas criticize each other's views of God.

In II.2.37–41 Śaṃkara's point is to criticize the idea of a maker God as an instance of poor reasoning, on grounds that may be summarized as follows. There is no coherent way to understand the variety of creation if a perfect Lord is the single, perfect efficient cause of it all. This perfect maker would make a world that is perfect like himself; there cannot be a coherent account of the relationship between a perfect maker God and the changing, effected world. Prime matter cannot be controlled by a God external to it, nor can a God stand in so intimate a relation to material nature as to govern it by way of sense organs, for example. Such a God would be limited in power or knowledge, in proportion to the finite world he seems to be making.

Although there is a place for reasoning in the inquiry into Brahman, such reasoning is secondary to revelation. On its own, reasoning is not a reliable source of knowledge about God. Even more clearly than in I.1.2, the critique at II.2.37–41 asserts that the logicians' induction cannot work and cannot provide reliable information about a world-maker. Rather, it can actually cause trouble by making efficient causality appear sufficient with respect to knowledge of God and suggesting that God can be known merely by reason and without the guidance of a specific religious commitment. In Vedānta, knowledge of Brahman is a religious event, which transforms and liberates the knower, and it ought not be confused with a merely correct induction. It is therefore better not to encourage any independent reasoning that might seem to leave one with sure knowledge about God.

A DEVOTIONAL CRITIQUE ACCORDING TO VEDĀNTA DEŚIKA'S *ĪŚVARA PARICCHEDA*

This religious skepticism about induction is explicitly stated in the Viśiṣṭādvaita Vedānta, a deeply theistic and devotional religious tradition. The theistic Vedānta, allied with South Indian Vaiṣṇavism, has complex roots in the Sanskrit tradition of the Upaniṣads as well as in the traditions of Tamil devotion. Its most influential early teacher was the eleventh-century theologian Rāmānuja, whose version of Vedānta is known as the Qualified Nondualist (Viśiṣṭādvaita) Vedānta. Unlike the strict Nondualist Vedānta of Śaṃkara, this Vedānta proposes that within the ultimate reality that is Brahman, who is the Lord, there continues to exist distinct and enduring insentient and sentient beings.[52]

Vedānta Deśika (1268–1369) was probably the most important theologian of this tradition after Rāmānuja. Two of Deśika's treatises, the *Nyāya Pariśuddhi* (The Purifying of Reasoning, 1324) and *Nyāya Siddhāñjana* (The Healing of Reasoning, 1334–1335), together comprise a thorough defense of the Viśiṣṭādvaita system of Vedānta according to norms of rational discourse shared with the logicians. The *Nyāya Pariśuddhi* clarifies and corrects principles of reasoning which will be of use in deliberations about God and re-

52. We will return to the question of the Vedānta debate about the relation of God and Brahman in chapter 3.

lated religious matters, while the *Nyāya Siddhāñjana* builds on this corrective work by focusing on the seven objects of right knowledge: inert material reality; the individual, dependent self; the Supreme Lord; the eternal spiritual/material abode of the Lord; understanding; the knowledge that is essential to conscious beings and not adventitious; qualities, which are real but not material.[53]

Deśika's position on the supreme Lord is stated succinctly in the third section of the *Nyāya Siddhāñjana*, the *Īśvara Pariccheda* (Delimitation of the Meaning of "Lord").[54] Here Deśika sets forth his understanding that there is a single such reality, who is Nārāyaṇa, the God of his particular tradition and some allied traditions. He defends this view against a series of opposing positions introduced by way of various objections. The *Īśvara Pariccheda* is argumentative, defending disputed theistic Vedānta positions about the nature of the Lord, the self, and the world.

Like earlier Vedānta theologians, Deśika insists that the Vedic scriptures (particularly the Upaniṣads) must be acknowledged as the primary, unquestioned authority, the only source of certain knowledge about God. While the logicians are right in asserting that there is a God, they mislead us when they argue that induction certifies that God exists. Arguments put forward by intellectuals such as the logicians will always remain open to further debate and can never provide the certainty believers require in their search for salvation. The Buddhists and Mīmāṃsā theologians are right in questioning the value and force of this induction, even if they are wrong in discarding the idea of God.

Deśika's critique of the induction is close to Śaṃkara's, and there is no need to repeat the arguments here. But two points are worth noting. First, Deśika directly asks why a theist would want to criticize the Nyāya defense of the existence of God. After all, this may seem to be a friendly position, which deserves support:

> Indeed, not only is there no good motive [for attacking the logicians], but we might actually cause those who have approached and adhered to the Lord on the basis of the induction to suspect that there is no God. This is a great injustice on our part toward them.

Deśika responds:

> Listen to our motive. To begin with, one must understand things as they really are. Just as hearing can refute what is grasped by smell, one who sees the speciousness of inference can avoid loss of faith in the Lord by acuity of mind. But the minds of the slow should not be disturbed by the understanding of the clever. That is the true way to show compassion. In this way one also avoids

53. The three constituents of reality, lucidity (*sattva*), passion (*rajas*), inertia (*tamas*); the five senses; conjunction (*saṃyoga*); potency (*śakti*).

54. Throughout, I use the edition of the *Nyāya Siddhañjana* that includes the *Ratnapeṭikā* of Sri Kanchi Tatacharya and the *Saralaviśada* of Sri Ranga Rāmānuja. The *Nyāya Siddhañjana* has not been translated into English.

the situation of having to interpret scripture in a secondary fashion in order to support a view that cannot otherwise be proven.[55]

Exceptionally intelligent believers will be able to see the flaws in the induction without thereby losing faith, but most people are slower and cannot make the distinction between reasoning and faith, and they weaken the latter due to uncertainties regarding the former. Real compassion means that one will not pretend that faith depends on reason. It is better not to defend reasoning as "proving" the fundamentals of faith.

Second, Deśika disposes of a compromise position: why not learn by reason that there is a God who is the efficient cause of the world and then learn by scripture that this divine maker is also the world's material cause? He responds that once reasoning has been allowed its desired scope and establishes a Lord who is the world's efficient cause, it will be a problem to incorporate scriptural claims about his role as material cause. If one is too respectful of reasoning's achievements, one might instead be inclined to reinterpret scripture to accommodate what seems more reasonable and thus be tempted to explain away the scriptural texts that claim that the Lord is the material as well as efficient cause of the world. It is correct, and easier too, to begin with scripture and think about causality only consequently in light of its teaching.[56]

The debate between the Nyāya logicians and their opponents was never really resolved. Even today we will find some Hindu theologians still willing to argue on rational grounds about God's existence. Others, in the Mīmāṃsā and Vedānta traditions, continue to assert the inadequacy of such efforts. Buddhists, from a different religious perspective, still insist that questions of ultimate religious truth cannot be resolved by appeals to reasoning and that the observable data of the world around us do not warrant the postulation of an intelligent and personal source responsible for them.

Yet all of these Hindu thinkers believe their positions to be more reasonable and more accessible to good reasoning than those of their opponents. Everyone involved (both before and now) seems to think they know what they are arguing about and what their opponents mean and are trying to accomplish. Logicians, ritual interpreters, scriptural exegetes, theistic devotees, and skeptics about traditions, gods, and rituals have been able to engage in a common conversation because of their commitment to the power and intelligibility of reasoned arguments.

We cannot discount the possibility that these disputants are arguing past one another, but neither is it obvious that we should dismiss their energetic efforts to demonstrate by inductive reasoning that God exists or, on the contrary, that no such induction can succeed. Differences notwithstanding, Jayanta Bhaṭṭa, Aruḷ Nandi, Dharmakīrti, Kumārila Bhaṭṭa, Śaṃkara, and Vedānta Deśika all believe that argument is worthwhile even in religious matters and that a critical assessment of reason's achievements would make clear the right

55. *Nyāya Siddhāñjana*, pp. 353–354.

56. This argument is set forth in the *Nyāya Siddhāñjana*, pp. 354–356.

conclusions while ruling out the false. Linked, believing and reasoning confirm one another; if one is undercut the other is threatened as well. Confidence in an induction of God's existence and faith in God are possibly allied commitments, but they are distinguishable. We can discern how faith sways logic and how logic constrains faith. We can decide whether the strengths and weaknesses of reasoning add up to a case where complementarity is advisable or instead to a clear assertion of the primary authority of revelation and faith. Of course, faith also affects how one judges reasoning. There may have been good reasons for doubting the Nyāya induction of God's existence, but the Buddhist, Mīmāṃsā, and Vedānta theologians also had religious reasons for not expecting the induction to work and for using logic to show the shortcomings of theistic reasoning.

Arguing the Existence of God as an Interreligious Theological Project

Some Christian and some Hindu theologians have argued that it is reasonable to investigate the causes of the world and on that basis to postulate that there is a God who is the world's cause. In both Swinburne's Western and Christian tradition of reasoning and Jayanta's Nyāya school of logic, questions about the nature and origins of the observed world and the expectations of reliable knowledge about it have justified discourse about God as world-maker. Moreover, Swinburne's keen interest in affirming the value of plausible demonstrations of God's existence is sufficiently akin to that of Jayanta and his fellow Hindu theologians, they can all be conceived as theological colleagues in a common project of reasoning about God. They share a strong confidence in reasoning, confidence in the power of the cosmological argument as an induction from perceived effects to a simplest cause, and willingness to bracket sectarian considerations as not immediately crucial to the determination of whether God exists. Jayanta and Swinburne argue similarly against a range of skeptics from Buddhists to Vaiṣṇavas to Barthians. In opposing skeptics and true believers alike, Jayanta and Swinburne agree that it is reasonable to assert that God exists because there is evidence that makes this assertion plausible and because it is reasonable to make and defend plausible assertions, even in religious matters. By extension, they also agree implicitly that a sound and well-expressed induction should be compelling for all thoughtful persons, regardless of specific cultural, philosophical, and religious peculiarities. The similarities that emerge also suggest that the conclusion that God exists is not merely the product of one philosophical tradition or one set of historical and cultural circumstances. It is broadly human to reason about the world's origins, and it is also plausible to conclude that there is a God who serves as the explanatory cause of the world. Reason survives cultural and religious differences, and in a comparative and dialogical context reasoning leads plausibly toward the conclusion that there is a God.

Consequently, Swinburne, a Christian thinker deeply committed to the power of reasoning, can be drawn into the Hindu conversation about God. Jayanta, a worshiper of Śiva, can be appealed to in support of Swinburne's argument with philosophers of religion in a Western and largely Christian context. Their reasoning brings them together, while their faith positions do not divide them.

It is therefore reasonable to see their positions as mutually supportive contributions to the single theological project of asserting that it is more reasonable than not to believe that God exists. While there are legitimate reasons that not every theologian can be a comparativist, the force of reason is on the side of theologians who enter into an interreligious conversation about God's existence and are willing to converse reasonably on theological issues; it makes little sense to reason about God's existence solely according to the habits of one's own tradition.

But neither must we get carried away by the similarities evident in the preceding pages. Nothing is definitively proven about God's existence simply by noticing that Richard Swinburne, Jayanta Bhaṭṭa, and others like them agree that there are reasonable indications of God's existence. That Jayanta and Swinburne agree is significant, but both of them could be wrong. The proponents of God's existence have not made a universally compelling case for their position. Obviously, disagreements can and do occur among theologians who agree that it makes sense to argue. Other theologians, both Hindu and Christian and Buddhist, still disagree on the value of the cosmological argument, and perhaps these critics (e.g., Buddhists and Mīmāṃsā ritual theorists in India, David Hume and his successors in the West) are correct. Thus, the simple and straightforward core argument about God's existence must continue even as the terms of debate have become more complicated as other theological voices, from other traditions, are allowed into the discussion.

Faith too is deeply influential even regarding the reasonable arguments that take place. Both the Hindu and Christian proponents and antagonists of the induction of God's existence know where acceptance of the induction leads and what could be gained or lost by denying it. Even in the course of the most reasoned arguments they are anticipating where the arguments might lead and accordingly steer the arguments toward conclusions they already firmly believe. The explicit argument may have to do with an assessment of empirical reality or of the nature of causality, but in the background the Buddhist remains always committed to the supremacy of the Buddha as the compassionate world-teacher, the Mīmāṃsā theologian to the exclusion of a Lord who might potentially rival the Veda's importance, and the logician to the existence of God as the foundation of the world's intelligibility. At every stage religious and cultural commitments and values affect how reasonable arguments such as the cosmological argument can be proposed, defended, and received. Faith does not render argument useless, but it does affect its tenor and purposes.

If one is inclined (as I am) to be more impressed by the common ground provided by religious reasoning, one will also be inclined to interpret even the contrary voices as welcome "adversaries" who, because they are willing to argue, confirm that there is a shared reasonable discourse that is religiously profitable.

In any case, both the agreements and the disagreements are cross-cultural events not defined solely in terms of specific religious traditions and their particular theologies. The sides in the debate about the induction of God's existence cannot be simplified to "the Hindu position" versus "the Christian position." There is no likelihood that all Christian theologians will agree on a position opposed by all Hindu theologians, nor vice versa. Some Christians and some Hindus favor the induction of God's existence, and others do not. Some Christian theologians and some Hindu theologians find reasoning a solid basis for interreligious conversation, and others do not. Swinburne and Jayanta are allies, while Mīmāṃsā and Vedānta theologians ally themselves with Western Christian thinkers suspicious of the charms of induction. Decisions on such matters have little to do with whether one is a Hindu or Christian, even if Swinburne may find that his argument is most conducive to Christian faith while Jayanta finds his to be most conducive to faith in Śiva. Since the arguments cross cultural and religious boundaries, theologians of all traditions regardless of their faith positions must decide where they stand on issues related to reasoning about God's existence. They must discern which theologians from which religious traditions are their real allies and then pose their arguments in forms that are comparatively and dialogically intelligible and credible. Nor do the sides, once recognized, remain entirely stable. Arguments may actually lead somewhere; persuasion may work; theologians may change their minds; intellectual and religious conversion becomes possible.

Impressed by the plausibility of their own reasoning, Christian theologians may be tempted to believe that they can think entirely adequately about God without paying any attention to how Hindu theologians have thought on the same topics and vice versa. Skeptics not so inclined may wish to assert that there is only the appearance of a shared discourse, arguments that only seem to engage thinkers in a single conversation that, from the start, is always doomed to inconclusiveness and an eventual reassertion of the faith positions with which one began. But if thinking about God really is *thinking*, then cultural and religious differences cannot be accepted as fixed boundaries. If faith positions are accessible to reason, even interreligious arguments will inevitably draw theologians into a broadened religious conversation.

As we saw in chapter 1, Roberto de Nobili believed that people who think clearly must eventually agree that there is a God, who is perfect, good, only one, and the maker of the world. It is unreasonable, he believed, not to see that the cause of the world is God, who is possessed of certain obvious perfections. Other views can be shown to be wrong or inadequate. Moreover, since thinking clearly about God's existence is a deeply religious activity, it can facilitate a reassessment of one's traditional religious choices and a conversion of life. In the long run, de Nobili says, proper thinking opens one to the prospect of becoming a Christian.

Many, probably most, theologians today are more skeptical about how far reasoning can progress in specifying correct ideas about God, and consequently they are less optimistic about determining which religion is more reasonable than others. But if we may judge from his reports, de Nobili seems to have succeeded in conversing with some Hindu theologians who agreed that he and they thought alike. They seem to have argued sensibly about theological issues, in terms that both sides understood. Although most of his interlocutors remained reluctant to convert, some were persuaded by his arguments and chose to change religions. Even today, there is no good reason to set aside entirely the religious value of reasoning and argument. These are invaluable in an interreligious context today, and the dialogue will not move forward if we abandon the possibility of a reasonable discourse on topics such as God's existence.

It is complex enough to balance reasoning with established religious beliefs, but the project we have been considering thus far is rather straightforward compared with the balancing acts that will be attempted in the following chapters. As we shall see, some Hindu and some Christian theologians also appeal to similar arguments that give credence to their views on God's identity (chapter 3), the possibility and nature of divine embodiment (chapter 4), and revelation's authority in the assessment of religions (chapter 5). At each step the fragile shared ground claimed in this chapter is increasingly shaken. The theistic consensus that there is a God who is the maker of the world and the conversation this enables may be short-circuited by these additional appeals to special claims about God's name, activities or special revelations. But if like-minded theologians agree to reason religiously even with those who disagree with them, they should be able to move forward in considering increasingly narrow arguments regarding God's identity, God's intervention in the world, and God's word, which judges the world. These more problematic considerations introduce new opportunities, which will sharpen our awareness of theology as a reasonable religious project shared across religious boundaries.

3

Debating God's Identity

"Because the world is a composite, it must have a maker capable of making it; that maker is God." Some Christian and Hindu thinkers find this a convincing argument and agree that it can be shown with some probability that God does exist. As we saw in chapter 2, there are also some Hindu and Christian theologians who, though believers in God's existence, dislike the idea of a minimal, rational apprehension of God and prefer instead to adhere more closely to scriptural evidence. Even those who disagree with the induction are able to understand the terms under discussion—world, product, maker, God—and the intention behind those words and the proposed induction of God's existence. Believers who base their faith on scripture or personal and communal religious experience may still be well disposed toward accepting this kind of induction as religiously useful.

But whatever their disposition toward reasoning in regard to knowledge of God's existence, believers also want to say more about God than "God exists." They want to be able to affirm that God is possessed of a particular, regular, and recognizable character as the perfect, omniscient, kind, and gracious Lord and even to call God by name. Although Richard Swinburne, for instance, intensely focuses on reasoning and its contribution to religious understanding, he does not conceal his further, strongly Christian commitments. He is willing to argue for the rational soundness of Christian beliefs and to refine his philosophical positions in specifically Christian ways. In *The Christian God*, his rehearsal of the probabilities regarding the existence and nature of God as a personal ultimate reality is followed by two chapters exploring the probability of the Trinity and the Incarnation. Although Swinburne does not pretend to prove that God is trinitarian and incarnate, he does assert that once the existence of God is accepted as probable, consequent Christian beliefs also should be considered probable.[1]

The shift to a richer confessional language that identifies God more specifically need not be devoid of rational persuasiveness. Even when specific faith claims about God are couched in language rooted in authoritative scriptural statements or in personal religious experience, such statements are rarely meant to be simply private matters internal to a particular faith community. Such claims are supposed to be true. Believers remain confident that their views are reasonable and validated by the expected nature, speech, and deeds of the one true God, and claims of this sort should be understandable in a wider context. By a proper theological mix of reasons, texts, and traditional expectations about God, one may wish to show that the divine world-maker is "this God, *our* God" and not "that God, *their* God."

To understand what happens when theologians presume that their specific beliefs can be explained reasonably and actually argue about God's identity, let us focus our attention on several instances where theologians make arguments in favor of the one true God. First we look at the Roman Catholic theologian Hans Urs von Balthasar, who argued a particularly strong case for Christ as the one and necessarily only complete revelation of God. As he presents the matter, once thoughtful believers understand something of what it means that God reveals himself in a way that is true to the reality of God and also accessible to humans, we will be able to see that this revelation can happen only once, in one particular way, and in a unique form, that is, in Jesus Christ. Thereafter, we move to the Hindu context and first examine how the identity of God became a topic of theological significance in a religious context where polytheism, atheism, and nondualism were real and respected options. We shall explore what happened when theologians such as Rāmānuja, Sudarśana Sūri, and Vedānta Deśika in the Vaiṣṇava tradition and Śrīpati Paṇḍita Ācārya and Aruḷ Nandi in the Śaiva tradition began to argue about whether Nārāyaṇa or Śiva is the true God, Lord of all. At the chapter's end, we consider the further problems and possibilities which now press upon Christian, Hindu and other theologians who continue today to think about who God is and how God has acted.

1. Swinburne's argument regarding the Trinity is typical. After discussing the place of love within the ultimate reality and the need for love to be relational, he draws this conclusion:

> Only fairly strong inductive arguments can be given for the existence of God. Given that, arguments for there being a God and God being "three persons in one substance" will be of the same kind. Our claim is that the data which suggest that there is a God suggest that the most probable kind of God is such that inevitably he becomes tripersonal. It is for this reason that the doctrine of the Trinity is not a more complicated hypothesis than the hypothesis of a sole divine individual. (*The Christian God*, p. 191)

Jesus Christ, the Form of Revelation: An Explanation of Christian Uniqueness According to Hans Urs von Balthasar

Von Balthasar's explanation of God as revealed uniquely in Jesus Christ is set forth clearly in "The Objective Evidence," a section of volume I of his *Glory of the Lord*. In a subsection entitled "The Need for an Objective Form of Revelation," he asks how it might be possible for humans to know the triune God, by what kind of mediation. Von Balthasar describes two polar positions and discovers that the Christian view stands neatly between the two extremes. On the one hand, the Christian understanding of God has nothing to do with "God in himself" as a total mystery toward which we strive as a largely unreachable limit of human knowing. On the other, the Christian understanding of God differs from the idea of an absolute that is really the same as the human self, for example, "in a system of identities in which Brahman and Ātman confront one another in their sameness."[2] For the Christian the situation is different, since Jesus perfectly mediates God to humans, who are not God. To be sure, God is from all eternity the interpersonal mystery of the Trinity, infinite freedom, and subjectivity and so can never be merely an available object of knowledge. But God is not entirely unknowable, since he freely chooses to communicate with humans and to give of himself in that communication. To be communicative, the divine form must be a form accessible to human knowledge but still appropriate to what is to be known, the mystery of who God is. But there is only one way to do this, since only God can be the adequate mediating form of his own self-communication:

> Now, what makes its appearance in Christ in no way presents itself as a *phainomenon* of the One as opposed to the Many, but as the becoming visible and experienceable of the God who is in himself triune. The form of revelation, therefore, is not appearance as the limitation (*peras*) of an infinite non-form (*apeiron*), but the appearance of an infinitely determined super-form, and, what is more important: the form of revelation does not present itself as an independent image of God, standing over against what is imaged, but as a unique, hypostatic union between archetype and image.[3]

This form, who is none other than Christ, is able to make God knowable because there is no separation between the message (God himself) and the messenger (Christ, the Son). Since Christ remains always the man who walked the earth and shared human experience, even to the extreme of dying on the cross, the self-communication of God also reaffirms the reality of what is human. Since Christ is God and God's own self-communication, the mystery of God is not lost in this manifestation. Von Balthasar postulates that by contrast all non-Christian forms of mysticism fall short since they are not focused entirely on Christ and thus cannot offer any plausible way to maintain the

2. Brahman as a kind of cosmic self, and ātman as the individual self (*Glory of the Lord*, p. 429). This is one of von Balthasar's only references to Hindu theological terminology.

3. Ibid., p. 432.

fullness of both human experience and the divine reality: "Christ's corporeal body is and remains the point of union (Ephesians 2.16), while all other 're-ligion' compared with his corporeality remains at best a 'shadow' (Colossians 2.17)."[4]

In "Christ the Centre of the Form of Revelation" (section C of "The Objective Evidence"), von Balthasar again emphasizes that Jesus Christ, the form by which God communicates to us, is incomparable, not an example of anything more general. He is the center with reference to which all else is measured, but he himself cannot be measured by any standard.[5] In him alone there is a complete unity of person and mission, identity and function, which comprise the communicative form of the divine, and only due to this unique form can God possibly be known by humans. This perfect self-communication of God is a unique and unrepeatable event: "the unique God can express himself in his ultimate totality and depth only once in a unique manner."[6]

Thus far von Balthasar's position is fairly reasonable. There is a successful communication from a perfect subject through a perfect medium capable of reaching an imperfect audience. He also moves from this understanding of God's self-communication to judgments regarding what other religions must be like. Every other supposed divine presence, because it differs from Christ, is to that extent inadequate to the unity of God's reality with its representation—the archetype united with the form—which alone makes it viable for humans to know God in some real sense. What needs to be known about religions is simply their clear failure and their approaching and inevitable disappearance:

> If God did not in himself possess form, no form could ever arise between him and man: *finiti ad infinitum nulla proportio*. What would occur, rather, is what *must* occur in all non-Christian mysticism: the finite is absorbed by the infinite and the non-identical is crushed by identity. In the non-Christian realm, therefore, consistent religion (in its mystical form) is in a state of unresolvable conflict with aesthetics (which then also includes religious and political myths), and this conflict can in the last resort be terminated *only* by a de-mythologization of religion and, consequently, also by the dying away of religion, for man cannot live without an interior image [*Inbild*]. *Only* Christianity can unite both things, because the appearance of the triune God can occur *only* within form.[7]

Positive arguments in support of who God is must include a representation and judgment on the "other" in order to reinforce the credibility of the faith position.[8]

4. Ibid., p. 433.
5. Ibid., p. 468.
6. Ibid., p. 435.
7. Ibid., p. 480. I have added emphasis to the words indicative of exclusion.
8. When it comes to actual judgments on religions, von Balthasar without hesitation proposes and defends an a priori position. There is little evidence that he studied other religious traditions directly or drew on sophisticated scholarly sources. In *The Glory of the Lord*, for example, he quotes several times from G. van der Leeuw's famous *Religion in Essence and*

The relationship of Christ to the religions must be both judgment, as occurs in the anti-idolatrous and iconoclastic tradition of Israel, and fulfillment, since everything non-Christian is illumined in relation to Christ.[9] The meaning of the "non-Christian" is therefore extrapolated directly from meditation on Christ, who alone shows us who God is. Non-Christian mysticism, reduced to a rather unimaginative and deracinated version of nondualism, is mentioned simply to provide a foil to the richness of the Christian truth.

"Quality" is a lengthy subsection of "Christ the Centre of the Form of Revelation" in which von Balthasar directly evaluates religions in light of Christ, the sole form.[10] Jesus is unique, since in him there is complete and lifelong identity of God's communication and the human person, but no such claim is made for the prophets of Israel or for Mohammed. Jesus is the perfect event of divine communication, God come down and speaking to humans; but the Buddha, the saints of India, and other such figures represent only the human effort to ascend to the divine. Other founders point the way, but Jesus is the way. Others have decisive conversion experiences and life journeys, but for Jesus none of that is needed, and we have only the narrative of his redemptive death. Their stories are recounted in naturalistic and cosmological myths, whereas the story of Jesus is historical. The others offer schemes for salvation in order to resolve the tension between the One and the many, by either abolishing the many (as happens in "all forms of non-Christian mysticism") or incorporating the One into the many (as happens in polytheism and pantheism) or standing in between the One and the many (as does Mohammed). By contrast,

> God's Trinitarian nature, which is revealed in Christ and is in itself an ungraspable light, enlightens the relationship between God and man in a wholly new manner which cannot be confused with any of the others. . . . The Son who is both the Word of the Father and a hypostasis, allows man to have a foreshadowing glance into the depths of God, and this glance enlightens man as to how God, at the same time, can be the One and Only (in his spiritual nature) and eternal love, without a shadow of that selfishness which weighs down on the other religions in the form of *fatum* or of *necessitas*.[11]

The superiority of Jesus to other religious figures is manifest in several ways. First, since the form of Christ is inseparable from its Old Testament

---

Manifestation, and this surely provided him with information on religions. He also translated into German a small book on religions by the French theologian Jacques-Albert Cuttat, *The Encounter of Religions*, a brief, general description and assessment of Eastern religions' search for the inner self and for the transcendent One. But van der Leeuw and Cuttat both work within a Christian theological framework, and neither engages Hindu nor Buddhist theological positions except in the most sketchy of ways. Since von Balthasar did not study any of the relevant theologies, it is not surprising then that he finds the religions theologically impoverished.

9. Von Balthasar (1982), pp. 507–508.

10. Ibid., pp. 481–525.

11. Ibid., p. 506. The section summarized here is on pp. 502–509.

antecedents, he is the promise and fulfillment of everything else that humans might propose as examples of holiness. Second, "insofar as Christ is supposed to recapitulate in himself everything in heaven and on earth, he is also the image of all images in creation and history, and to that extent he fulfills the partial truths contained in the religious myths of all peoples"—myths that are simply variations on the human effort to ascend toward God.[12] Third, Jesus is of course a historical figure, who therefore can be studied, compared, and fit into typologies along with religious founders and teachers. But in the end and by the eyes of faith the intelligent observer will recognize Jesus as the apex of history and fulfillment of everything to which Jesus might have been compared on a merely historical basis. In reality, he is like no one and nothing else. In the short run, all kinds of comparisons can be illuminating, but if pursued thoughtlessly they may encourage "a blindness for the particularity of the revealed religion and for its uniqueness which sets it apart from all others. But the fact is that true uniqueness in the end can be seen only by the believing eye."[13] Comparisons must therefore always be cautious lest superficial similarities gain undue importance. Benevolent comparisons that stress fulfillment but neglect judgment do great harm. Yet neither should religions be trivialized nor treated with contempt, since this attitude might thereafter cause contempt to be heaped upon Christianity itself.[14]

The strength of von Balthasar's position lies in his deep sense of the significance of knowing God and his claim that God does indeed show us God's own self. He sees how this self-communication is made possible in Jesus Christ, and he appreciates why this form of communication can be exchanged for no other. Once one discerns clearly how God is uniquely revealed in Jesus Christ, then one truly understands; nothing of importance remains to be said on this topic. His position has a certain logic to it: God is mystery; God cannot be known except should he reveal himself in a way that humans can apprehend; but this revealing cannot be effective unless it is somehow adequate to who God is; this requires that the revealing form be God himself; Jesus Christ is that form, God himself; and since God's self-revealing in Jesus Christ is adequate, there neither can nor need be another such self-revealing of God.

Von Balthasar and similar Christian theologians base their judgments about the divine identity and the worth of religions on nothing but the core Christian idea that God is known in Jesus Christ. We are no longer thinking about whether the world has a maker. Now we are asking who God is and who it is that reveals God to us, and von Balthasar both believes and thinks that the

12. Ibid., pp. 496–497.

13. Ibid., pp. 498–499.

14. Such problems arise even when "the gods" are ignored or dismissed as unreal, since the same reductionist method may hurt the Church too. Moreover, we will lose sight of elements of genuine worth. It can be put positively: the Church (and before it Christ) inherit "the interior realities of the religions of all peoples, in so far as these contain theophanies and not demonologies" (p. 502).

answer is Jesus Christ. This question of personal communication and the specific form of God raises questions that are uncomfortably more specific.

Von Balthasar's approach may seem to bring theological dialogue with the theologians of other religious traditions to a dead halt. But his arguments are not unreasonable, and what is reasonable can be discussed. He explains his positions not only in terms of who Jesus Christ is but also in terms of what is reasonably implied by a single, necessary, and perfect communication between God and humans. One can therefore step back and assess this proposed model of divine communication, ask why this might be considered the best or only way of thinking about the encounter between God and humans, and ponder whether von Balthasar has not leapt too far too fast in his conclusions about religions. As we shall now see, other theologians in other religious traditions, specifically the Hindu traditions, offer other serious and well-developed models for God's identity in relation to the world, models that cannot be swiftly disposed of by a quick measurement against the standards von Balthasar proposes. There may indeed be a convincing and rationally cogent path from von Balthasar's understanding of Christ as God's self-revelation to his judgments on religions. But his manner of explaining this revelation and the form, Christ, needs to be chastened in an interreligious, comparative, and dialogical conversation with theologians whose writings will call into question his reading of their theological views and who offer a different theological portrayal of the divine–human relationship. But as we shall now see, many Hindu theologians share his basic concern about how God can be encountered in a way appropriate to both the divine nature and varied human capacities.

Hindu Apologetics: Identifying the True God in a Constructed Monotheistic Context

Let us begin our consideration of Hindu theological perspectives by recalling several points from chapter 2. As we saw, it was only gradually that the question of God's existence became an important topic that could be argued by Indian religious thinkers. Although the debate with atheists did not require Jayanta and the Nyāya logicians to elaborate ideas regarding divine activity, graciousness, and the worship of God, certain minimal claims about the divine nature were nevertheless implicit in his argument about God's existence. As one thinks about God, certain identifying attributes come to the fore as intrinsic to the discourse in which God's existence is established. Thus, the induction of a world-maker entails a minimal list of qualities that are essential to any maker: intelligence, because he must know what is available and how to use it; will, because he must have an intention regarding what is to be done; and effort, the power to act, since the making of things requires the effort to bring them about. In turn, these minimal qualities are shown to be unlimited perfections in the special case of the world-maker, since it is clear that no ordinary maker would be capable of making the world. God is omniscient and possessed of a comprehensive, eternally present knowledge and thus does not need the apparatus of memory. Since he is the world-maker, God must have unrestricted knowledge and power. Since bodies, as material, are impermanent, limited, and in need of makers, God cannot have a body. Because this God is omnipotent and always succeeds in whatever he intends and undertakes, one can also posit that his will is always perfectly satisfied, and he is never in want nor is he ever frustrated. Accordingly, there can only be one such God, since it would not be possible for there to be several—potentially competing—omnipotent Lords. But Jayanta and the other Nyāya logicians, despite their probable Śaiva affiliations, chose not to argue further that God has a specific name and identity as opposed to all others. It suffices to assert that there is a God, maker of the world and author of the scriptures, and this theology remains open to multiple views of God's identity. Whatever else might be said about God, however, can presumably be left to the insights of specific religious communities whose views, as local, need not be thought to conflict with one another.

The early Vedānta theologians are more interesting for our purposes since they constructed a theological framework for thinking about God, which made it plausible to investigate further who God really is, how God is to be named, and how God relates to the world in particular ways and acts within it. As the Vedānta theologians focused philosophical and exegetical arguments on more specific claims about God's character and activity, sectarian argumentation—for or against Nārāyaṇa or Śiva—could then become a legitimate intellectual enterprise. It is reasonable to call upon God by one name and not by other names.

First we describe the beginnings of this Vedānta argumentation about God through some key passages from the *Uttara Mīmāṃsā Sūtras* as explicated by the moderate Nondualist theology of Rāmānuja. Then we explore a more sectarian Vedānta theology in the writing of Rāmānuja's disciple, the twelfth-century theologian Sudarśana Sūri. Finally, we look at parallel developments in the theology of Śrīpati Paṇḍita Ācārya, a Śaiva commentator from approximately the same time period.

How It Becomes Theologically Interesting to Name God

The *Uttara Mīmāṃsā Sūtras*, the foundational Vedānta text, is deeply theological in the concerns that structure its four books. These books deal with the proper interpretation of contested texts from the ancient Upaniṣads, right and wrong philosophical positions on the origins of the world in relation to God (Brahman) as explicated in the Upaniṣads, the proper use of Upaniṣadic texts in meditation, and the cosmological framework within which the meditator can reach Brahman after death. Although the *Sūtras* and commentaries thereon are not organized as a treatise on God, the case can easily be made that Upaniṣadic speculation about the source of the world—including "self" to "Brahman" to "God" to "person"—leaves room for theistic theological considerations. While exegesis and language, ritual and meditation, epistemology and cosmology were debated early on, gradually the discussion focused on the nature of the highest reality and hence on the nature of God.[15]

The Upaniṣads themselves, as well as the *Sūtras*, militate against conceding intellectual significance to God's particular names, deeds, or personality. We have already seen in chapter 2 how the commentators used *Uttara Mīmāṃsā Sūtra* I.1.2 as the occasion for debate over whether inductive reasoning reliably supports the claim that there is a God. The *sūtra* itself simply announces that Brahman, the primary object of efficacious religious knowledge, is that reality "from which the world originates"—and by which it is preserved and into which it is dissolved. Ambivalent about induction, the Vedānta theologians argued that this *sūtra* points simply to a scriptural definition of Brahman found in the *Taittirīya Upaniṣad* III.1. The claim about God is minimal, and even those who agree that the world-cause is established in the Upaniṣad and in the *sūtra* still differ regarding the nature of the cause, whether it is prime matter, a maker who is an agent within the world and a celestial enjoyer of the benefits and demerits of activity, or a Lord with definable personal qualities.

The Nondualist Vedānta theologians were famously committed to a reality beyond all anthropomorphic images of the divine, and it is not surprising that Śaṃkara's early and influential Nondualist exposition of the *Sūtras* left little room for a discussion of God's identity. But even Rāmānuja, whose Qualified Nondualist Vedānta ceaselessly confesses that Brahman is God and God is Nārāyaṇa, did not use *sūtra* I.1.2 as the occasion for arguments against the importance of other gods. Even when Rāmānuja asserts that there is a permanent threefold differentiation in reality (Brahman, conscious beings, and nonconscious beings) and argues that Brahman is none other than the Lord, he does not interject particular comments that would make clear his belief that God, the world-maker and Brahman, is Lord Nārāyaṇa.[16]

But Rāmānuja does once make a claim about the identity of Brahman and the Lord, in his commentary on *sūtra* I.1.1, "Now then is the Inquiry into 'Brahman.'" Near the beginning of his explication of the *sūtra*, he explains that Brahman possesses a set of qualities that cannot be surpassed and that these are the qualities of a highest person:

> The word "Brahman" denotes "highest person," one who by his own nature is free from all imperfections and in possession of [a] host of innumerable auspicious qualities of unsurpassable excellence.

15. On the structure of the *Sūtras*, see Clooney, 1993b, chap. 2.

16. Elsewhere in the *Sūtras* the Vedānta theologians argue with the Mīmāṃsā theologians about the nature, function, and importance of the gods, who are insubstantial beings in Mīmāṃsā. In *Uttara Mīmāṃsā Sūtras* I.3.26–33, the Vedānta theologians argue for the reality of the gods as embodied beings, who need liberation and are able to study the Upaniṣads, and against the functional attitude of the Mīmāṃsā theologians, who are willing to reduce the gods to mere names, simply linguistic realities. It is strategically useful for the Vedāntans to posit that the gods are real, embodied beings, since as such they too would be motivated to seek some better, more permanent status and thus desire liberation by knowledge of Brahman. Without bodies, they would merely be content and have no interest in seeking anything more. See Clooney, 1988a, 2000a; and also chapter 4 of this book.

But only the Lord can meet the high standard of possessing this maximal set of qualities:

> The word "Brahman" is everywhere used in conjunction with anything possessed of the quality of greatness, but it primarily denotes that which possesses greatness in its essential nature as well as in its qualities, in unsurpassable excellence. Only the Lord of all can thus be denoted, and "Brahman" primarily denotes him alone. It applies only figuratively to things which possess [some of] his qualities. For it would be inappropriate to assume several meanings for the word. It is similarly the case with "the fortunate one."[17]

Rāmānuja defends his identification of "Brahman" with "Lord" on two grounds. First and most important, scripture does not permit a figurative interpretation of Lord; rather, it requires a real distinction between self and Lord and a real identification of Lord and Brahman.[18] Later in his lengthy exposition of *sūtra* I.1.1, Rāmānuja draws out a practical consequence of great religious importance:

> The doctrine that Ignorance is put to an end only by the cognition of the oneness of Brahman and the Self is not fitting. Bondage, which is something real, cannot be ended by knowledge. Bondage consists in the experience of pleasure and pain caused by entering into divine and other kinds of bodies, by a connection which springs from good and evil actions; how can anyone assert that it is something false?

Accordingly, a personalist language must be introduced:

> The cessation of bondage of this sort is to be obtained only through the grace of the highest Person who is pleased by [a] worshipper's meditation, which is devotion.[19]

If Brahman is not a person who can respond to devotees, nothing will happen; liberation is not going to occur spontaneously. Recognizing that Brahman is the Lord therefore has both philosophical and religious implications, but Rāmānuja and Sudarśana Sūri do not, in this context, further identify the Lord as Nārāyaṇa.

We can more deeply understand the nature of the sectarian Vedānta arguments about God's identity by examining the interpretation of *Uttara Mīmāṃsā Sūtras* II.2.37–45, where Sudarśana Sūri extends Rāmānuja's thinking in a critique of Śaiva theology. We have already seen in chapter 2 how section II.2.37–41 served primarily to occasion a critique of the Nyāya induction of

17. P. 4. Sudarśana Sūri explains the reference to "the fortunate one," *bhagavān* (often translated simply as "Lord"). In both scripture and ordinary experience various people may be described as possessed of good fortune, and a person may be called "the fortunate one." But this title belongs preeminently only to God, who possesses all fortunate qualities in their fullness (Sudarśana Sūri, *Brahmasūtra-Śrībhāṣya*, pp. 21–22).

18. In Rāmānuja's Vedānta, conscious and nonconscious dependent realities preserve their distinct identities within the comprehensive reality of the Lord.

19. P. 145.

God's existence. This was a criticism of a particular induction and also a rejection of the idea that one can know by reason that there is a personal agent/deity who makes the world. But these *sūtras* were located in a more sectarian framework. Traditionally Śaivas (of various schools) were said to be prominent among those holding that God is an agent, maker of the world (II.2.37–41; II.2.36–39 in Rāmānuja's numbering). The next section (II.2.42–45; II.2.40–43 in Rāmānuja's numbering) examines the view that there are four gradations in God's self-manifestation and explores philosophically whether it is possible to attribute change—evolution—to the eternal world-maker. The commentators give this view too a sectarian identification, marking it as the position of the Pañcarātra Vaiṣṇava school.[20]

On the foundation of that rational critique—the presumed basis for all that now follows—Sudarśana Sūri builds a more specifically religious critique of the Pāśupata religious system, which holds that God is the efficient cause of the world.[21] One might argue, Sudarśana Sūri concedes, that *sūtras* 36–39 refer only to the inference and do not criticize devotion to Śiva. The induction of a God who is efficient cause may be taken as the only point requiring correction. Sudarśana Sūri explains that since this view of God as efficient cause is deeply embedded in the Yoga and Pāśupata religious systems and buttressed by scriptures considered authoritative by proponents of those religions, the rejection of the induction cannot avoid becoming a critique of related, specifically religious views and scriptural interpretations. Nor can one dismiss the Śaiva position simply on the ground that it contradicts the Veda on the issue of God's causality, since this narrower critique might leave intact its related set of religious practices, which lend credence to the allied philosophical views. The Śaiva religious position must be criticized.[22]

By the Vedānta consensus the Yoga school was refuted earlier (II.2.3). Consequently, Sudarśana Sūri says, it is appropriate now to criticize the Pāśupata theological stance regarding the world-maker, including even its faith that Śiva is God. After explaining why it is justifiable and important to criticize systems of religious beliefs, Sudarśana Sūri dismisses a series of intriguing theological strategies that, if accepted, would obviate the need for debate about God's identity. First, he says, it is not right to suggest that the Śaiva viewpoint is an exceptional case with respect to general Vedic theoretical and practical principles. Were it an exception, this would mean that while the Vaiṣṇava reading of the Veda is generally true, the truth of the Śaiva religion also retains a special place. But exceptions are valid only under specific conditions and certainly not when the consequent contradictions would be numerous and important.[23] Second, one

20. Śaṃkara and Rāmānuja number these *sūtras* differently. Śaṃkara's older and more accepted division leaves us with the enumeration II.2.37–41 (on the Pāśupata system) and II.2.42–45 (on the Pañcarātra system), whereas Rāmānuja counts II.2.36–39 and II.2.40–43, respectively.

21. His lengthy critique follows Rāmānuja's comment on *sūtra* 41.

22. *Brahmasūtra Śrībhāṣya*, pp. 316, 321.

23. Ibid., p. 316.

cannot make the excuse that the scriptural words referring to Śiva refer in the final analysis to Lord Nārāyaṇa and therefore can be used religiously as long as this proviso is kept in mind. While it is true that all words, even those naming other gods, ultimately refer to Nārāyaṇa, this does not excuse continuing to use those words incorrectly, as merely naming other gods. So tolerant an attitude would open the door to the acceptance of just about all religious claims, even those of Buddhists and others who deny God's existence altogether.[24] Third, one cannot elude conflict by claiming that the contexts of conflicting texts differ, as if claims about Śiva have one purpose and claims about Nārāyaṇa another. This attitude too would open the door to an unlimited acceptance of just about anything that could be said religiously.[25]

On the surface, it seems reasonable that if the Pāśupata position regarding divine agency and Śiva is to be rejected because of some basic flaws, one might reject the Pañcarātra Vaiṣṇava tradition for similar reasons, since it too draws on popular beliefs and practices and is not entirely Vedic. But the situation is different, according to Sudarśana Sūri, because the Pañcarātra religion can be interpreted as never contradicting the Veda. It is therefore legitimate to make smaller corrections regarding Pañcarātra, when needed, without rejecting the entire religious system. Such leniency cannot be afforded the Pāśupata Śaiva position because it fundamentally contradicts the Veda.[26] Thus, arguments about causality, the coherence of scripture, and God's identity all converge with fundamental faith dispositions and judgments for or against systems and coalesce in settled apologetic stances about who God is and is not.

Sudarśana Sūri's lengthy exegesis of a passage from the *Varāha Purāṇa* deserves particular attention. Like other *purāṇas*, the *Varāha* is a complex synthesis of myth, cosmology, philosophy, and ethics; it seems to have been a familiar text respected by both Vaiṣṇavas and Śaivas.[27] Since it is explicitly concerned with the relationships among the gods, it is pointedly quoted and argued in the course of the debate about the status of the Pāśupata path.

Chapters 70–71 of the *Varāha Purāṇa* are known as the *Rudra Gītā*. Here Śiva speaks about the nature of his devotees and the origins of the Pāśupata version of Śaiva worship. Sudarśana Sūri cites a defender of the Pāśupata view as saying that this text gives divine authorization to the *Niḥśvāsa Collection*, a set of Pāśupata scriptures and thus too recognizes the Pāśupata way of life as appropriate for the current age. But Sudarśana Sūri responds that the *Rudra*

24. Ibid. Sudarśana Sūri notes also that the principle of substitution does work with Vedic references to Indra, the ancient king of the gods, who was in effect replaced by Nārāyaṇa, because nowhere in the Veda was it claimed that Indra was superior to Nārāyaṇa. But when such claims (of supremacy) are made regarding Śiva, the Śaiva faith conflicts with correct Vedic and Vaiṣṇava faith and hence cannot be approved.

25. *Brahmasūtra Śrībhāṣya*, p. 316.

26. Ibid., p. 321.

27. *Purāṇas*—"old" texts—were not classed as revelation in the old orthodox calculation, but in the wider and more popular reckoning many are traced to divine or inspired authors. In any case they were highly respected sources that recollected items of importance, such as cosmogony, the origins of dynasties, and the deeds of important deities in the world.

Gītā gives only relative value to the Pāśupata path; it is merely less flawed than other, more deviant paths. Though not quite so bad as the others, the Pāśupata faith mixes together properly Vedic elements with non-Vedic elements. Lord Nārāyaṇa directed Śiva to promulgate this inferior Pāśupata path in order to accommodate inferior people according to their capacity and, in the long run, to improve them and turn them toward proper religion. But the fact that there are useful elements in Pāśupata theory and practice does not validate the whole religion. Whatever is good actually points to Nārāyaṇa, and only on that basis is there any truth or practical value in the Pāśupata way.[28] What is good in the Pāśupata way is not peculiar to it; what is peculiar is wrong.

When the Pāśupata advocate appeals to the *Rudra Gītā* in support of the Śaiva viewpoint, he is also introducing a genetic theory of nature and religion: there are three fundamental constituents that, in various combinations, comprise every reality. The Pāśupata representative cites a passage from chapter 66 of the *Varāha Purāṇa*:

> O best of the twice-born, know that all the gods worship me in the form of Viṣṇu, and theirs is known as the pure form of my behavior, O eminent sage. But, wearing the braided locks, crown, and surrounded with snake beings, I was honored as Rudra by the followers of the "Novel Doctrine." Know theirs to be the passionate form of my behavior, best of the twice-born.[29]

The references to the "pure" and "passionate" forms of behavior evoke naturalistic, religious, and social calculation as old as the Upaniṣads, systematized in the Sāṃkhya philosophical system, and repeated with variations in the *Bhagavad Gītā* and various other *purāṇas*. By this theory, all things are composed of three constituent elements: pure being (*sattva*), passionate energy (*rajas*), and dark lethargy (*tamas*). Religions and their gods can be sorted out as pure, passionate, or lethargic. Some suggested that the Supreme God is beyond all three of these, but others held that insofar as God is involved in the world God too must in some way share the elements, even if only what is pure (*sattva*). Passionate behavior is inferior but not condemned outright. The religion of the Pāśupatas and their God, Śiva, belongs to the second category, the passionate, and attracts people in whom the passionate constituent predominates.

This defense of the Pāśupata path concedes an inclusive hierarchization of the religious universe. It distinguishes the more orthodox worshipers of Nārāyaṇa, who are pure, from the worshipers of Śiva, who are passionate; both are legitimated, though they are ranked differently. It can therefore be conceded even by Vaiṣṇava theologians that the "new religion" of the Pāśupatas is put forth by Śiva at Nārāyaṇa's behest for the sake of a lesser and passionate group of people. This is a naturalistic and scripturally warranted explana-

28. *Brahmasūtra Śrībhāṣya*, pp. 319–320.

29. Cited by Sudarśana Sūri (*Brahmasūtra Śrībhāṣya*, p. 317) but not found in the editions of the *Varāha Purāṇa* to which I have had access.

tion of religions and their gods. The differences are genetic, since that is the way God made people and their religions.[30]

Sudarśana Sūri acknowledges differentiation and ranking but emphasizes the negative aspect of this genetic account of religion. As an exegete he argues that the opponent has failed to read carefully and to notice the main point of the relevant passages, that is, the mention of the proper divine qualities of the Lord, who is the material and efficient cause of the world, recipient of all worship, and composed entirely of pure being. Sudarśana Sūri says that the chapter actually criticizes the Pāśupatas when Śiva is described as constituted of passionate energy. According to the *Rudra Gītā* chapters of the *Varāha Purāṇa*, Śiva is a genetically inferior god, suited to inferior people who naturally worship that sort of god. Even the allotment of this modest role to Śiva is part of Nārāyaṇa's larger plan, since he delegated Śiva to undertake the ignoble though necessary work of confusion: "In this last age, people who adhere to me are very rare. I emit confusion, and it will confuse people. You, mighty Rudra, should produce [seemingly] instructive scriptures which confuse. By just a little effort produce a large result!"[31] The new religion of Śiva confuses those who need to be confused in order to diminish their influence and to prepare them for future improvement by having them suffer now the ill effects of their confusion.[32] The religion of Śiva therefore has some status and a role to play, but this cannot be taken as certifying it to be true or even honorable.

Commenting on II.2.37–41 (II.2.40–43 in Rāmānuja's numbering) Sudarśana Sūri as usual follows Rāmānuja's lead and presents the Pañcarātra positions generously and in a positive light. While he attacked the Pāśupata position despite some apparent points in its favor, he now defends the Pañcarātra position despite apparent weaknesses. Texts and evidence from religious practice and social description are adduced to show that the Pañcarātra arguments should be construed as orthodox, and, if properly understood, as essentially correct.[33] One can therefore favor this system even in its more controversial aspects. But since other systems are essentially incorrect, recognition of their positive features need not translate into sympathy with their philosophies and religions as wholes. Sudarśana Sūri had to develop a nuanced relationship between religious theory and practice, lest his generous attitude toward

30. Below we shall see a similar move to explain other people's religions in Aruḷ Nandi's *Śiva Jñāna Siddhiyār*.

31. *Varāha Purāṇa* 70.35–36. Translations of the *Virāha Purāṇa* are my own, but I have consulted the available translations (1981, 1985).

32. "It was for the delusion of those outside the Vedic fold that I introduced the instructive scriptures called the New Religion. . . . Such is the rope [*pāśa*] which binds men as beasts [*paśu*]. But insofar as it is seen as coming from the Lord [*pata*, "from the *pati* (lord)"], on that basis this *Pāśu-pata Śāstra* can be called Vedic" (*Varāha Purāṇa* 70.42–43).

33. Here too, Sudarśana Sūri draws heavily on passages from widely accepted texts, such as the "Mokṣadharma" chapters of the *Mahābhārata*, the *Śrīkālottara Purāṇa*, and as above, the *Varāha Purāṇa*. He appeals to these texts simply as informative about what was said and done in times past.

Pañcarātra also entail a similarly tolerant view of Śaiva and Buddhist religious ideas and practices. Sympathy or lack thereof changes how one reads the traditions one favors, while other traditions are held to stricter standards.

Let us now look briefly at the Śaiva explication of the same *Uttara Mīmāṃsā Sūtra* passages. Much of the reasoning is the same, but the sympathies are reversed, now for Śiva and against Nārāyaṇa. In his commentary on *sūtra* I.1.1 in his *Śrīkara Bhāṣya*, the Śaiva theologian Śrīpati Paṇḍiṭa Ācārya similarly draws a theistic conclusion, except that he begins with the belief that Śiva is Lord and reads accordingly. He cites passages from the Upaniṣads and Purāṇas[34] to show that Śiva alone is the perfect, unlimited God. There must be a Lord, since alternative agents such as insentient matter and finite persons cannot guarantee that actions come to fruition; they themselves are the products of action. Of course, scriptural texts also give us a viable definition of "Lord" and set criteria that one can affirm reasonably, even aside from whatever authority one might recognize in scripture. For example, the lord and world-maker is unobstructed by the limitations of time, the inner controller of all, the cause of all, the referent of all words, the Lord of all and self of all, and Brahman. There can only be one such Lord, since the idea of multiple lords conforms neither to revelation nor to the consensus view of the Vedānta schools that there is but one Lord. Nor would it be reasonable to assert multiple lords. The Lord is the cause of the origin, continuation, and dissolution of the world, and there can only be one such being.

Moreover, based on what we understand reasonably and know from revelation about the nature of Brahman and the Lord, we can also conclude that Brahman must be identical with the Lord. Although there are multiple views about the Lord's identity, intelligent exegesis clears up the difficulties. By an established principle drawn from Mīmāṃsā exegesis,[35] we know that general claims are specified by particular claims, and therefore texts establishing the fact of a Lord in general are specified by texts that assert that Śiva is the Lord and the source of liberation. What we know of deities like Nārāyaṇa indicates that they cannot function in those roles nor can we conflate "Nārāyaṇa" and "Śiva" as if these were synonymous names of God.[36] It is simpler and more sensible to confess that Śiva alone is Lord.

The logic of *Uttara Mīmāṃsā Sūtras* II.2 is that each heterodox system introduced is in some way less objectionable than those treated earlier in the section, so it seems difficult to interpret the *sūtras* as defending the Pāśupata views over against the Pañcarātra views. Nevertheless, Śrīpati Paṇḍiṭa Ācārya is vigorous in his Śaiva explication of *sūtras* II.2.37–45,[37] and he explains that the section clearly asserts the supremacy of Śiva. Nevertheless, Śrīpati

34. Literally, the "old texts," texts that combine elements of mythology, genealogy, cosmology, theology, ritual, and ethics into arguments for particular sectarian religious views.

35. *Pūrva Mīmāṃsā Sūtras* VI.8.30–42.

36. Commentary on I.1.1 in the *Śrīkara Bhāṣya*, pp. 26–28.

37. Śrīpati Paṇḍita Ācārya numbers the *sūtras* in the same way as does Śaṃkara, *sūtras* 37–41 (on the Pāśupata system) and *sūtras* 42–45 (on the Pañcarātra system).

Paṇḍita Ācārya offers an unhesitating defense of the Śaiva position that there is a Lord (*pati*) who frees eternal but bound conscious beings (*paśu*) from their bondage (*pāśa*), and that this Pāśupata position is identical with the authoritative Upaniṣadic viewpoint. He accepts the Vedānta consensus that II.2.37–45 confirm that the Lord is the material and efficient cause of the world, but he also believes that this Vedānta view is most perfectly articulated in his Vīraśaiva sect of Śaivism. Contrary sectarian views are intertwined with erroneous philosophical positions, and they also wrongly favor other deities. God is one, and there is a simple proper explanation of who God is.[38] The true reality, philosophical and religious, does not bear multiple, contrary interpretations. Śiva alone is God, and this truth is vindicated by experience, scripture, and reason.[39]

Śrīpati Paṇḍita Ācārya's analysis in II.2.37–41 and II.2.42–45 therefore weaves together rational arguments with selected scriptural citations, utilized to support specific Pāśupata views. The reasons elucidate scripture, and scripture confirms proper reasoning; both together confirm that Śiva is Lord. Indeed, the coherence of scripture and reason is an important measure by which religious and philosophical positions can be judged. Even dubious ideas can be afforded serious consideration—friendly interpretation, improvement, or partial correction—if they are conformable to scripture in one way or another. If respected texts seem to support erroneous philosophical positions, those texts should be reinterpreted properly so as to exclude such positions. In general, texts that might be thought of as applying either to Śiva or Nārāyaṇa must be interpreted as referring only to Śiva. That heterodox systems are partially correct does not warrant the approval of those systems. The Śaiva position already includes everything that is true and good in them, but even that inclusion does not excuse or validate its errors.

In the course of his commentary on the *sūtras* in support of his Śaiva position, Śrīpati Paṇḍita Ācārya offers a number of arguments that make clear the trajectory of his apologetic theology. First, it is to Śiva that the scriptures ascribe the proper and supreme divine attributes (omniscience, omnipotence, and so on) not Nārāyaṇa.[40] Passages that seem to favor Nārāyaṇa must be reinterpreted as referring to Śiva; otherwise, if taken at face value, they would contradict more authoritative texts, which favor Śiva.

Second, even Vaiṣṇavas admit that Nārāyaṇa has a body and repeatedly becomes embodied in various divine descents (*avatāras*). Since Nārāyaṇa is therefore encumbered with a gross physical form, he cannot be the inner,

38. Because their views are contradictory to scriptural texts, traditions "other than the Pāśupata Śaiva tradition are incoherent and, some say, lack authority" (II.2.37, p. 234). At II.2.40, p. 237, Śrīpati Paṇḍita Ācārya reaffirms that because God's double causality (as efficient and material cause) is not properly explained in traditions other than the Pāśupata Śaiva tradition, those traditions are refuted both as intellectual and as religious systems. Philosophical and religious correctness cohere.

39. Śrīpati Paṇḍita Ācārya does not explain how experience is a criterion.

40. *Śrīkara Bhāṣya*, p. 234.

guiding spirit upon which material things depend. As embodied, created, and inferior, he cannot be the transcendent God. Indeed, even Nārāyaṇa's capacity to become embodied indicates that he must always have possessed a subtle physical body and must always have depended on subtle physical senses for his knowledge. He has consequently always been prone to the same passions that limit other embodied beings and cannot be said to be perfect. By contrast, Śiva's own engagement in physical reality is a wondrous activity that in no way compromises his perfection.[41] The Pañcarātra idea that God might evolve into the world in stages, according to the theory of the four gradations, does not help; there is still no way to avoid admitting some perishability in a Lord from whom a perishable world evolves.[42]

Third, Vaiṣṇavas also admit that Nārāyaṇa is only a second-caste (*kṣatriya*) God, whose teachings therefore cannot command the same respect merited by Śiva's superior teachings. Moreover, the proponents of Pañcarātra Vaiṣṇavism are persons of dubious character whose rituals and customs are irregular, and their testimony does not inspire respect. On the whole, Śrīpati Paṇḍita Ācārya says, it is simply impossible to marshal an array of evidence sufficient to persuade an objective observer to view Pañcarātra sympathetically.[43] Apparent similarities to true (Śaiva) positions must be scrutinized carefully, lest true positions be dragged down to the level of false ones. The apparent similarities of the Pāśupata and Pañcarātra positions must be critiqued from the perspective of the integral and complete Pāśupata perspective.

Both Sudarśana Sūri and Śrīpati Paṇḍita Ācārya claim the support of reason and scripture for their faith positions. They cite older authoritative texts, such as the Upaniṣads, plus other, explicitly sectarian texts and argue about the correct interpretation of texts such as the *Varāha Purāṇa* to which both traditions lay some claim. Without due attention to scripture, reasoning will be inconclusive and can go astray. On their own, theological hypotheses rarely convince but instead merit severe criticism; scriptural texts can be decisive, but they must be read intelligently. It is possible and reasonable to argue about who God is, since scripture and tradition inform us about what is real, and reason helps clear away erroneous ideas. God (Brahman), known from scripture, can also be thought about as the maker and sole source of the world and guarantor of religious practice and knowledge. For both, God has become *the* central theological topic, worth explaining and defending.

Because the sum total of arguments includes numerous judgments about smaller issues interpreted in light of the whole, those who do not share the Vedānta starting points and have not worked their way through the Vedānta exegesis may not be immediately persuaded by the Vedānta arguments and conclusions about God nor by the particular Śaiva and Vaiṣṇava specifications of the Vedānta position. Christian theologians may understand some of

41. Ibid., pp. 235–236. The differing Vaiṣṇava, Śaiva, and Christian views of divine embodiment are the theme of chapter 4.

42. Ibid., p. 239.

43. Ibid., pp. 242–250.

the reasoning and some of the exegesis but balk at the idea that the Vedānta sectarian conclusions are really compelling. After all, understanding the positions might lead to changes in faith and worship; if it makes sense to argue in this way that Śiva or Nārāyaṇa is God, perhaps it also makes sense to worship Śiva or Nārāyaṇa. Nevertheless, almost all theologians should be able to recognize what these theologians are doing; even the heirs of von Balthasar should be able to admit that these Vedānta positions are not, on the face of it, any less plausible than their own.

Arguing God's Identity in Two South Indian Theologies

Thus far we have considered Vaiṣṇava and Śaiva arguments as stated in commentaries on the *Uttara Mīmāṃsā Sūtras*, where reasoning is evidently constrained by the boundaries of scripture and commentary. Here we take one further step and examine several more systematic, noncommentarial theologies of the one true God and false gods in the Vaiṣṇava and Śaiva traditions. For this I draw on Vedānta Deśika's *Īśvara Pariccheda* and Aruḷ Nandi's *Śiva Jñāna Siddhiyār*, which were both introduced in chapter 2. The *Īśvara Pariccheda* accentuates the logical force of arguments favoring one Supreme God, while the *Śiva Jñāna Siddhiyār* expounds a quasi-genetic theory of the interrelationship of nature and religion; it explains religious diversity while also defending the fact that there is one God, Śiva, who is sovereign over all. While both the *Śiva Jñāna Siddhiyār* and the *Īśvara Pariccheda* are rooted in scripture, they are not commentaries but theological treatises that draw on scripture to support reasoned positions. Let us consider them in turn.

NĀRĀYANA AS THE TRUE GOD IN VEDĀNTA DEŚIKA'S *ĪŚVARA PARICCHEDA*

As explained in chapter 2, the *Īśvara Pariccheda* is the section of Vedānta Deśika's *Nyāya Siddhāñjana* that deals with a number of disputed issues regarding the nature of God.[44] In it Deśika argues primarily on philosophical grounds to support the truth of scripture with concise reasonable arguments. Scripture tells us that Nārāyaṇa alone is Lord, and it is reasonable to make this claim. In making his arguments Deśika does occasionally appeal to scriptural texts, since he is arguing with opponents who agree that the Upaniṣads give information about the nature of reality, that the correct meaning of the Upaniṣads can be determined, and that what is known by reason and what is known by scripture are harmonious. But the distinctive contribution of the *Īśvara Pariccheda* has to do with the reasoning not the exegesis.

Like Rāmānuja, Deśika presumes that a proper notion of "Lord" entails an ample set of divine qualities, which he lists at the beginning of the *Īśvara*

44. As noted in chapter 2, the *Nyāya Siddhāñjana* is a Sanskrit-language defense of the Vaiṣṇava religion according to the Rāmānuja school's interpretation of Vedānta.

Pariccheda: the Lord is ruler over all, perfectly conscious and omniscient; everything depends on him totally; he is propitiated by all religious actions and gives all the fruits that accrue to all kinds of worship; he is the foundation for everything, the generator of all things that are made; all things other than his own knowledge and own self are his body; and all that he wishes is realized due simply to himself.[45] Deśika does not further explain these qualities but focuses instead on a series of more controversial issues, including (as we saw in chapter 2) why God's existence cannot be known by inference and (as concerns us here) why there can be only one Lord, who is Nārāyaṇa. Deśika believes that the beliefs of devotees of other gods are misplaced and connected with inevitably flawed philosophical positions.

In section 2 an adversary proposes the concept of *trimūrti*, which states, that the original divine power differentiates into three forms: Brahmā, Viṣṇu, and Śiva. Deśika rejects this view on several grounds, including that the division of the divine identity and power into three functional aspects is inconsistent with the claim of the Upaniṣads that the Lord is infinite, one without a second, the greatest, the supreme self, and so on.[46] Likewise, texts that seem to give independent status to Śiva or Brahmā merely reflect the traditions of a ritual polytheism in which multiple gods are invoked for multiple purposes. Such texts are not directly informative about God's nature and must be interpreted figuratively. The highest, perfect divinity is integral and whole and cannot be subdivided into specific deities with more limited roles. If there were a *trimūrti*, none of its three member gods, nor all three together, could reasonably merit the title "Lord."

After criticizing variant forms of the *trimūrti* theory—there are three equal gods; the three gods are all one self; and all three are surpassed by a still higher consciousness or by a greater God—Deśika concludes section 2 by stating, "It is proven that Nārāyaṇa alone is the highest cause, the object of meditation for those seeking liberation, the inner controller of all, etc. Thus too are rejected the theories that there are three forms which are equal, or oneness [of Self], or some different [higher reality] or yet another [superior] individual."[47] Once reason has corrected wrong ideas, what one learns from scripture—that God's name is Nārāyaṇa—will be accepted as decisive by reasonable people.

45. We can add these additional claims, which are defended in the course of the *Īśvara Pariccheda*: God is perfect and complete, one Lord beyond all sectarian distinctions, such as the trinity of Brahmā, Nārāyaṇa, and Śiva. God is both the material and efficient cause of the world. God is the all-encompassing reality; everything is his body, yet both conscious and nonconscious realities remain distinct within him. Although God is beyond human comprehension, language is not entirely useless, and God can be spoken of in terms of his strength, beauty, kindness, and so on. His eternal consort is the goddess Lakṣmī. In these statements, Deśika is echoing the beliefs of his Śrīvaiṣṇava community, beliefs elaborated elsewhere in Sanskrit and Tamil sources.

46. *Nyāya Siddhāñjana*, pp. 273–275.

47. Ibid., p. 284.

In section 3 Deśika considers the objection that no name can apply properly to God. Although the Lord is always complete and perfect, his specific relations to a finite world might nevertheless be multiple and in each case seemingly incomplete, since every worldly reality must be less than full or complete. What is perfect can never be fully present in any particular, limited context. Since perfect representation is impossible, multiple and diverse representations of the divine are therefore appropriate. Religious symbols, which present the divine in limited, partial ways, such as the image of three cooperating deities, can be respected as legitimate partial expressions of this always-partial presence of the divine. But no name or image is ever truly appropriate, and people can therefore rightly choose from the array of inadequate names, including Śiva, Nārāyaṇa, or Brahmā.[48]

This important opposing position seems to be drawn from the Nondualist Vedānta. Although the theologians of this school would agree on many issues with Deśika, they deny that it makes sense to attribute any particular name and personality to God. A brief explication of this view is worthwhile before returning to our explication of Deśika's position. In the *Advaita Dīpikā*,[49] Nṛsiṃha Āśramin takes up the topic of God—Brahman or Lord—at the end of a discussion of ultimate reality. An unnamed opponent says that it is appropriate to think of Brahman as really possessed of certain glorious qualities. There are authoritative texts that describe Brahman not only as omniscient and perfect in being, but also as possessed of more specific iconic signs, such as Nārāyaṇa's conch shell and war discus, his four arms, and so on. According to this theistic view, texts that deny that Brahman has qualities are merely correcting false views about the Lord and are not intended to rule out correct speech about God. This theistic adversary argues too that Śiva and other gods cannot be God and asserts that Brahman, the ultimate reality, Lord, and world-maker, is none other than Nārāyaṇa.

Nṛsiṃha Āśramin responds that the sectarian symbolizations of the divine found in Śaivism and Vaiṣṇavism are secondary, figurative, and do not merit heated debate; as secondary they are all permissible, but none is decisive. Such portrayals of God by positive words and images, common in sectarian traditions, are naive and overly literal. Sectarian devotees rely on misreadings of the Upaniṣads, wrongly favoring texts that attribute qualities to God over texts that deny such qualities. But texts that attribute qualities even like omniscience to Brahman are merely corrective of misconceptions and not positively informative about real qualities existing in Brahman. Texts that describe God positively with attributes must be interpreted in conformity with primary texts that deny that Brahman has qualities; sectarian texts apply to the higher reality, which can only be described in terms of perfection and cannot be reduced to the object of the material symbols of one or another sectarian group. So too, while a literal attribution of ornaments and weapons to Brahman pictured

48. Ibid., pp. 285–290.

49. Introduced in chapter 2, n. 47.

as Nārāyaṇa might be favorably received in devotional audiences, such attribution is of no use to a person seeking ultimate reality and liberation. The attributes must be relegated to a secondary place and consigned to the interest of lesser, ordinary people. In truth, Brahman is always identical with the qualities seemingly attributed to him, and the multiplicities suggested by language should not be interpreted as really indicative of actual distinctions in God. Because Nondualist Vedānta is not committed to particular names and forms but seeks Brahman beyond them, it occupies an advantageous higher ground, a vantage point from which sectarian debates seem profoundly mistaken.[50]

This line of Nondualist reasoning has the advantage of ending sectarian competition by relativizing all sectarian claims. But Deśika rejects it, refusing to accept that God has either an endless number of provisional names or no name at all. The Lord is indeed Nārāyaṇa, Viṣṇu. Deśika argues that the idea of "divine fullness" does not require imagining this divine reality to subsist in multiple, partial modes nor are we required to imagine that this reality can never be communicated in any enduring, successful human speech. Nothing about the idea of a perfect Lord requires one to postulate that this Lord is present only in partial forms, as multiple gods, for the sake of lesser people. The limitations of time, space, and human perception do not introduce limitations into God, who is not constricted by human limitations; he can enter into relationships with finite beings without himself being limited. As we shall see in chapter 4, Nārāyaṇa's divine descents into the world are taken by the Vaiṣṇava theologians as perfect examples of how the Lord does actually enter into relationship with humans under limiting conditions without surrendering divine unlimitedness. It is neither necessary nor plausible to assert that there are multiple deities sharing a single divine life nor that there is a higher transcendent reality beyond all imagination. It is more useful and makes better sense to believe in one God possessed fully of all the positive attributes appropriate to the highest reality. What is known from scripture is quite reasonable: Nārāyaṇa is the only God, and he enters time and space without detriment to his transcendence. This view makes sense, conforms to proper reasoning, and leaves neither room nor need for alternative views.

The Vaiṣṇavas, like many Christian theologians, give great importance to narrowing down and fixing God's identity: God is one, and Nārāyaṇa is God's name.[51] It makes sense to claim that God is one, perfect, and full even during divine interventions in the world, while alternative views are not as satisfying reasonably. Scripture and tradition tell us that this God is Nārāyaṇa. God

50. This position is spelled out in the third *pariccheda* of the *Advaita Dīpikā*, pp. 447–463. See Sharma on a modern version of the nondualist view of religions.

51. Ayyangar defends apologetics and offers a detailed refutation of Tamil-language writings, mostly from the 1970s, which in his view distorted Vaiṣṇavism and the religious history of Tamil Nadu.

can to some extent be known, and we know enough to rule out all kinds of mistaken representations of God.

While Christian theologians may hesitate to agree that God's name is Nārāyaṇa, on the whole the Vaiṣṇava principle should be familiar even to von Balthasar's heirs: "Our theological position is the most reasonable, coherent with scripture, adequate to what we know of God. Therefore other views are unreasonable, incoherent, and inadequate."

This is so even if Deśika's path to this conclusion is not the same as von Balthasar's. He does not identify a single unique form through which God is manifest and (to some extent) knowable by humans in an interpersonal encounter. While the Vaiṣṇava tradition was in fact aware of the importance of personal encounters with God, theologians like Deśika did not choose to argue the questions related to God's identity on the basis of interpersonal relationship and in accord with theories about primal divine self-expression. But such differences again indicate a common theological style. Deśika too is motivated by fidelity to his scriptures, the Upaniṣads. By his reading they point to a single material and spiritual world source inclusive of all human reality. To this he adds his own reasoned position as to why the essential divine attributes indicate that the one denoted by "God" cannot be differentiated into "gods" nor relegated to an ineffable and undifferentiated higher truth. In the end, he names this reality and cause "Nārāyaṇa," just as von Balthasar named the perfect form of God's self-manifestation "Jesus of Nazareth." On the whole, von Balthasar and Deśika are theologians like-minded enough that they can actually disagree.

ŚIVA AS GOD OF GODS IN ŚAIVA NATURAL THEOLOGY

Aruḷ Nandi's *Śiva Jñāna Siddhiyār* presents the Śaiva position on how the one true God stands in relation to the "natural" gods of the various religions. When Deśika focuses on the cogency of the philosophical claims in favor of the one Lord who can be positively identified as Nārāyaṇa, Aruḷ Nandi offers a cosmological and epistemological context for specific claims about Śiva as God and offers reasons why there might exist counterviews and practices. His exposition of the internally coherent true religion includes an inclusive but sharply hierarchical theory about why there are other religions and for what purpose. We highlight five features in the positive exposition of the Śaiva world view in *Śiva Jñāna Siddhiyār*'s *Supakkam* section, that is, its constructive account of Śaiva beliefs.[52]

First, from the start Aruḷ Nandi makes strong claims about Śiva. In the prologue to the *Supakkam* he introduces Śiva as the comprehensive source, savior, and foundation of the world:

52. As explained in chapter 2, *Śiva Jñāna Siddhiyār* is divided into two major parts, *Parapakkam* (Section on Others' Positions), which critiques other religious systems, and *Supakkam* (Section on Our Own Position), which sets forth a positive exposition of the religion of Śiva.

> [The Lord] who has no beginning, middle, or end, the infinite light whose form is grace and knowledge, and at whose side is the mother of everything; he is the prime jewel in the crown of the gods, praised by all the world, adorned with hanging coral braids and the half-moon, the highest one dancing in the arena where light pervades all. I place his lotus feet, adorned with pollen, on my head, and I let blossom my unfading great love for him.[53]

After the prologue, the first verse of the *Supakkam* defines Śiva as the source, sustenance, and end of everything, yet ever transcendent:

> As he, she, and it, altogether, the whole world comes, abides, then goes again, and therefore there must be one who gives it all. He is the cause in the beginning, he ends it, he creates it again. He is beginningless, free, in form pure consciousness, he alone remains and abides.[54]

Aruḷ Nandi's Śaiva theology begins with the recognition that Śiva alone is the explanatory principle for the world—beyond whom, by implication, no other is needed—and the rest of his treatise is dedicated to stating convincingly the coherence of this already-established faith.

Second, and to preview a theme we will return to in chapter 5, Aruḷ Nandi identifies the true religion as the one that is comprehensive and noncontradicted:

> The systems put forward along with their doctrines and doctrinal books are many, but they conflict with one another. One may ask which is the true system, which the true doctrine, and which the true book. The true system, doctrine and book is the one about which one does not argue, "This part is true, that part is not," and which includes everything within itself in right order. Hence, all these [systems, doctrines, books] are accounted for [in] the rare Vedas and Śaiva Traditional Texts, and these two are placed beneath the sacred feet of Hara.[55]

Other religions are fragmented; they can find coherence only outside themselves and only with reference to Śiva.

Aruḷ Nandi's third and most complex point is that the world is an integral reality differentiated on natural, psychological, social, and religious levels, which parallel and reflect one another. Distinctions regarding true and false religions and their various gods are not merely conventional but are deeply rooted in the nature of reality. True religion—Vedic, Śaiva—is from the start inscribed in the nature of the world itself and so too the norms by which one

53. I.1, p. 113.

54. I.1, p. 117.

55. VIII.2.13, p. 229.

56. In the third topic under *sūtra* 2 (see *Śiva Jñāna Siddhiyār*, pp. 178–183), Aruḷ Nandi elaborates his account of the genesis of the world, following in most respects the analysis worked out in the old Sāṃkhya school of philosophy. This genetic account of religious and theological differences can be compared with the argument in the *Rudra Gītā* considered earlier in this chapter.

delineates and specifies the world religiously. The gods are among the "natural phenomena" and so is the inclination to worship them.[56]

The world can thus be explained in a way that also accounts for the variety of religious beliefs as part of the overall natural way of things. Accordingly, Aruḷ Nandi's account of the genesis of the universe as a natural and religious whole is rather complicated; it takes into account these physical, psychological, intellectual, religious and spiritual differences, as well as the differences among deities. Reality is divided into a number of elements, which are in turn subdivided in various ways; the total number of elements is thirty-six. There are five pure, real elements: Śiva, Śiva's consort power (Śakti), Sadāśiva (Śiva's auspicious form), Maheśvara (Śiva's identity as Great Lord), and his pure knowledge. Secondary but closely related to these is his marvelous creative power, the one *māyā*. This *māyā* generates three further realities: time, order, and component intellectual powers.[57] In turn, these generate a sequence of three more: knowledge, which generates passion, which generates person.[58] The one *māyā* plus the six generated realities (time, order, intellectual powers, knowledge, passion, and person) exist in both pure and impure forms, generating additional elements: time generates nature in its constituent qualities, (consciousness, understanding, ego, and mind) to which then are added the five basic elements, which are, the essential forms of sound, touch, visible form, taste, and smell. Ego then differentiates into three levels of increasingly gross nature: the five organs of knowledge, the five organs of action, and the five material elements in their basic (and then manifest forms). We therefore end up with thirty-six elements—five pure, seven mixed (pure and impure), and twenty-four impure:

Five pure elements: Śiva, Śiva's consort power, Sadāśiva, Maheśvara, Pure Knowledge
Seven mixed elements: Māyā, time, order, component intellectual powers, knowledge, passion, person
Twenty-four impure elements: consciousness, understanding, ego, mind, plus the five basic elements, five organs of knowledge, five organs of action, five material elements

The five basic elements generate manifest forms:[59]

Basic Elements	*Manifest Basic Elements*
essence of sound	ether
essence of touch	air
essence of visible form	fire
essence of taste	water
essence of smell	earth

57. That is, *kalā*. Thus we have this sequence: Śiva, Śiva's consort power, his auspicious form, his identity as Lord, pure knowledge, *māyā*, time, order, component intellectual powers, knowledge, passion, and person.

58. II.3.54, p. 179.

59. This chart is based on VIII.2.64–68, pp. 181–182.

In turn, each manifest element differentiates in a series that is perceptual, linguistic, and theological:

Manifest Basic Elements	*Shape*	*Color*	*Sacred Sound*	*Image*	*Genetic Status*	*Deity*
ether	circle	blue	a	ambrosia	pure *māyā*	Sadāśiva
air	hexagon	black	ya	six points	pure *māyā*	Maheśvara
fire	triangle	red	ra	svastika	mixed *māyā*	Rudra
water	crescent	white	va	lotus	impure *māyā*	Viṣṇu
earth	square	gold	la	sword	impure *māyā*	Brahmā

Religions and their gods are parts of this complex network of manifest elements both as natural phenomena and social phenomena (sectarian communities). The manifest, lower forms of Śiva himself (Sadāśiva, Maheśvara, Rudra) and also rival gods Viṣṇu and Brahmā are accounted for as parts of the larger, more complex natural and social reality. Those gods, their devotees, and their religions are natural components of reality, traceable back to ever-simpler forms and, ultimately, to Lord Śiva. Cults of deities other than Śiva are a predictable consequence of the same generative process that shapes the other features of creation:

> The several false systems are based in the fundamental elements, from the several material elements up to the confusing power.[60] The six true ways of knowledge, beginning from the Śaiva, have their respective places in the real elements, knowledge and the others. But the Lord himself is beyond all of this.
>
> Śiva, his Consort Power, the pure Sound, the pure Point,[61] Sadāśiva, the shining lord [Maheśvara], the rejoicing Rudra himself, and Viṣṇu and Brahmā: though only one, he becomes each one, four without form, four with form, one as both; the one Lord thus divides into nine and becomes manifest.[62]

Aruḷ Nandi does not spell out the specific correlation between erroneous religious world views and the constituent natural elements, but the idea seems to be that the more or less erroneous systems—criticized in the apologetic section of the *Śiva Jñāna Siddhiyār*, the *Parapakkam*—can be coded and located according to corresponding levels of material grossness, for instance, on charts such as above. Only the highest form of Śaivism is entirely beyond material limitation and defect.

As in Sudarśana Sūri's treatment of the *Varāha Purāṇa*, here too we find a naturalistic and genetic interpretation of religions. Description and genetic theory undergird theological judgment. The gods and their worshipers are constituted as component parts of reality as it now is. In the future, of course,

60. That is, *māyā* in its deluding form.

61. That is, *nāda* and *bindu*.

62. II.4.73–74, p. 184. The four without form are Śiva, his consort power, pure sound, and pure point; the four with form are Maheśvara, Rudra, Viṣṇu, and Brahmā; the one with and without form is Sadāśiva.

changes in their natural makeup will enable them to advance to more sophisticated levels of being, deity, and worship.

Once the various gods and their religions are plotted on this natural map of reality, they can also be ranked socially as more or less "inner" or "outer" in terms of their distance from the truth of Śaivism. Aruḷ Nandi arranges them concentrically around Śaivism. Those most different and thus most in error are located farthest away from his own Śaiva theology, while the less erroneous are placed closer to the inner cosmos and the realm of truly efficacious religious practice:

> People leave the outer systems, enter the orthodox fold, and move through the paths of the traditional texts, the various stages of life and their duties. They practice hard asceticism, learn many difficult sciences, master the Vedas and reflect on the Purāṇas. Thus they come to understand very clearly the truth of the Veda, and attain the Śaiva way. After practicing right behavior, right action, and right integration, by means of knowledge they reach the feet of Śiva.[63]

Sketching a clear and comprehensive account of other beliefs does not render them all satisfactory, nor does it render the plight of other believers hopeless. Aruḷ Nandi believes that movement inward from the outer paths to the Śaiva way is possible, even if the journey is difficult and slow.

Finally, Aruḷ Nandi drives home the point of Śiva's superiority by specific references to Śiva's chief divine rivals, Brahmā and Viṣṇu. They are denied glorious deeds, which might establish them as truly potent divine figures. Like Vedānta Deśika, Aruḷ Nandi rejects a compromise *trimūrti* and instead attributes everything to Śiva's (Hara's) power:

> If one asks how the gods Brahmā and the rest can also be forms of Hara, we respond that it is because of his creative Power that these gods perform their functions at all. Should one object that since these gods do perform such functions, no additional god such as Hara is needed—we respond that each god performs only one function.[64]

We close this section by noting one further polemical development in the other part of the *Śiva Jñāna Siddhiyār*, the *Parapakkam*, which is a serial presentation and refutation of positions that diverge from the Śaiva viewpoint. In the *Parapakkam* Aruḷ Nandi's attack on Pañcarātra is not limited to a critique of the idea of God's fourfold and gradual involvement in the world nor of other Pañcarātra doctrines. Rather, as we shall see in chapter 4, it deals primarily with the folly of the narratives of the divine descents of Nārāyaṇa into the world. Aruḷ Nandi directly criticizes the Vaiṣṇava belief that the divine descents are God's salvific interventions in the world. Such descents serve no good purpose and do not reflect a proper understanding of God. They show only the weakness of Nārāyaṇa, who is both dependent on Śiva and seemingly cursed to continue being born into undesirable bodily forms.

63. VIII.2.11, p. 227.
64. I.3.60, p. 157.

As a theologian, Aruḷ Nandi holds a two-edged sword. He is inclusive in his *Supakkam* account of why other religions continue to exist, and he is polemical in his *Parapakkam* critique of Vaiṣṇava religiosity. Everything and everyone is accounted for in a way that makes clear the supremacy of Śiva. The gods are diminished, but their existence is not denied. Perhaps a few unbelievers will get the point and change their ways, but on the whole Aruḷ Nandi may be simply vindicating the Śaiva community's own faith by criticizing others. The wise will be able to see that both reasoning and scripture point to Lord Śiva. Others, those who disagree, are mentioned primarily in order to explain who "we" are. The beliefs of the Śaiva community are true and convincing, while the error of alternative views will be evident not only to the faithful but also to all reasonable persons.

Naming God in an Interreligious Theological Context

Steadfast believers who are theologians persist in asking who God is, how God relates to the world and acts within it, how God is best named and invoked, and how the truth about God is to be presented in terms recognizable to reasonable persons. Differences aside, the same activity and the same goal—identifying God—seems to be at stake in both the Hindu and Christian traditions. These are fellow theologians engaged in the same activity, faith seeking the terms of an adequate understanding of who God is and how God is to be named.

Von Balthasar, Aruḷ Nandi, and Vedānta Deśika agree in seeking to demonstrate the coherence, plausibility, and scriptural foundation of specific claims about the religion that is true and dedicated to the true God. All three firm up their theologies by relegating other religions and other gods to secondary status. They are willing to discount the authority and status of the competing gods, even if Hindu theologians usually stop short of denying their existence altogether. Von Balthasar argues that Jesus Christ alone can be the true revelation of God. The Hindu theologians argue similarly that only Nārāyaṇa, or only Śiva, is the true God. For von Balthasar and these Hindu theologians, God is at the center, the measure of all else; competing religious personas are peripheral at best. None is unaware of popular and elite tendencies toward compromise positions–that various Gods are members of a *trimūrti* or that all religions symbolize the same underlying truth—and none accepts such compromises.

These examples indicate a limited but significant theological ground shared by some Hindu and Christian theologians; there are large areas of agreement as well as some significant disagreements. Since they want to name God and say something about God's character, they share more than a generic philosophical conviction that a world-maker exists. On the whole, von Balthasar, Deśika, and Aruḷ Nandi are fellow theologians engaged in the recognizably similar theological and apologetic project of defending their community's view of God by similar methods: "Our view makes perfect sense, while your view surely does not." Had the three been familiar with each other's works, they would have had no problem understanding each other's projects, even if they name God differently and agree that the difference is significant.

Once we admit that there is a shared interreligious theological inquiry into the topic of God, which goes beyond the question of the existence of God, we can consider the nature of God and God's behavior in a comparative and dialogical theology. We can attend to similarities and differences and examine more closely how theologians in different traditions reflect on the topic of the one true God.

Many Christian and Hindu theologians agree that properly used the term *God* indicates a person with certain qualities, such as pure consciousness, omnipotence, independence, benevolence toward the human race, and a lack of imperfections. To speak of God is really to speak of "the one God," the person who is "Lord of all." One can argue about which religion most appropriately and adequately identifies God, but at some point provisional judgments have to be made. These Hindu and Christian theologians seem to agree that such arguments and judgments should be attempted and that compromises should be rejected: God is not merely an absolute beyond all names nor a transcendent godhead knowable in multiple forms.

Von Balthasar is of course not entirely like his Hindu colleagues. Proposing that true religion has to do with the issue of God's self-communication to humans—we know God as God reveals himself to us, not otherwise—von Balthasar believes that everything has to do with understanding how it is that God, who can be known only when he freely communicates himself, can be encountered within the limited confines of human capacities. Self-disclosure is the key, and God chooses to be fully self-disclosive and communicative only in Jesus Christ. Therefore, von Balthasar reasons, no imaginable alternative form, if in any way different from Christ, could be complete or correct, and of course no alternative is needed.

Unlike von Balthasar, Deśika and Aruḷ Nandi do not formulate the argument for true religion and the recognition of the true God in terms of an encounter with the revealing God. The portrayal of the divine–human relationship is clearly interpersonal for Vaiṣṇava and Śaiva theologians too, but they do not rely on a theology of divine self-disclosure for their determination of who God is. Rather, they seek the best possible explanation of the world in relation to God and accordingly the most adequate identification of the God who is explanatory of the world. They begin with a sense that the world, human beings, and every human religious formulation already exist within the reality of God, and their concern is to trace a plausible path from variously limited human religious experiences back to the God from whom all have come forth. True religion has to do with recognizing one's proper place within the whole that is God's own reality.

By Aruḷ Nandi's calculation, there is not just one special way of knowing God. Since everything exists within God, one begins to know God by knowing one's own immediate reality as best one can. Although Deśika thinks that God can be most completely known by humans only through a gracious revelation, he also believes that God *is* Brahman, which is the material cause of the world and hence the most immediate object of our every experience.

From von Balthasar's vantage point, one can easily fault the theologies of Sudarśana Sūri or Aruḷ Nandi for a lack of openness to divine transcendence and the utterly gracious self-communication of God to humans in a perfect divine–human form of communication. Similarly, if Sudarśana Sūri and Aruḷ Nandi lived today, both might have similarly deeply considered doubts about von Balthasar's blindness to the idea that all natural and social realities already exist within God and manifest God in the specific details of their natural and social reality. But if such judgments are merely stated and not thought through in a comparative and dialogical context, they tell us nothing decisive about these theologians. As we learn more and recognize common theological ground, a priori judgments are more clearly seen to be provisional and insufficient, starting points and not conclusions in the interreligious theological conversation.

Rather, all these positions are to be taken seriously. There is a powerful coherence and consistency to von Balthasar's argument about Christ as the unique, adequate form of God's person, but he makes it depend on the model of divine self-revelation he puts forward as central to the divine–human encounter; if God is to be known, Christ is the one form through which that knowledge is possible. Aruḷ Nandi is persuasive in explaining how the world, composed of all conscious and nonconscious beings, coheres in relation to the one Lord, Śiva, but this persuasiveness too presupposes that everything does indeed stand in an evolving, dependent relationship with God. Deśika is forceful in arguing against confining the human apprehension of the divine to what seems possible within the boundaries of ordinary human knowing, and so he disposes of simpler alternatives, which leave the divine necessarily indeterminate. In the end, Deśika really knows that Nārāyaṇa is Lord.

Some who ponder our treatment of von Balthasar and the Hindu theologians may conclude that apologetics, in Christian or Hindu forms, is not intellectually cogent. People know what they know on religious topics and rarely if ever change their minds significantly. Studying a different theological tradition is not likely to change anything. Apologetics then is for the most part merely preaching and poor preaching at that. Even more than the arguments aimed at demonstrating God's existence, these arguments may seem to satisfy only believers and have little compelling force for outsiders.

We can certainly agree that believers like von Balthasar, Rāmānuja, and the other Hindu theologians studied here do not begin their inquiries in order to explore uncharted territory nor do they process data neutrally. They want to affirm answers already known within their believing communities. Nevertheless, one cannot so simply dispose of the matter. The point of apologetics is in part to demonstrate the plausibility of one's beliefs in a way that is comprehensible even to persons who do not share those beliefs. Reasonable believers are inclined toward apologetics, since they think that a good case can be made for believing some fairly specific things about God. The divine character and likely mode of behavior can be described in certain ways, and other ways can be ruled out as not true. The theologian who puts forward theological arguments seriously is also seriously proposing that his or her beliefs are reasonable. In turn, it is this serious reasonability that saves the beliefs from a splendid isolation in which they are immune to the questions and critiques of outsiders. One can make a plausible theological case for naming and characterizing God in a certain way: God is manifest in Jesus Christ, who is the form; Śiva is the Lord, who is always known when reality is finally clearly perceived; Brahman is Nārāyaṇa, the perfect reality, who alone is the maximal object of human apprehension. Such arguable claims help make possible a theology that crosses religious boundaries. But once they start to make the case for the truth of what they believe, they are risking dialogue with all thinking persons, including believers from other religious traditions. The truth of my beliefs opens rather than closes the way for dialogue.

Theological confessions can be plausible today only in an interreligious context and therefore must be argued with comparative and dialogical sensitivities. However mysterious God may be and however frail human language about God, it is still possible to speak of God's character, and God's way of acting and thus to give some content to the project of naming God. God is very near to humans, accessible and gracious; if one approaches God, who is manifest and accessible, one is enabled to overcome the frailties and flaws of the human condition. To say that God is manifest in Jesus, or that God is Nārāyaṇa, or that God is Śiva, is actually to agree on this divine condescension. This point is not attenuated by the outstanding differences that divide the Hindu and Christian faiths.

To participate in today's interreligious theological conversation, those making confessional claims about God's identity must therefore allow them to be examined in light of other such confessional claims. Even core beliefs about God's identity, if argued theologically, can profitably be assessed in terms of the reasons put forward on their behalf. Thereafter, they can still be reaffirmed but only as reexpressed intelligently in awareness of others' theologies, similarities among the claims made, and the reasoning behind them. To do this, theologians will have to learn to make their case without caricaturing others' beliefs or assuming them to be more theologically naïve than their own. Believers need not be less firm or articulate in their beliefs; they just need to be better informed, including about where the uniqueness of their beliefs does not lie.

Perhaps one theology is correct, and others are in error. How can God be the Father of our Lord Jesus Christ *and* Śiva *and* Nārāyaṇa? Roberto de Nobili thought that one could make claims about the true God that would be cogent even in interreligious contexts. He believed that there was sufficient common ground upon which one might explore God's identity, rule out inadequate conceptions of God, and thus reasonably draw listeners at least to the edge of faith. In the end, he thought, it is simply more reasonable to believe in the Christian God than in a Hindu god. He thought too that he could present the proper and reasonable way of divine action in the world in a way that any reasonable Hindu could understand. For if God meets the standards implied by the term *God* then, on the whole, God can be expected to act in ways we find reasonable and morally responsible. Because the presentation of God in the Christian tradition is more coherent and responsible than any other such representation, it is reasonable to assert that the Christian God is the true God.

Up to a certain point, de Nobili's reasoning is likely to have resonated well with his Hindu audience, since many Hindu theologians would agree on the validity of reasoning about God, God's likely action, and hence God's name as well. To a certain extent, we can know and name God, and likewise we can exclude unlikely characteristics and erroneous names. As I admitted at the end of chapter 2, in retrospect de Nobili's project of conversion through reasoned argumentation may seem to place too much confidence in reason's ability to clear the way to the Christian truth. Nevertheless, he rightly saw that reasoning offers a real basis for interreligious theological communication and that it cannot be left aside in considerations about God and God's existence. If one starts to talk reasonably about God's existence, further questions about God's character, God's deeds, and God's identity arise and can hardly be avoided. Provided a theologian is willing to do the work, there is no reason not to discuss and argue God's identity in an interreligious, comparative, and dialogical context.

If the examples adduced in this chapter are significant, it seems evident that there can be a sufficiently rich set of shared criteria and methods so that Hindu and Christian theologians can converse and argue profitably about who God is, and the expectation exists that some theologians might change their minds and their allegiances. Most Hindu theologians believe firmly that ignorance can be eliminated, and most Christian theologians come from traditions that attest to the possibility of conversion. It would be ironic if theologians in either tradition thought that interreligious conversations about God's name and character could never inform anyone nor persuade anyone to change their theological positions.

Even today then, whenever God's name and character form a topic of serious theological inquiry, well-informed theological reasoning should command our attention. The obligation to think about God's identity and argue the possibilities in an informed interreligious context is urgent today and, I hope, not easily postponed or deferred. Indeed, only if we share something of de Nobili's confidence in the value of reasoned, informed argumentation will theologians be able to construct an account of God's identity that might actually be persuasive in today's interreligious realm.

To put it simply then, the fact of an interreligious common ground requires us to think in different terms about the quest to know God. We must not ask only whether theologians who believe in different gods and judge religions accordingly can nevertheless talk reasonably to one another about what they have in common as theologians. We must also push further and ask whether theologians, some of whom are Hindu and some of whom are Christian, can draw on shared theological resources in order to make lucid and even compelling to one another those specific faith claims that seem to divide them.

There are still other issues to be considered in thinking about God in an interreligious Christian and Hindu context. The comparison put forward in this chapter was not entirely symmetrical. Von Balthasar's meditations on Christ as the perfect form of God's encounter with humans are not exactly parallel with the Hindu meditations on human reality as inscribed within God's own reality; von Balthasar's God is manifest in Jesus of Nazareth in this world, while the Hindu theologians are reflecting on the world within the reality of God. Such differences could be major, but in fact even at this point the Christian and Hindu traditions have much in common. Many Hindu and most Christian theologians believe that God can enter the world in specific ways. In chapter 4 we will introduce another degree of intensity to the theological conversation across religious boundaries as we examine how a Christian theologian and some Hindu theologians defend and explain what it means to say that God enters the world and assumes an embodied human form.

4

Making Sense of Divine Embodiment

Many Christian and Hindu theologians agree that there is a God, maker of the world, and that there is only one such God, possessed of certain superlative qualities and likely to act in certain proper ways. Though God is mystery, God can be known well enough that he can be named; God is the Father revealed in Jesus Christ; God is Śiva; God is Nārāyaṇa. Such theologians agree in principle that it is possible and valuable to name God, even if they disagree on what God's proper name actually is.

Many of these same theologians (along with those who disagree with them about God's creative activity and God's identity) also hold that there are advantages and problems connected with asserting further that the God who makes the world could or should also have a body, as a necessary instrument for making things or for other kinds of activities in the world. In chapter 2 we saw that divine embodiment is an issue upon which people in different religious traditions can form opinions, take sides, and argue within and across religious boundaries. For those not disposed to accept the idea of a maker God known inductively from the world, the problems connected with divine embodiment serve as convenient obstacles with which to cast doubt on the induction itself. Even sympathetic theologians can agree that most notions of embodiment do not cohere well with the idea of a perfect God.

We also saw several efforts to construct a plausible attitude toward embodiment that would be satisfying at least to theists. Richard Swinburne, in agreement with Jayanta and other Nyāya logicians, affirms that by definition "God" indicates a being who is incorporeal and free from the various material limitations to which embodied beings are subject. But he adds that a principle of divine incorporeality does not rule out the possibility that God might freely assume a body: "By saying that God is essentially bodiless, I mean that, although he may sometimes have a body, he is not dependent on his body in any way."[1] When Swinburne takes up the topic of the Incarnation later in the same work, he denies that there are good reasons for saying divine embodiment is impossible. As God's free choice, incarnation is possible without upsetting the definition of God's perfection both metaphysical (omnipotence, omniscience, etc.) and moral (sinlessness, non-temptation to evil, etc.).[2]

The Hindu and Buddhist theologians who argue for and against the existence of God likewise argue about whether it makes sense to say that God has a body. The charge that a maker God must have a body is recognized as a possibly fatal flaw in the argument for a world-maker. An embodied God would be constricted by the inevitable limitations of material form and would be dependent on whoever made the divine body. Jayanta, our representative logician, counters simply by saying that there is no rule to the effect that only an embodied maker can manipulate material things. The soul affects the body without relying on yet another body in order to do this, and analogously, God can be appreciated as an incorporeal controller of corporeal things.[3]

In the Vedic tradition of worship, particularly as formalized in Mīmāṃsā theological texts, gods were not pictured as having bodies, and it was not important to imagine them that way. On the contrary, as admitted in *Pūrva Mīmāṃsā Sūtras* 9.1.4–10, various inconveniences arise if one supposes that gods actually have bodies. These supposedly embodied deities never actually seem to eat the offerings made to them. Moreover, if the gods were embodied beings located in time and space, they would not be able to attend more than

1. Swinburne (1994), p. 127.

2. In *The Existence of God*, Swinburne defends the propriety of divine embodiment as follows: Given what one can know reasonably about God and God's benevolent attitude toward the world, it is also reasonable to think that this God might decide to become effectively involved in human affairs by taking a bodily form. God may decide that the lamentable state of human affairs requires atonement. Since there is no human who is in fact capable of making the atonement or of whom it can be demanded, God may likewise decide to become incarnate in order to carry it out. To solidify the results of the atonement, the human race requires a supreme leader and inspirer who can found the necessary institutions in which his work would be continued, and God may decide to come as that leader. Finally, God may decide that it is good to share the burden of suffering imposed for good purposes on the human race. Swinburne proposes these points as rational criteria by which one might judge which scenarios and candidates for incarnation are more probable. But, I speculate, he would also not object to identifying the Christian version of divine incarnation as more probable than competing views. See *The Existence of God*, pp. 239–240. Drawing approvingly on Thomas Aquinas, Swinburne offers five reasons for the Incarnation: human nature is good, and it is fitting that God adopt it; by adopting it, God shows the great dignity of the human; by adopting it, God shows the greatness of his love; in adopting it, God gives a good example as to how humans should properly live; and finally, although God can teach the truth in other ways (e.g., by prophets who are not divine), the teaching is strengthened when taught by God incarnate. Swinburne adds another reason: if, as he believes, a plausible theodicy suggests that suffering can have positive value, God's incarnation allows him to demonstrate this by suffering in his embodied form (pp. 218–220).

3. See chapter 2 of this volume.

one sacrifice at a time. Nor should Vedic texts be read as intending to indicate that gods do have bodies. Texts that seem to indicate divine corporeality by pointing to the "swift feet" of one god or the "mighty arm" of another do not intend to inform us about divine physiques but rather serve only to inspire people to believe that gods are swift and strong in responding to prayers, for example.[4]

Agreeing with the Mīmāṃsā theologians that the gods are secondary but reusing this tenet for their own purposes, at *Uttara Mīmāṃsā Sūtras* I.3.26–33 the Vedānta theologians take a contrary position and argue that it is necessary that the gods undergo embodiment. They ask whether the gods are eligible for knowledge of Brahman and for the required Upaniṣadic study leading up to that knowledge, and they decide that gods do have bodies. Although the Nondualist Vedānta theologians had no special interest in gods or in sacrifices to gods, they chose to argue this way because they wanted to include gods in the Vedānta economy of salvation. Gods too needed to be saved by knowledge of Brahman learned from the Upaniṣads, but the desire to learn becomes urgent only when one is upset by the unpleasant, painful, and limiting experiences that accompany embodiment. If they are troubled by the inconveniences of bodily experiences the gods will, like everyone else, be motivated to learn the meditation practices that lead to liberation.[5]

All these Christian and Hindu arguments about divine embodiment are significant, but of themselves they do not lead to serious reflection on the positive importance of asserting that God—as opposed to gods—has a body. In theistic environs, the topic demands and eventually receives more ample consideration. I therefore turn now to a Christian theologian and several Hindu theologians who pursue a more developed theology of divine embodiment and assert that it is religiously important to affirm that God, though uncompromised in divine qualities, can assume a body. For an appreciation of divine embodiment in the modern Christian theological tradition, we turn to the influential German theologian Karl Rahner. Thereafter we will examine several Hindu theological views of divine embodiment.

Devotion to the Incarnate God: Karl Rahner on the Sacred Heart

The core of Rahner's theology of the Incarnation is spelled out in an important essay, "On the Theology of the Incarnation." Two points are key. First, the Incarnation is a superlative act of the gracious God, a mystery that could never be merely deduced. Second, however, Incarnation should not be misunderstood mythologically as an alien intrusion on the world of humans. To be human is already to be open to the infinite, by one's very nature expectant of the gracious act of divine incarnation:

4. See *Pūrva Mīmāṃsā Sūtras* 9.1.4–10; Clooney, 1988a.
5. On this Mīmāṃsā-Vedānta debate, see Clooney, 1988a.

> One can only say what man is by expressing what he is concerned with and what is concerned with him. But that is the boundless, the nameless. Man is therefore mystery in his essence, his nature. He is not in himself the infinite fullness of the mystery which concerns him, for that fullness is inexhaustible, and the primordial form of all that is mystery to us. But he is mystery in his real being and its ultimate reason, in his nature, which is the humble, conscious state of being referred to the fullness, the form of the mystery which we ourselves are.[6]

Our human mystery opens into the mystery of God, and divine embodiment demonstrates to us the fullness of who we are. The fundamental choice before humans therefore is "the acceptance or rejection of the mystery which we are."[7]

In light of this human openness, the Incarnation is to be understood not as "an incidental activity which could perhaps be left aside" but as the fullness and completion of the meaning of being human "when the nature which surrenders itself to the mystery of the fullness belongs so little to itself that it becomes the nature of God himself. The incarnation of God is therefore the unique, supreme case of the total actualization of human reality, which consists of the fact that man is insofar as he gives up himself."[8] As humans are, so Christ is par excellence. In Christ humans see the divinely accomplished fullness of the meaning of being human. The Incarnation is thus both a mysterious work of God and the most human of all events. It is also the occasion for a deeper sense of God's nearness, which evokes a devout response:

> But when the longing for the absolute nearness of God, the longing, incomprehensible in itself, which alone makes anything bearable, looks for where this nearness comes—not in the postulates of the spirit, but in the flesh and the housings of the earth: then no resting place can be found except in Jesus of Nazareth, over whom the star of God stands, before whom alone one has the courage to bend the knee and weeping happily to pray: "And the Word was made flesh and dwelt among us."[9]

Rahner's well-known essay "The Theology of the Symbol" begins and ends with reference to the traditional, several centuries-old cult of the Sacred Heart of Jesus as the symbol—in Jesus, in the flesh—of God's love for the human race. In the essay Rahner proposes the heart as a true symbol, truly expressive of God's embodied love for humans. The Heart of Jesus, the embodied Word of God, is a fleshly symbol truly expressive of God's identity. Near the end of the essay Rahner distances himself from the vaguer and easier view that heart somehow symbolizes "the inner center of the person, which realizes itself and expresses itself in the bodily existence." Instead, he evokes a richer and more vivid older sense in which the heart is a concrete and powerful symbol:

6. Rahner, "On the Theology of the Incarnation," *Theological Investigations* 4:108.
7. Ibid.
8. Ibid., pp. 109–110.
9. Ibid., p. 120.

> In medieval tradition and in St. Margaret Mary, "heart" is used spontaneously in the broad sense; it does not designate simply the "bodily heart," nor does it designate simply the "inwardness" of Christ in the metaphorical sense. It is used as a "primordial word" of religious speech, and signifies from the start the unity of both [i.e., bodily heart and inwardness]—a unity which has not to be created subsequently, as when an object is linked to a sign exterior to it as its symbolic representation.[10] In this Heart we encounter God as present, since "reality and its appearance in the flesh are forever one in Christianity, unconfused and inseparable."[11]

In volume 3 of Rahner's *Theological Investigations* we find three essays related to the cult of the Sacred Heart. Two essays are brief and in the form of notes,[12] but the third, "The Eternal Significance of the Humanity of Jesus for Our Relationship with God," offers a more complete consideration of God's incarnate presence. In it Rahner explains the problem of finding the divine in the world as a problem of balance between extremes. Jesus Christ is the mean between two one-sided possibilities. When there is too strong a sense of the sacredness of the world, not balanced by a powerful enough sense of God's transcendence, we end up with the extreme situation in which every material thing is considered divine. An overly vivid sense of the numinous, the sacred-in-things, promotes a multiplication of the divine, in what Rahner calls polytheism. Things are invested with a power not properly connected back to God but in a sense replacing God: "A polytheistic, or polytheistically tinged, enslaving veneration of the powers and forces of this world is merely the other side of the same guilty dilemma: the numinous nature of the world without the one, living God."[13]

This is bad enough, but it is just as dangerous to place too much emphasis on God's difference from the world. Too strong a sense of God's otherness threatens to strip the world of its embodied, created holiness and substitutes instead a superimposed "false, basically unchristian, pantheistic or theophanistic conception of God."[14] Intriguingly, Rahner here makes one of his rare allusions to Indian thought and uses the Sanskrit word *māyā* to name

10. "The Theology of the Symbol," *Theological Investigations* 4:251–252. In taking up the specific piety and theology of the Sacred Heart, Rahner presupposes, of course, that his readers are already familiar with the tradition of Sacred Heart devotion; the seventeenth-century private revelations to Margaret Mary Alacoque, the ubiquitous pictures of Jesus with his Heart exposed, which were common in Catholic households and (to some extent) still are; and various theological interpretations of the devotion as in some way symbolic of God's love for humans. The fact of this familiar piety must be kept in mind, as a center of gravity in relation to which Rahner balances his more elaborate reflection on the relationship between God and the world and on the more specific question of how the incarnate form of the Son, Jesus of Nazareth, figures essentially and centrally into how humans relate to God. Because Rahner believes it, he can begin to explain it.

11. Ibid., p. 252.

12. "'Behold this Heart!': Preliminaries to a Theology of Devotion to the Sacred Heart" and "Some Theses for a Theology of Devotion to the Sacred Heart."

13. P. 41.

14. P. 40.

this danger of pantheism and theophanism. *Māyā* seems to mark the cheapening of the reality of created things to which a crudely exaggerated sense of God's transcendence leads:

> [God] is not "the truly real" which like a vampire draws to himself and so to speak sucks out the proper reality of things different from himself; he is not the *esse omnium*. Things created by him are not *maya*, the veil, which dissolves like mist before the sun the more one recognizes the Absolute, i.e. the more religious one becomes.[15]

One might love such a God, Rahner admits, but only as one might love the absolute, which is elsewhere and beyond heaven and earth. It is quite different to love the God who made heaven and earth.

On the one side a world sacred and devoid of God; on the other, a God entirely separate from the world. After constructing this scenario, Rahner discovers that the Christian position stands between the extremes. He urges his readers to resist disassociating a sense of God from a sense of the holiness of the world. The Christian goal is a proper *latria*, an ability to worship the one transcendent God even in and through this-worldly, material realities. The goal of the Christian understanding of the world is to render this *latria* to the God who is fully and uniquely present in Christ, who is the apex of human development:

> For, according to the testimony of the faith, this created human nature is the indispensable and permanent gateway through which everything created must pass if it is to find the perfection of its eternal validity before God. He is the gate and the door, the Alpha and Omega, the all-embracing in whom, as the one who has become man, creation finds its stability. He who sees him, sees the Father, and whoever does not see him—God become man—also does not see God.[16]

On this basis Rahner offers a clear-cut judgment on the difference between encountering God in Christ and all other ways of encountering God. The way of Christ is contrasted with the way of an impersonal absolute, which remains always an unattainable horizon beyond human reach:

> We may speak about the *impersonal* Absolute without the non-absolute flesh of the Son, but the *personal* Absolute can be truly *found* only in him, in whom dwells the fullness of the Godhead in the earthly vessel of his humanity. Without him every absolute of which we speak or which we imagine we attain by mystical flight is in the last analysis merely the never attained, objective correlative of that empty and hollow, dark and despairingly self-consuming infinity which we are ourselves: the infinity of dissatisfied finiteness, but not the blessed infinity of truly limitless fullness. This, however, can be found only where Jesus of Nazareth is, this finite concrete being, this contingent being, who remains in all eternity.[17]

15. Ibid.
16. P. 43.
17. Pp. 43–44. Emphases in the original.

Here too, Rahner recognizes the Sacred Heart as a powerful symbol which captures what is at stake in every Christian's encounter with God in Christ: "If the 'Heart of Jesus' means the original center of the human reality of the Son of God, then there must be a basic religious act which is mediated by and goes through this center to God." This heart is not merely "the indefinable, nameless reality of God alone"; it really does indicate the human heart.[18] But human language fails at this point, so one must rely all the more on the simple mystery the Heart presents to us:

> One can be a Christian without ever having heard anything in human words about the Sacred Heart of Jesus. But one cannot be a Christian without continually passing, by a movement of the spirit supported by the Holy Ghost, through the humanity of Christ and, in that humanity, through its unifying center which we call the heart.[19]

Aside from the disparaging allusion to *māyā* and the affirmation of the superiority of the encounter with God that occurs in Christ, in these essays Rahner never asks explicitly what this focus on Jesus as God incarnate might mean regarding how we are to think of non-Christians. But it is clear that Rahner is passionately committed to the highest possible estimation of God's self-expression in the incarnate Son, Jesus of Nazareth. Other religions cannot adequately replicate the reality that occurs in Jesus Christ. How his appreciation of the Incarnation is to be connected with an estimate of the world religions is more explicitly indicated in Rahner's essays on "anonymous Christianity," essays that echo the understanding of the Incarnation we have already been considering. Here we look briefly at the first in the series, "Anonymous Christians."

Rahner says that the fact of the Incarnation means that every human being, as human, is open to the mystery of God and is always at least implicitly faced with the mystery of God-made-human.[20] Because of this deep involvement of God in human nature, it follows that to be human—regardless of religious affiliation—is always to be in encounter with the God of Jesus Christ. Some humans may not recognize this encounter, but nonetheless every legitimate act of self-appropriation is an encounter with the Word made flesh:

> Accordingly, no matter how he wants to understand and express this in his own reflective self-understanding, he is becoming thereby not merely an anonymous "theist," but rather takes upon himself in that Yes to himself the grace of the mystery which has radically approached us. "God has given himself to man in direct proximity": perhaps the essence of Christianity can be reduced to this formula.[21]

Likewise, if a person does not go out of his way to deny the existence of God, he or she is truly graced with the experience of Christ, even if this encounter

18. P. 46.
19. Ibid.
20. "Anonymous Christians," *Theological Investigations* 6:393.
21. Ibid., p. 394.

is never properly named and the person remains instead an "anonymous Christian."[22] God is present in the man Jesus and in this way defines the specific meaning of every human identity. Jesus is God embodied, so Jesus is the standard and depth of every act of human self-appropriation.

None of this enables us to predict anything specific about Hindu religious and theological positions, but the material specificity of Rahner's own faith is splendidly clear. We can see how this faith instigates and authorizes him to judge everything according to what he knows of God embodied in Christ. Because God is so compellingly embodied in Jesus, it seems evident, in advance and without further discussion, how ethereal or misplaced other notions of divine presence must be. The faith position—God is embodied in Christ—is clear, but as we shall now see, the theological extension, which states that other understandings of divine embodiment obviously miss the mark, requires a great deal more comparative and dialogical analysis before it can hold up as an arguable position in an interreligious context.

Hindu Theologies of God's Body

Rahner the theologian is in fact like some of his colleagues among traditional Hindu theologians, especially, Aruḷ Nandi and Vedānta Deśika. They too believe in God's embodiment and nearness to humans and likewise hold this proximity to be the gracious measure by which everything is to be judged. They too demonstrate a passionate commitment to God's embodied form and similarly interpret everything else according to that primal commitment. By noticing how several Hindu theologians have thought about God's embodiment, we will be able to reconsider Rahner's Christian theological position—and theirs too—in a more nuanced theological light. Methodologically, this experiment will confirm the position I have been stating throughout: no theological topic, even the most seemingly concrete and tradition-specific, profits from being considered in isolation from comparable theological reflections in other traditions. The event of divine embodiment can be thought of in a comparative theological perspective, and even this most specific of religious and theological claims is more richly appreciated in an interreligious theological context.

The reality of this body, this form, is defended as plausible; as Swinburne might put it, it makes sense for God to act in this particular way. And, as Rahner might add, divine embodiment encapsulates the most precious of religious truths. We begin with the Śaiva position, which offers a view on divine embodiment interestingly different from what most Christian theologians might expect, and thereafter turn to the Vaiṣṇava position, which is interestingly similar to Rahner's position.

22. Ibid., p. 395.

The Śaiva View of God's Body in Theology and Worship

The Śaiva theologians defend God's particular involvement in the world and hold that God can assume physical forms.[23] Their particular understanding of embodiment serves also to obviate alternative explanations, which would demean divine perfection. To gain a sense of this rather complex Śaiva theology, we first return to Śrīpati Paṇḍita Ācārya's *Śrīkara Bhāṣya* and Aruḷ Nandi's *Śiva Jñāna Siddhiyār*, and thereafter we examine several passages from a traditional Śaiva manual of theory and practice, the *Mṛgendra Āgama*.

In his *Śrīkara Bhāṣya* comment on *Uttara Mīmāṃsā Sūtra* II.2.40,[24] Śrīpati Paṇḍita Ācārya argues that Śiva does not have an ordinary body, vulnerable to weaknesses and suffering, but rather a special, auspicious body, which actually enhances his glory. To the objection that it is incoherent to suggest that God becomes embodied, Śrīpati Paṇḍita Ācārya responds:

> Śiva's form is auspicious and generated for the sake of play. It is "auspicious" because it is not subject to the flaws of other bodies; that it is "generated for the sake of play" indicates that the Lord assumed it freely and not out of compulsion.
>
> Even if he has no body, texts such as "without hands and feet he runs and grasps, without eyes he sees, without ears he hears" indicate nevertheless that he is the cause of everything.[25] Moreover, he does not bear the same characteristics as does Nārāyaṇa—birth, death, etc.—and he has no connection with the kind of body that is a mere effect. So there is no fault or blame in Śiva's having a form which is auspicious and generated for play.[26]

Śrīpati Paṇḍita Ācārya defends as reasonable his own Śaiva understanding of appropriate divine embodiment, while yet pointing out the intellectual weaknesses in the Vaiṣṇava tradition's view of the same. It is plausible to claim that God can take on forms freely and at opportune times, but competing conceptions of divine embodiment are not reasonable because they demean the divinity. Śrīpati Paṇḍita Ācārya does not comprehensively explain the purposes of Śiva's material forms; he seeks only to defend correct views and ward off misinterpretations. He asserts that Śiva is not constricted by bodily limitations but can,[27] at will and without detriment, assume various more or less subtle forms suited to the varying capacities of human knowers. His acts of embodiment are not liable to the weaknesses that Nārāyaṇa suffers in his corporeal forms.[28]

23. In the following pages there are a number of Śaiva Sanskrit and Tamil terms that refer in some way to physical form, shape, or body. Throughout, I use the following translations for the sake of uniformity and simplicity, although overlap is inevitable: (in Sanskrit) *vigraha*, figure; *śarīra*, body; *vapu-* and *mūrti*, form; *kāya*, physical body; and *rūpa*, visible appearance; (in Tamil) *uru*, *uruvu*, *uruvam*, and form; *aruvam*, without form; *mēni*, body; and *vaṭivu*, figure.

24. We also examined parts of this section in chapter 3.

25. *Śvetāśvatara Upaniṣad* 3.19.

26. II.2.40, p. 236.

27. For example, at *sūtra* II.1.13.

28. For example, at *sūtra* I.1.1.

In Aruḷ Nandi's *Śiva Jñāna Siddhiyār* we find a richer and more detailed consideration of Śiva's embodiment. In section I.2 of the constructive part of *Śiva Jñāna Siddhiyār* (the *Supakkam*) Aruḷ Nandi defends the idea that the Lord can have a body, for the simple reason that he is all-powerful and can do anything he chooses. Śiva alone is the source of the world though never compromised by the limitations of the world he makes. Aruḷ Nandi takes up several questions regarding the Lord's physical form:

> "What is the figure of this maker of whom we speak? Is he without form, or is his form devoid of both no-form and form, or is he possessed of a visible form?" If you pose such notions, I respond: all three options belong to the one of whom we speak. He is without form, is devoid of both no-form and form, and appears in visible form.[29]

He too firmly asserts that the perfection and freedom of Śiva are preserved even as he chooses to assume forms:

> You may object that if form is ascribed to God, then another maker like the one who made our bodies will be required; or, if God wills his own body, you object that many other selves too might similarly will their own bodies. But we cannot assume any body we like, while the great God assumes any form he thinks of, just as those perfected in yoga do.[30]

Śiva aptly chooses special forms of embodiment appropriate to his salvific role in the world; his forms are the instruments of his intention to save. If the Lord did not externalize himself and assume a body, no one could experience him. His body is the instrument by which he communicates his salvific teaching and ultimately himself to humans who are confused about the order and purpose of material and spiritual realities:

> Assuming the Vedas and Śaiva Traditional Texts as his form by grace, the Cause was gracious. Otherwise, no one could have progressed, and there would have been no succession of teachers to impart instruction to Nārāyaṇa, etc., to humans, and to the residents of nether regions.[31]

Without any necessity, Śiva (Hara) chooses to become embodied out of love:

> The Lord's form is grace, his attributes and consciousness are grace, the action appearing in his form is grace. The organs of Hara—hands, feet, etc.—are grace, as are all his accessories. His form achieves nothing for himself, and he takes form out of grace for living beings. This is beyond our comprehension![32]

Śiva's assumption and manipulation of physical forms is more comprehensive and practically useful than skeptics can conceive in their limited imagination:

29. I.2.38, p. 135.
30. I.2.39, p. 135. In verse 40 he adds that those "perfected in yoga" assume multiple forms only with the Lord's consent.
31. I.2.46, p. 139.
32. I.2.47, p. 139.

> They call him one of the gods, he who has the Goddess as his form. They do not understand that he abides as all three of the gods, or that neither Nārāyaṇa nor Brahmā was able to comprehend his form. They do not comprehend how he was half a woman, they do not know how his form grew to fruition. They do not understand that he became an enjoyer in order to grant enjoyment to individual selves. By his spiritual discipline he grants perfection to the practitioners of yoga; when he seems fearsome he is getting individuals to consume their deeds. When they call him one of the gods, they lack discernment and are fools. They do not understand that when he wears these varied, different disguises, this means that he abides beyond this world, that these disguises are all his gracious work, and they do not understand that even his act of destruction is the act by which he destroys deeds.[33]

In this way his body differs from other bodies, since they arise from the combined energy of the distorting power, which deeply obscures reality, and the compensatory projecting power which adjusts to the effects of the distorting power:

> The figures assumed by those who have become impure are nothing but effects of the projecting power. For all these people, knowledge and action are limited by the distorting power. But because the Lord is first, full in knowledge and in action, his physical body is not due to the projecting power, but rather only to his own power.[34]

Since there are no distortions, which could entangle the Lord in embodied forms not of his choosing, "by his own grace, the pure one can assume any body he decides on" (I.2.45).

Even while seemingly confined in a physical form, Śiva remains free, pure, and unrestricted. He thus can be described only paradoxically, in terms of the three possibilities already mentioned above:

> Once we admit that the Lord takes a body with form, we see that he still has a rare body without form, and we can also derive a body, both with and without form; together there are three. See how he has come with a figure of compassion, that our bodies might be cut away![35]

Śiva's mysterious play of form and no-form is part of a divine pedagogy that leads humans through the mystery of their own physical and spiritual reality, away from a crude identification with material form and toward a deeper understanding of self, form, and body. By turning to the supremely free Śiva, humans discover their own freedom; by encountering him in his embodied form, they learn to see their own bodies as potentially nothing but instruments of their inner spiritual lives.

The *Mṛgendra Āgama* is a Sanskrit-language Śaiva text from before 1100. It explores multiple aspects of Śaiva theology, ranging from a treatment of the philosophical problems related to divine embodiment to a practical and

33. I.2.49–51, pp. 140–142.
34. I.2.41, p. 136. The distorting and projecting powers are, respectively, *āṇava* and *māyā*.
35. I.2.55, p. 155.

explicitly ritual explanation of how one is to respond to Śiva's embodiment. In its four sections the *Mṛgendra Āgama* gives a succinct and systematic presentation of the religion of Śiva: Knowledge Section (*Vidyāpāda*), Ritual Practice Section (*Kriyāpāda*), Meditative Practice Section (*Yogapāda*), and Proper Behavior Section (*Cāryapāda*). Each expounds, from its particular angle, the key Śaiva positions on the Lord (*pati*), conscious though usually bound beings (*paśu*), and the bonds (*pāśa*) from which the Lord liberates conscious beings. Here we focus on several passages from the Knowledge and Ritual sections, which discuss the pedagogical value of Śiva's assumption of material forms and of the soteriological efficacy of his exemplary embodiment.

In the first chapter of the Knowledge Section the issues are addressed in the course of a discussion between the deity Indra and a group of sages favored by Śiva and selected for spiritual advancement. In the ancient Vedic pantheon Indra had been king of the gods but here he is a kind of divine pedagogue, and his task is to prepare the sages for a deeper understanding of Śiva. To provoke and stimulate their minds, Indra argues against the idea of a Supreme Lord, for a moment adopting the position of the Mīmāṃsā theologians, whose views we examined in chapter 2: "There appears to be no means of right knowledge which permits one to prove, in a manner that is not contradicted, that there is such a divinity."[36] As the commentator Bhaṭṭa Nārāyaṇa Kaṇṭha explains, Indra's prima facie point is that even the maker God, as God, should not possess a material body; he therefore cannot be the object of perception. If knowable at all, he would have to be known indirectly, by induction. But since the induction of God's existence cannot be made to work properly (as the Mīmāṃsā theologians argued), one can never have sure knowledge about this hypothetical God.[37]

In response to this deliberately provocative assault on their theologies, the sages assert that the Lord does have a body, which can be apprehended so that we can know him. But this body is different from ordinary human bodies and must be assessed by different standards: "The bodily form of the divinity

36. Knowledge Section, I.9a. Throughout, translations from the *Mṛgendra Āgama* are my own, but in every case I have profited by consulting the French translation. Page references are to the French translation.

37. Bhaṭṭa Nārāyaṇa Kaṇṭha concludes his provocation of the pious sages with this summation:

> The reasoning invoked for knowing that the world is an effect ends in attributing to the one under discussion [the Lord] a nature opposed to his proper nature. Only if the divinity possesses a body as we do, will it be able to create, dissolve the world, etc. This body will be made, either by itself or by another agent. If it constructs itself, [one will ask whether] at the moment of creation [the deity] is already provided with a body, or not. But no one ever observes an effect caused by one who has no body or senses. If he already has a body when he makes bodies, one can ask who made that [first] body. Whether it is made by itself or by another, the objection that there is an infinite regress still pertains. So there is no irrefutable means of right knowledge which serves as a proof [of the existence of the divinity]. (Knowledge Section I.9a, p. 27)

is not in any way comparable to the bodies of beings like us. It possesses a particular lordly power. That is why your comparison [with other bodies which would diminish the Lord] is not valid" (I.11). As Bhaṭṭa Nārāyaṇa Kaṇṭha explains in commenting on I.11, God's body need not be subject to the same rules that govern a human body, for example, the inability to be present in more than one place at a time. Even lesser divinities and sages can control the measure of their physical manifestation so that humans sometimes can, and sometimes cannot, see them. All the more, then, the Lord can make use of material presence as he wishes. Indeed,

> it is a fact that the corporeal form of a divinity is never like a body such as ours. Never is the divine form subjected to suffering, to the ripening of actions, to mental impressions. The divine form is never not all-pervasive. It is provided with a lordly power which consists in the power to create, to conserve, and destroy beings such as ourselves, entirely at will. If it takes on a corporeal form, it does this in order to protect individual souls plunged into stupor. Its embodiment is therefore very different from our embodiments, so it follows that you are ineffective in putting forward "embodiment" in refutation of the idea that the divinity might be omnipresent.[38]

After emphasizing further the supreme power of the Lord, who is not to be bound by human limitations, Bhaṭṭa Nārāyaṇa Kaṇṭha concludes his comment on I.11 by observing that those who unimaginatively compare the Lord as world-maker to a pot-maker create for themselves unnecessary difficulties when they attempt to imagine how the Lord's body is really like that of a pot-maker, when they go on to compare his instrumental power with that of the pot-maker, and so on. He cites approvingly from the *Siddha Cūḍāmaṇi*:

> They want to know, "In virtue of what desire, with what body, by what means, thanks to what support, with what material cause, did the Organizer create the triple world?" This poor argumentation is poorly applied to You whose lordly power is beyond reasoning! It makes those people ramble on, and leads to confusion in the world.[39]

The first chapter of the Knowledge Section concludes dramatically. After his rhetorical and argumentative buildup, Indra reveals his own divine self to the sages. By numerous proper sacrificial acts Indra had become pure, so that he can now show himself fully and without any obscurity. Aghora Śivācārya, a second commentator, says that when the sages see this true, purified form of Indra, omnipotent and omniscient, they themselves become like Indra. Their capacity to learn is maximized, and they realize their own inner, true Śiva-nature, which had previously been obscured by impurities. To see God with spiritual eyes includes seeing oneself as primarily spiritual.

In the third chapter of the Knowledge Section we find another version of the debate over the inference of God as maker. Here the author rehearses

38. Knowledge Section I.11, pp. 31–32.
39. Ibid., p. 32.

arguments now familiar to us: as maker, Śiva must be one who can act physically, and for this he assumes a body. But he is not confined by his body as are other embodied beings, whose bodies signify their bondage. Verse 7b in the third chapter proposes, "In ordinary life we observe that visible effects proceed only from an agent endowed with material form. This must be true [of the Lord] as it is for us."[40] The response in verses 8–9a is that even when embodied the Lord remains pure, because his embodiment is verbal:

> The corporeal form of the omnipotent one, comprised of his powers, is not like our bodies. Most notably, it lacks the primal stain. His corporeal form, his head, etc., is composed of the five mantras proper to his five functions: the Lord [*Īśa*], the Person-Within [*Tatpuruṣa*], the Unfrightening One [*Aghora*], the One Casting-Down [*Vāma*], and the Unborn One [who makes others to be born well].[41]

Though somewhat elusive, the reasoning follows from points already made. Material realities are instruments, made to be used in communication with others. In this case, "body" is the instrument by which Śiva communicates with humans. But words too are a primary form of communication, so sacred words, in the form of mantras, can rightly be termed "the body of Śiva."

In his comment on 9a, Bhaṭṭa Nārāyaṇa Kaṇṭha explains that Śiva can be known through the mantras that he reveals. In this way, he can be said metaphorically to have a body, even if it is not a literally physical body such as can be seen by ordinary eyes. Moreover, for the sake of meditation aimed at visualizing Śiva, who cannot ordinarily be seen, one mentally constructs for Śiva a body correlated with the "mantra body" mentioned in verse 9a:

Physical Feature	*Mantra Body*
Śiva's head	Lord (*Īśa*)
Śiva's face	Person-Within (*Tatpuruṣa*)
Śiva's heart	Unfrightening One (*Aghora*)
Śiva's inner organs	One Casting-Down (*Vāma*)
Śiva's torso	Unborn One (*Aja*)

Perceptible sound transmutes into perceptible sight, as one first hears and then learns to see Śiva. At the end of chapter 3 of the Knowledge Section Bhaṭṭa Nārāyaṇa Kaṇṭha comments:

> In reality, one must say that the supreme Lord has no body. His power is called "body" because it produces the same effects as a body. It is only one but it is divided according to names such as "the One Casting-Down" according to the diversity of what is to be done. [Śiva's power] is like the power of fire which,

40. Ibid., III.7b, p. 118.

41. Ibid., III.8–9a, pp. 119–120. These are five names of Śiva, which indicate the five mantras by which he can be invoked; they are also correlated with his five powers: to create, to preserve, and to dissolve the cosmos; to conceal; and to graciously reveal. I have based my explanatory translations of *Īśa*, *Tatpuruṣa*, *Aghora*, *Vāma*, and *Aja* on Bhaṭṭa Nārāyaṇa Kaṇṭha's commentary on verses 9b–14a.

> though multiple with respect to its action in cooking and illuminating what must be cooked or illumined, yet remains essentially one.[42]

One further nuance regarding the Lord's efficacious physical form occurs in the fourth chapter of the Knowledge Section. There we are told that the Lord has a body due to the power by which he creates the world.[43] He differentiates this power into the eight superintendent beings,[44] into particular acts of sacred language,[45] and then into the 108 beings,[46] from whom he creates lower beings which are bound by deeds.[47] The world and the higher and lower beings that, populate it are all manifestations of Śiva's power through which he makes the world and does his work in it. Because "body" indicates "instrument of action," when Śiva acts through sacred words and through intermediate beings ranging from gods to gurus, he is rightly said to have a body even when he has not assumed a particular manifest form that ordinary people can perceive.

In the third chapter of the Ritual Section the instrumentality of body is further emphasized. The "body" function can be legitimately filled by various means; the ordinary physical body is just one possible way. This is why Śiva, though purely spiritual and unconstrained by matter, can nonetheless have a body, which becomes the object of meditation:

> [In truth, Śiva] has no specific form. But for whichever task he accomplishes his form is in accord with that which an ordinary agent would require for such an act. Since each form presents a particular visible appearance, and that feature of the Lord is a function of the task, in our tradition the wise describe both [the Lord's] general features and other features.[48]

Bhaṭṭa Nārāyaṇa Kaṇṭha explains:

> It is certain that in ultimate reality the Lord is without form. But previously we also explained with arguments that he does everything. Since we know that the accomplishment of an action is impossible without a body, [we can add that] when Śiva accomplishes an action, whatever it is, his form becomes like an agent's body for that action. Those meditating will see him with beneficent features when he accords his grace or acts similarly, with furious features in actions suggesting anger, or as dripping nectar for rites aimed at fattening. As it says in the *Sarvasrotaḥ Saṃgraha Sāra*, "the Lord is like the jewel that satisfies all desires; on whichever form the practitioner focuses his remembering, the Lord takes that form."[49]

42. Knowledge Section III.15, p. 124.
43. Ibid., IV.1, p. 125.
44. Ibid., IV.3–4 and 9, pp. 128 and 131.
45. That is, in recited mantras; ibid., IV.6, p. 129.
46. Ibid., IV.9, p. 131.
47. Ibid., IV.11, pp. 133–134.
48. Ritual Section III.41–42, p. 63. Each feature of the Lord presents a different important aspect—graciousness, immobility, terrible nature, and so on—which is marked by a mantra form. Graciousness, immobility, and terrible nature are, respectively *Īśa*, *Tatpuruṣa*, and *Bahurūpa* (*Aghora*) (see Ritual Section III.43–44, pp. 64–66).
49. Ritual Section III.43, p. 64.

By meditating on the Lord in various forms, one gradually achieves various intermediate goals, which lead to greater union with him. He takes on forms that become the appropriate objects of meditation at the various stages. By virtue of these, he is "embodied."

Although this kind of embodiment—free, communicative, and instrumental—is true most clearly for the Lord, it can also be realized by all individuals who engage in worship and meditation. This is vividly shown at the beginning of the same chapter of the Ritual Section, where the practitioner is urged to immolate his body in preparation for worship of Śiva, so as to be able to take on a new body made of knowledge and activity: "Turned toward the east or toward the north, he undertakes the mastery of breathing three times, and so immolates his animal body by the fire of this weapon which reaches the place of Sadāśiva."[50] The material body is immolated in the inner breath; when the meditator blows away its ashes, he glimpses his true, inner body:

> Blowing on the ashes with the wind of [divine] power, he should contemplate the form of the sphere of the sun as the sphere of seeing and doing. Such alone is his body. But it is also evident that a form which does not possess distinct members cannot be effective. He must therefore remember himself with mantras as his members, his head, etc.[51]

The meditator then imagines in himself the same five mantra forms (Lord, Person-Within, etc.) in relation to the same five bodily features (head, face, etc.) that were correlated with respect to Śiva. He thus mentally constructs a new body for himself.[52] Bhaṭṭa Nārāyaṇa Kaṇṭha gives an interesting interpretation of the reality of this process by asking, at verse 4, whether this self-immolation is to be taken literally. He responds that the immolation is very real indeed, on a deeper level, since this ritual process destroys the residue of deeds that had led the performer to bear his (or her) current and particular body.[53] The impure is really burned away, and what is left is really the inner, illumined instrument, the body made of knowledge and action. Part of this real liberative process is this transformation of the ritual performer's self-consciousness even of the body, which is no longer merely physical matter but also, and more important, recreated in knowledge and action and expressed in mantra form. That is, the ritual process leads the performer into similitude with Śiva, as he or she acquires a spiritual and verbal body like Śiva's. This body still meets the definition of body-as-instrument, since by it every need of the self is met. Śiva is everywhere, but the goal of ritual and meditative practice is the transformation of the performer/meditator into a person who can actually see Śiva, with heightened spiritual sense, and see himself as Śiva. Ultimately, what is true of Śiva is the ultimate truth of human nature; as humans are, so Śiva presents himself. No form represents Śiva directly, but when

50. Ibid., III.4, pp. 38–39.
51. Ibid., III.5 and 6, pp. 39 and 41–42.
52. Ibid., III.7–10, pp. 42–45.
53. Ibid., III.4, p. 41.

properly utilized, every material form becomes a vehicle for the realization of Śiva's presence.

Some of these material forms are the result of exquisite reflection and planning and, like the Sacred Heart, can evoke a powerful response. The most famous and interesting is the *liṅga*, a cylinder usually made of simple stone devoid of carving.[54] It is an aniconic representation of the present but unseen Śiva, who is "seen" yet eludes direct sight. Richard Davis has helpfully elaborated the place of the *liṅga* in Śaiva theology and spiritual practice;[55] he cites this passage from the ancient *Liṅga Purāṇa*:

> They say there are two types of *liṅgas*, exterior and interior. The exterior *liṅga* is tangible, O excellent sages, while the interior one is subtle. Persons devoted to the external rituals and sacrifices, and those gratified by worshipping a tangible *liṅga*, are themselves gross. The tangible form is only for those unable to visualize. The inner *liṅga* is not perceptible to the dull-minded person who considers that exterior reality is everything and that nothing else exists. The unstained, unchanging subtle *liṅga* is just as evident to persons of knowledge, however, as a gross *liṅga* made of some material like mud or wood is to those who are not practiced in yoga.[56]

Davis observes that the *Liṅga Purāṇa* favors interiorization more than most Śaiva texts, which ordinarily do not shy away from claiming that Śiva is manifest more straightforwardly in external and material forms. He also notes the wide range of possibilities created by various kinds of plain and carved *liṅgas*:

> An austere, upright cylinder, the *liṅga* is physically nonpartite. An image, by contrast, is an anthropomorphic form with all the characteristic parts and marks of a body. Intermediate between these two forms, the *liṅga* with faces is in its basic shape and dimensions a *liṅga*, but with one or, more often, five faces partially emerging from a central shaft to the four cardinal directions. The fifth, upward face is not discernible to humans of limited visual acuity. . . .
>
> The undifferentiated *liṅga* is considered superior and the fully partite image is inferior. Moreover, the texts assert that these different types of icons parallel the three levels or aspects of Śiva's totality. The undifferentiated *liṅga*, appropriately, corresponds to Śiva in his most encompassing, transcendent, and undifferentiated aspect, Paramaśiva [highest Śiva]. At the other end, the various human-like images of Śiva, depicting him iconographically as he has acted in the world and appeared to his devotees, correspond to the level of embodiment called Maheśvara [great Lord]. In between, where Śiva is seen halfway between transcendence and manifestation as it were, with five faces appearing from the once-undifferentiated *liṅga*, the *mukhaliṅga* [the *liṅga* with faces] clearly parallels the five-faced Sadāśiva [ever-auspicious Śiva].[57]

54. The *liṅga* is sometimes carved with faces or other representations of Śiva, while in some myths it clearly represents the phallus of Śiva.

55. In *Ritual in an Oscillating Universe*, 1991.

56. *Liṅga Purāṇa* 75.19–22, as cited by Davis, pp. 120–121.

57. Davis, p. 121.

If Śiva does not limit himself to a single, confining human form neither does he shy away entirely from involvement with body. Symbols such as the *liṅga* test the boundary between what can be seen and what is never seen. Objects like the *liṅga* embody—make manifest and articulate—the Lord, who graciously chooses to enter the realm of embodiment.

As in Rahner's theology of the Sacred Heart, here too we find an intense devotional core, a theology of Śiva's body that stands in complementarity with devotion to the cult of the *liṅga*. Mutually confirming, the theology and the cult together comprise a most plausible account and representation of the human encounter with God. As in Rahner's thought, here too one finds the terms for a complete theology of divine embodiment, even if the theology works out differently than Rahner's. Here too, divine transcendence and freedom are not jeopardized, yet graciousness is emphasized. The reality of divine embodiment is stressed but according to technical theological conceptions of "body as instrument" and "body as word." Kinds of body and materiality are studied and differentiated with great subtlety. As in Rahner's theology, the truth of the gracious divine embodiment illumines the truth of the embodied human. According to the *Mṛgendra Āgama*, Śiva is a purely spiritual being who for a time usefully associates with matter. This temporary association is true of humans as well, but the latter mistakenly identify themselves in a more permanent way with the bodily resources they habitually use for self-expression. To know Śiva in his embodied forms enables one to see more clearly what it means to be human, body and soul.

The Theology and Piety of Divine Descent (Avatāra) in Vaiṣṇava Theology

For Vaiṣṇava theologians too a preliminary requirement in the discussion of body was the exclusion of models of divine embodiment that would constrict God in ways inappropriate to the divine perfection. They too explored divine embodiment in terms of its salvific purposes. But regarding other important features the Vaiṣṇava theology of the divine body is rather different from the Śaiva theology, since Vaiṣṇava theologians are more open to the idea that God can assume specific bodies, either animal or human, and take on at least the circumstances of limitation that accrue to such bodies.

For Vaiṣṇava theologians, the problem of body-as-limitation is counterbalanced by a theory of the soul/body relationship understood by analogy with material causality. Material and spiritual realities both arise from a single source, Brahman, which in its primordial form includes them both. We already saw in chapter 2 that the Vedānta and Vaiṣṇava rejection of the induction of God's existence in part concerned the need to defend the Upaniṣadic doctrine that Brahman/God is not only the efficient cause of the world but also its material cause. Though intended primarily as a plausible explanation of the origins of the world, the attribution of material causality to Brahman (God) also enabled Vedānta theologians to see materiality in the highest reality but without the unacceptable consequence that Brahman (God) is crudely, deficiently material. In Rāmānuja's theistic Vedānta, it also became possible to say that the world is God's material manifestation, God's body. Just as the soul informs and gives life to the body without suffering material limitation, so too God informs and gives life to the world without suffering material limitation. From this perspective it is easier to imagine that God can assume specific material forms.

Rāmānuja believed that in addition to bearing the entire world as his body, the Supreme God, Nārāyaṇa, also assumed more specific material forms, divine bodies, during those divine descents (*avatāra*) renowned in poetry and myth, including the fish who came during the great flood and saved the human race from destruction; the dwarf who grew large and tricked Bali the demon king by striding the earth in three steps; Rāma, who gave up a kingdom and suffered numerous tribulations in exile; and Kṛṣṇa, who taught the *Bhagavad Gītā* and (in related myths) also lived as a village child and danced with the neighboring cowherd women. Rāmānuja and his successors explored the nature of these divine descents in order to interpret them in a way consonant with their general understanding of God.

The basic principle of divine descent occasioned further questions: How can it be possible for God to assume particular bodies and act in the world in specific ways? If God descends into the world, is God thereby bound by bodily weakness, the limitations of deeds, and so on? Is God's embodied presence in the world merely an appearance of embodiment? In response, the Vaiṣṇava theologians argue that while karma—bad and good deeds from a previous life—normally necessitates embodiment and determines the nature of one's embodiment in the world, karma does not govern Nārāyaṇa's freely chosen divine descents. Rather, divine embodiment and activity are undertaken freely and out of compassion for the human condition. God's activities during these divine descents are real but always free and consonant with divine perfection.

The opening of chapter 4 of the *Bhagavad Gītā* provides the occasion for Rāmānuja and his successors, such as Vedānta Deśika, to elaborate the classical Vaiṣṇava account of divine descent. According to Rāmānuja, *Gītā* 4, which explains detached action in general, particularly in verses 5–11, explains divine descent as God's own and exemplary detached action:

5. Many births of mine have passed away, Arjuna, as well as many of yours. I know them all, but you do not, O slayer of foes.
6. Though I am unborn and inexhaustible in my own nature, though I am the Lord of all things, yet abiding in my own nature I am born due only to my own self.
7. For whenever righteousness withers away and lawlessness arises, then do I generate myself [on earth].
8. For the protection of the good, for the destruction of evil-doers, for the setting up of righteousness I come into being age after age.
9. Whoever thus truly knows my godly birth and mode of operation, leaving his body behind, is never born again; he comes to Me.
10. Freed from desire, fear, and anger, absorbed in me, many, purified by the austerity of knowledge, have obtained my state.

11. However people take refuge in me, in that way do I favor them, O Arjuna; humans travel my path in all ways.[58]

In introducing verse 5, Rāmānuja lists questions about divine descent. If, as scripture says, the Lord is "the opposite of all that is evil," "the sole seat of auspicious qualities," "omniscient," possessed of a "will that always accomplishes its goals," and "one whose desires are always fulfilled," then one may ask:

> Is his birth the same as that of gods, men, and others who are subject to the influence of deeds? is it false like a magic illusion, etc.,[59] or is it real? if real, what is the manner of his birth, what is his body made of, and what is the reason for his birth? when does his birth take place and for what purpose?[60]

Rāmānuja's questions can, for our purposes, be simplified to three: Are the divine descents real? Are the divine corporeal activities free? Does divine embodiment have a purpose that could not be otherwise fulfilled? In what follows we shall see that the answer to all three questions is yes. Though not like ordinary human embodiments, nevertheless God's births are real; God's embodied activities are entirely free; and God thereby makes the divine presence immediately accessible to human beings.

By Rāmānuja's reading, verse 5 ("Many births of mine have passed away, Arjuna, as well as many of yours") asserts that Kṛṣṇa, like Arjuna, does undergo births. Both Kṛṣṇa and Arjuna are born but not in exactly the same way. Verse 6 ("I am born due only to my own self") stresses the Lord's freedom in being birthed, without the compulsion of deeds:

> Without giving up my own nature as Lord of all, being possessed of all auspicious qualities, being without sin, etc., and making his very form similar to those of men and gods, etc., then I am born in a condition like that of gods, men, etc., due only to my own self. The revealed text, "He who is never born is born many times" [*Taittirīya Āraṇyaka* 3.12.7], teaches the same thing. I.e., without making his birth the same as that of other beings, he is born in the form of gods, etc., in the manner described here, by his own free choice.[61]

Verse 7 ("whenever righteousness withers away") emphasizes the primary intention of divine descent: the defense and restoration of righteousness (dharma) in times of crisis. But in his interpretation of verse 8 ("for the protection of the good") Rāmānuja adds a second purpose for divine embodiment: Nārāyaṇa comes in visible form so that humans may be able to come near him and see him:

> As they will become weak and unnerved in every limb [on account of separation from me] I am born from age to age in the forms of gods, men, etc., for

58. *Bhagavad Gītā* 4.5–11. I have used Sampatkumaran's translation as found in his *Gītābhāṣya of Rāmānuja*, with adaptations.
59. "Magic illusion": literally, "Indra's net," the rainbow.
60. *Bhagavad Gītā* 4.6, p. 103.
61. Ibid., p. 105.

> the sake of protecting them by giving them opportunities of looking, talking, etc. in regard to my proper nature and my activities. [I am born] also for the destruction of those who are the opposite of these; and for the firm establishment of the Vedic righteousness when it is in decline, a righteousness which is of the nature of worship of me, by showing my form which is the worthy object of adoration.[62]

According to verse 9 ("he . . . is never born again"), those who really see the Lord become free, since knowledge of the Lord—who is now knowable in this visible, embodied form—leads to liberation:

> Whoever knows truly that unique birth, which is divine and not comprised of material Nature, and those deeds which are intended solely for the protection of the good and making them take refuge with me, a birth and deeds which belong to me who am free of that birth which is caused by actions and which is characterized by contact with material Nature made of the three constituents, and who is endowed with all auspicious qualities such as Lordship over all, omniscience, capacity to achieve what one intends—such a person, when he has given up the present body, gets no more rebirths, but obtains me only. Through knowledge of the truth about my divine birth and work, all the sins that stand in the way of his resorting to me are destroyed, and in this birth alone he takes refuge in me in the manner already stated, and having me only as the object of affection and thinking of me only, he obtains me alone.[63]

At verse 11 ("however people take refuge in me, in that way do I favor them") Rāmānuja summarizes the double purpose of divine descent, the restoration of righteousness and the promotion of divine accessibility:

> Not only do I bestow protection on those who desire refuge with me, by descending by the forms of gods, humans, etc., but also, "however," i.e., in whatever manner do they imagine me and in accord with that desire, "in that way," i.e., in that human form do I share myself with them. What is more, all men who are desirous of following me on my path shall, with their own eyes and other organs of sense in all ways, i.e., in every manner desired by them, keep on experiencing my form, my essential character, even though this is beyond the range of speech and thought of those who are expert in yoga.[64]

According to Rāmānuja, then, the descents are real, although their particular circumstances are unique and appropriate to the perfection of the divine nature. They are acts of divine freedom aimed at the defeat of evildoers and the uplift of the good. Most important, they provide devotees with more immediate access to the Lord. This access is a distinct end, good in itself.

Vedānta Deśika's *Tātparya Candrikā* commentary on Rāmānuja's *Gītā* commentary confirms and elaborates Rāmānuja's reading. As Deśika explains at *Gītā* 4.4, the challenge is to balance the two values. Divine descent in no

62. Ibid., 4.8, p. 106.
63. Ibid., 4.9, p. 107.
64. Ibid., p. 108.

way compromises the Lord's perfection but also divine descent is not entirely different from the embodiment undergone by lesser living beings. God's births are truly divine yet not merely the appearance of birth.

Two of Deśika's technical points are noteworthy. First, he insists that "body" can be used in an analogical fashion and as applicable to both divine and human bodies, yet without the further conclusion that all such bodies are alike in every respect. Second, he interprets the activity that occurs during a divine descent as "dramatic gesture" (*abhinaya*). Let us consider these strategies in turn.

In introducing *Bhagavad Gītā* verses 5–11 (at verse 4), Deśika asks directly whether divine descents should be called real births or not. Were the Lord to remain lord of all, omniscient, able to accomplish his will simply by wishing it so, and already possessed of all he desires, it would appear that he is so unlike other embodied beings that his "birth" is merely apparent. Deśika responds that this conclusion follows only if one posits a necessary connection between "birth" and "necessity, limitation, pain." But it is possible to define *birth* simply as "having [or taking on] a body," without defining it in terms more exclusively appropriate to ordinary births. In introducing verse 6 ("Many births of mine have passed away, Arjuna, as well as many of yours"), he reaffirms Rāmānuja's position by pointing out that Kṛṣṇa does not say "many appearances of birth" but distinguishes "births of mine" and "births of yours." This distinction makes clear that the Lord's births are real even if not the same as Arjuna's. No ordinary or impure matter is present in the body of a divine descent, but its material is nonetheless real matter.

Deśika adds that when the *Bhagavad Gītā* says in 4.6 "yet abiding in my own nature"—as distinct from "human nature" or "nature in general"—a distinction of two modes of nature, ordinary and divine, is intended. Ordinary, human nature is confined by material nature, which is composed of the material constituents of reality. But the Lord is not confined by that kind of nature when he becomes embodied. Rather, God's nature indicates his proper divine nature and, in keeping with that divine nature, the particular forms he assumes in each divine descent. Hence the emphatic "my own."

At verse 11, Deśika reviews various criticisms, and his major points may be summarized as follows. It may appear that in his births the Lord takes on limitations contrary to his divine nature. But there is no contradiction between his substantial perfection and these limitations, since he freely chooses to be born, without the compulsion of deeds and without thereupon assuming ordinary, flawed matter as his body. That the Lord's birth cannot be compelled by deeds rules out only ordinary births, not perfect, free acts of birth. Since the Lord is not burdened with good and bad deeds, he is not under the compulsion of some other agent or force but acts freely. Therefore there is nothing lacking in the reality of his births, even if he does not have good and bad experiences such as others endure. Although he has no personal needs to be satisfied during his embodiments, those births are purposeful and aimed at protecting good people. The fact that the Lord experiences just some joys in each birth—not all joys in all births—does not indicate that his joy is limited, but only that he has made choices regarding which joys to experience in which births.

Deśika's second key idea has to do with determining the significance of the actions and experiences that occur during divine descents. Here too he sees a balance to be maintained, to preserve divine dignity while yet allowing for real action and real experience. Deśika concludes his defense of the reality of the divine body with a new but at least initially unsettling comment, which seems to undercut the reality of what happens during divine descents: "In various texts it is mentioned that the Lord experienced suffering, grief, and fear during his divine descents. But due to the fact that he is not afflicted by sin, etc., and in light of texts such as 'In this way he deceived the worlds,'[65] it must be understood that these [apparent sufferings] are simply *abhinaya*." *Abhinaya* more commonly refers to theatrical or dramatic performance and gestures, that is, the physical movements made by an actor or dancer in the course of a performance, to express emotions. These are often highly refined and subtle gestures, which perfectly coordinate the spiritual and intellectual, psychological and physical dimensions of action. As a Vaiṣṇava theological term, *abhinaya* is used to characterize the Lord's real and free engagement in difficulty and suffering during his embodiment—an involvement that is entirely free and that leaves him perfect and untainted.[66]

Deśika has nothing more to say in the *Gītā* context, but in a parallel discussion at *Uttara Mīmāṃsā Sūtra* I.1.21 (where the term is introduced first by Sudarśana Sūri) Deśika elaborates his understanding of *abhinaya*. In the course of explaining the nature of the Lord's body as distinct from other human and divine bodies, Rāmānuja says:

> He is a boundless ocean of compassion, favorable disposition, tenderness, generosity, and lordly power, in whom the scent of *all* that is undesirable is *annihilated*, who is the highest Brahman, not afflicted by sin, the highest Self, the supreme person, Nārāyaṇa. In order to gratify his devotees he individualizes his form so as to render it suitable to their apprehension.[67]

In explaining the Lord's qualities, with reference to the second part of this statement, Sudarśana Sūri adds:

> By mentioning *annihilated* he is indicating the Lord's transcendence. I.e., both his transcendence and accessibility support his role as an object of meditation. But in order to indicate that in his shared nature with humans, etc., he is still untouched by the grief, confusion, etc., which they experience, he uses the word *annihilated*.
>
> When one enters into the condition of humans, then grief, etc., pertain to the portion which is an individual self. But clearly, in the divine descents grief,

65. A citation, not further elaborated by Deśika, from *Udyoga Kāṇḍa* (67.15) of the epic *Mahābhārata*.

66. This theological usage is reflected in the *Viśiṣṭādvaita Kośa*, where *abhinaya* is defined as "the highest one's acting as if impotent during the times of his divine descents" (vol. 1, p. 360). Throughout, I translate *abhinaya* as "dramatic gesture."

67. *Śrībhāṣya* I.1.21, p. 240. My emphasis.

> etc., are simply dramatic gestures. *All* refers to the flaws which pertain to both conscious and nonconscious beings.[68]

From an ordinary human perspective, the Lord appears to be suffering various hardships, but from the divine perspective these are only dramatic gestures. Although the Lord is born and does act, neither in his birth nor in his deeds does he suffer or experience the limitations that arise from prior evil deeds.

In his comment on this passage from Rāmānuja's commentary, Deśika explains dramatic gesture a bit more fully:

> Objection: because [the Lord's body] is a body and because it has parts, it must also have the seven physical components, the three impurities, flawed and painful; and it must be the cause of suffering and destined for destruction.
>
> Not so, we reply. That view is contradicted by authoritative knowledge about the possessor of that body. There can be no contradiction regarding the one who is known only from scripture, since otherwise there would be the extreme danger [of uncertainty about scripture and the scriptural truth necessary for liberation]. Whatever his dramatic gestures during his divine descents, all of them are freely intended, by his own will, for the overthrow of demons.[69]

The commentator Vaiśvamitra Śrīvarada Guru adds:

> These demons are Kaṃsa, etc. They think that when Kṛṣṇa and the other divine descents act as children, etc., that is the complete truth about them, so again and again they move against them; but when they act thus they themselves perish. As it says, "For the destruction of evil-doers" [*Bhagavad Gītā* 4.7]. Thus the Lord's behaving like a child, etc., has as its fruit the destruction of evil-doers.[70]

According to Vaiśvamitra Śrīvarada Guru, the Lord's mundane body is distinctive, neither merely a flawed, limited human body nor merely the Lord's eternal, transcendent body:

> Is that body comprised of material Nature or is it not material Nature? If it is merely natural it will be burdened with all the flaws and constraints of other bodies; if it is simply the eternal divine body, how could it then be subject to change? Nor can it be some third possibility, neither divine nor natural, since there is no other kind of matter. . . . It is pure-being,[71] that is, a kind of divine

68. Ibid., I.1.21, p. 245.

69. *Adhikaraṇa Sarāvali* verse 65, p. 125. Deśika's exposition reaffirms Rāmānuja's and Sudarśana Sūri's positions, which of course echo those stated in the context of *Bhagavad Gītā* 4. He reasserts Rāmānuja's view that the Lord's body cannot be attributed to deeds. In a way that interestingly parallels the Śaiva notion of body-as-instrument which we considered above, he redefines body as that which is a support for the self, not merely that which is material. The Lord's body is devoid of the merits as well as the demerits of ordinary human existence (verse 62) and made of a special substance, unlike ordinary bodies (verse 63). Yet it also bears ordinary appearances so that it can be seen by people, since the point of divine descent is the benefit of righteous people who seek the Lord (verse 64).

70. In his *Adhikaraṇa Cintāmaṇi* comment on *Adhikaraṇa Sarāvali* verse 65. The evildoers are King Kaṃsa and other figures who worked against the Lord during the various divine descents.

71. As explained in chapter 3, *sattva* is one of the three constituents of material reality.

> substance which is pure-being without passionate energy (rajas), and dark lethargy (tamas). . . . The result is that the Lord's actions (during divine descents) are actions modeled on grief, confusion, etc., just as performances on a stage occur for the sake of enjoyment.[72]

Vīrarāghava Ācārya, a second commentator on Deśika's *Adhikaraṇa Sarāvali*, begins his discussion of verse 65 by charging that the real adversaries here are "orthodox scholars who are infatuated by reasoning; they accept that there is a God, but despise the divine forms."[73] He then rehearses the problems connected with divine embodiment as a seeming limitation of God and asks whether the Lord really suffers:

> [Objection:] But even so, it must be admitted on the basis of scripture that the Lord does experience some powerlessness and some suffering. [We respond that] it is known authoritatively that he suffers due to the suffering of others, as in the text, "He was sorely grieved . . . ,"[74] and with respect to his own self, as in the text, "Exiled from his kingdom, living in the forest, [Sītā lost, a brahmin killed: such is my misfortune that it could burn even fire]."[75] Were divine descents dependent on deeds, then deeds would be the cause of his suffering. But his divine descents are by his own will. Nor would he wish his own birth as the cause of his own suffering. So it is certain that this suffering is simply dramatic gesture. What is its use then? Its use is that demons see his suffering and his impotence, etc., and think him inferior. They become particularly hostile toward him, refuse to approach him, and instead go to the lowest place.

Vīrarāghava Ācārya notes that this enactment of suffering also aids good people. When Rāma or the child Kṛṣṇa suffer, for example:

> devotees see him suffering in ways that are unlimited and without precedent, etc. Then they cry out, "How could this little one suffer in this way?" Seeing his dramatic gestures of suffering and his exhaustion, and not realizing that it is performance, even his friends are distressed. But this confusion is due to their affection and is for their protection. By contrast, the confusion of others is due to their hatred and leads to their overthrow in confusion. Reflection [on a series of texts cited here] . . . indicates how tradition informs us that the Lord really has a body, is born, etc., but also that he lacks the affliction, weakness, etc., of a body made of flesh and blood, ordinary material Nature. Thus it is agreed that only certain aspects [of embodiment] are ruled out, but not form, etc., in themselves.[76]

Just as the body assumed during a divine descent is real, yet different from that of ordinary humans, so too the activity of God descended to earth is real

72. Verse 64 of the *Adhikaraṇa Sarāvali*, pp. 123–125.

73. In his *Sārārtha Ratna Prabhā* commentary on the *Adhikaraṇa Sarāvali* verse 65, p. 125.

74. Unidentified.

75. *Rāmāyaṇa, Āraṇya Kāṇḍa* 67.24. The fuller citation is found in another text, the *Padayojana*, which is quoted in the *Viśiṣṭādvaita Kośa*, vol. 1, p. 425.

76. *Sārārtha Ratna Prabhā*, pp. 126–127.

and effective activity, which helps good people and punishes the evil. It confronts human ignorance and the inability to understand who God is, by bringing humans into proximity with a God involved in human activities. Humans view the Lord who is engaged in human activity and have to decide what they are seeing—whether to despise it, as do demons, or to admire it, as do worthy people. Like the moods and gestures of an actor on the stage, the actions of the embodied Lord are always freely chosen, neither compelled nor detrimental to God's perfection. God remains God throughout and chooses to engage in dramatic conflict with those who are evil in order to bring about the triumph of righteousness. His action is real, effective, persuasive, engaging, and divine.

The notion of dramatic gesture is used to explain how someone can be involved in a series of events, while always free with respect to what others do and never genuinely hurt by what happens. Dramatic gesture is more profound and deeply engaging than a mere show, just as a powerful theatrical performance can be truly transformative or wrenching even if no one is "really" drowned or murdered loved or saved. Of course, theologians from other traditions will have different opinions about the value of this theory. The less sympathetic will be inclined to interpret dramatic gesture as proving that divine descents, as understood in Vaiṣṇava theology, are merely apparent and therefore of little significance to Christian theologians, who long ago dismissed such errors. Those inclined to more respect for other theological positions will be inclined to interpret divine descent and dramatic gesture as plausible theological strategies that affirm the reality of divine embodiment and divine activity. But in any case one can rightly observe that this Vaiṣṇava position does not attribute redemptive power to the suffering itself. The deeds of Kṛṣṇa and Rāma are deeply effective because of the powerful way in which God communicates through these actions and transforms the "audience" of devotees but not because God is suffering as humans suffer. The Vaiṣṇava presentation of divine descent appreciates the importance of moral correction but focuses on the sheer power of the divine visibility. At stake is an iconic and sacramental presence that eventually turns out to be prized more highly than the original task of protecting the righteous and overturning the unrighteous.

To portray more vividly the intense devotional and emotional realism that Vaiṣṇavas have actually attached to the divine descents, I conclude by noting several verses from Śaṭakōpaṉ, an important eighth-century Vaiṣṇava saint who composed in Tamil. Verse VII.5.5 in his *Tiruvāymoḻi* praises an animal descent of Nārāyaṇa, in which he came as a boar and lifted the earth out of the cosmic ocean into which it was sinking:

> Will the people who have meditated on these skillful exploits embrace the
> feet of anyone
> but the Marvelous One who took the form of a boar
> when the earth was drowning in the great deep waters
> and held it on His horn so that it wouldn't sink
> —after they have heard and thought about all this?

In his discussion of the verse, the influential fourteenth-century commentator Naṃpiḷḷai emphasizes the reality of Nārāyaṇa's boar form:

> He wanted to take on a perishable form—see what that means: for the sake of protecting those who took refuge in him, he did not care for himself at all but took on this state. As it says, "he took the honorless form of a boar," and he took on the soiled form fitting to that, a "filthy, dripping" form,[77] without chasing after his lordship.

Naṃpiḷḷai stresses the reality of this boar form; unlike the disguises worn by demons, the Lord's boar form convinces the other boars:

> When animals see an illusive animal form they realize, "There is the scent of demons here," and they move away from it. [During Nārāyaṇa's boar descent] the boars believed, "He is one of us." This is because the brilliant god, when he took on the form of the boar, gave up all his brilliance. Compared to his glory in the assembly of the eternal ones, this lowering of himself is his excellence. This is what is to be "heard and thought about."[78] "Will the people who have meditated on these skillful exploits embrace the feet of anyone but the Marvelous One?" Indeed, which is greater glory: to make the world by his will alone and without any diminution at all of any of his qualities, or to give up his form and take on another one in order to help the world in its time of dissolution?[79]

The divine descent is material and real, and Nampiḷḷai recognizes it as a great divine achievement. These deeds are in keeping with the Lord's transcendent divine identity yet also are as mundanely real as the lives and actions of animals.

The affective power of the Vaiṣṇava sense of divine self-debasement is made clear in one of the few anecdotes about Śaṭakōpaṉ. In verse I.3.1 of *Tiruvāymoḻi* the saint sings movingly of how the child Kṛṣṇa allowed himself to be bound to the grindstone by his mother, who was trying to control her mischievous son:

> Accessible to those who love him, hard for others to find, he is amazing;
> the Lady in the lotus delights in him, yet for us his feet are so hard to gain;
> now he is bound to the grindstone, his firm waist tied,

77. This verse is from Āṇṭāḷ's *Nācciyār Tirumoḻi* XI.8, "Once long ago, for the sake of the maiden earth, forlorn in moss-ridden body, he took the honorless form of a boar, filthy, dripping. That radiant one, famed lord of holy Āraṅkam—the words he spoke to me can never be erased from my mind." In his commentary on Aṇṭāḷ's verse, Periyavāccāṉpiḷḷai stresses that without shame or hesitation the Lord became a wild boar and, giving up his usual food, ate the things that boars eat. In support of this divine condescension he also quotes a passage from the *Viṣṇu Purāṇa* where Kṛṣṇa assures the cowherd men, who consider him an extraordinary alien visitor or a god, that he really is their kinsman and brother (*Viṣṇu Purāṇa* 5.13.12). Another passage from the *Rāmāyaṇa* (*Yuddha Kāṇḍa* 120.11) tells how Rāma had to be reminded of his divine identity, since he was so immersed in his human form that he forgot who he was. He gives up his accustomed divine self-identity and does so freely.

78. In the text, the Tamil words "having heard" (*keṭṭu*) and "having thought about" (*unarṇtu*) are glossed with the Sanskrit words "hearing" (*śravaṇa*) and "thinking" (*manana*) found in *Bṛhadāraṇyaka Upaniṣad* 2.4.5, the classic text that interconnects reception of the sacred word, reflection, and meditation.

79. From Naṃpiḷḷai's *Īṭu* commentary on *Tiruvāymoḻi* VII.5.5, in Śaṭakōpaṉ Vol. 8.

because he stole the butter from the churn:
what is this? how pitiful, how vulnerable!

The commentators recount that in singing this verse the saint was so deeply moved by the Lord's humility in becoming human and subjecting himself to another's will that he went into a trance and could not speak for six months. People had to beg him to resume his composition and sing the remaining 1,080 verses of *Tiruvāymoḻi*. This recollection makes clear that divine descent bears a real emotional force. First defended as possible and appropriate, divine descent is now positively praised as the occasion for pious insight into the intense love the Lord showers upon the world as he willingly lowers himself and becomes subservient to humans.[80]

Like its Christian and Śaiva counterparts, this Vaiṣṇava theology invites and perhaps even requires some appropriate symbolic representation to complete it practically. For Vaiṣṇavas there is a range of such possible completions, but perhaps the most important is the idea of surrendering at the Lord's feet, a place of refuge. In narratives such as the epic *Rāmāyaṇa*, devotees bow down at the feet of Rāma and take refuge there, and refuge at the Lord's feet is frequently represented in popular art. In temples people frequently touch the feet of images of Nārāyaṇa, his Goddess, and related saintly figures, who themselves are holy because they too are at the Lord's feet. Linguistically, the customary pious name by which devotees call themselves is *aṭiyēṉ*, "I who am at the feet [of the Lord]." The songs in *Tiruvāymoḻi* cited above refer to the importance of taking one's place at the Lord's feet, for example, "Will the people who have meditated on these skillful exploits embrace the feet of anyone [else]" (VII.5.5) and "his feet are so hard to gain" (I.3.1).[81]

As in Rahner's Catholic theology and in Aruḷ Nandi's Śaiva theology, we find in Vaiṣṇavism a vigorous defense of divine embodiment, understood in a mode that is both fairly literal and yet hedged around with protections intended to deter reductive conclusions about a God who becomes embodied. For Vaiṣṇava theologians, the total set of beliefs—the critique of the crude imagery of a physical world-maker but also awe at a divine self-humbling, which is nevertheless compatible with the divine nature—constitutes a faithful theology of divine embodiment, a rational account of how God acts, which is preferable to other comparable explanations of how God might become human. Theologians in other traditions can certainly recognize as familiar the combination of piety and argument operative in this particular Vaiṣṇava reasoning.

A Note on What Śaiva Theologians Thought about the Vaiṣṇava Understanding of Divine Embodiment

Theology is rarely irenic, and here too it is helpful to notice that not everyone in South India was impressed with the Vaiṣṇava view of divine embodi-

80. Clooney 1996, p. 320, n. 4.

81. In *Tiruvāymoḻi* alone, the word *feet* occurs 258 times in 1,100 verses.

ment. The Śaiva theologians lacked the sympathy that would have been required for them to be satisfied with the Vaiṣṇava mix of piety and reasoning. In the *Parapakkam*, the apologetic section of his *Śiva Jñāna Siddhiyār*, Aruḷ Nandi rather sharply dismisses the Vaiṣṇava conception of embodiment and makes criticism of it the center of his critique of Vaiṣṇavism. From Aruḷ Nandi's perspective, Nārāyaṇa is burdened with a body he does not control. This is shown, he says, in the myth where Nārāyaṇa attempted to fill Śiva's begging bowl with blood from his own forehead but then could not stop the flow of blood,[82] and in the myth in which Nārāyaṇa was decapitated by Śiva's servant and could not restore his head without Śiva's help.[83] More generally, Nārāyaṇa (Māl) does not take on bodies just for the sake of devotees, and neither does he have the power to create nor even to teach others to create, as Śiva (Hara) does:

> Māl was born like ordinary mortals, from various individual wombs. You assert that he is God, born by his own will in order to protect the world. But at that time when Brahmā failed to create in imitation, though he was the God of the Vedas, he came to praise Hara's feet, and Hara burst forth from Brahmā's forehead and taught him how to create.[84]

The troubles experienced by Nārāyaṇa in the divine descents are taken as signs of his painful embodiment—real and not merely apparent weakness—as this comment on the boar descent, taken so seriously by the Vaiṣṇavas, shows:

> As the boar, he cleaved the seven worlds and bore them on his tusk, and then he put himself forward as the only light to be worshipped by the world. But then the Lord, who delights to dance in the jungle where demons swirl about, came and knocked down the boar, and tore off the tusk and wore it himself.[85]

Nārāyaṇa is an ignorant victim of *māyā* and lacks the wisdom to be Lord. As Rāma, for example, he is constantly deceived, tricked, exiled, and outwitted by demons.[86] On the whole, his descents exemplify a path quite the opposite of that which leads to liberation:

> The pure Traditional Texts declare that liberation is obtained when the "beasts" [*paśu*] rid themselves of their "bondage" [*pāśa*] and join with the Lord [*pati*]. But you senselessly say that your pure Māl becomes ignorant and takes on impure Māyā. Won't wise people feel ashamed, and leave this confusing book to you?[87]

The descents of Nārāyaṇa (Hari) are actually a curse, not an act of divine favor:

82. *Parapakkam* 14.2, p. 114. For a paraphrase and elaboration of these verses, see also Gopalakrishnan.

83. *Parapakkam* 14.3, p. 114.

84. Ibid., 14.6, p. 115.

85. Ibid., 14.12, pp. 115–116.

86. Ibid., 14.15, p. 114.

87. Ibid., 14.25, p. 118.

> He was bound by the curse of Bhṛgu to be born ten times; he thus endured sorrow and pain, and is not spotless. What can I say but that this Hari cannot be Lord! Be advised of this, and worship the lotus feet of Śiva, the Dark-Throated God of gods.[88]

A concerted polemic perspective makes it easy to observe the beliefs and theologies of others without sympathy, to see gaps and inconsistencies where believing theologians see plausible connections between what is believed and what can be explained logically. For Śaivas, the Vaiṣṇava theology of divine descent is too real and crude to be accepted as a respectable theory about what God does. Whatever the Vaiṣṇavas may hope, the critique goes, their account of Nārāyaṇa's embodiment in divine descents condemns Nārāyaṇa to confinement and limitation within embodied existence. According to the Śaivas, the imagery of divine descent as mythological still confuses "body as matter" with "body as instrument of purpose" and fails to indicate that the former is not necessary while the latter is entirely appropriate. The Vaiṣṇavas want to defend both real embodiment and the divine perfection, but in the Śaiva view they disrespect the divine nature by attributing to it a crassly material embodiment. By contrast, Śiva is manifest, perceptible, and graciously possessed of the verbal and subordinate instrumental "body" by which he really encounters those whose salvation depends on him, yet he is not inappropriately mired in matter.[89] The Vaiṣṇava response, we may conjecture (for we seem to have no direct rejoinder to Aruḷ Nandi), is that God is ever more gracious and condescending than outsiders can imagine. As Śaṭakōpaṉ sang, the mystery is both simple and remarkable:

> By nature abiding as light, radiant, griefless splendor,
> the Lord endured afflictions and thereby made his divine state enter this world,
> appearing in human birth with its abundant griefs;
> he came to be seen by our eyes, excellent, griefless Kṛṣṇa, the marvelous one:
> when I shout his praises, I have no sorrow.[90]

God's Body: Arguing the Obvious—and the Inarguable

Some Hindu and Christian theologians thus share a basic disposition to agree that divine embodiment is possible and can be defended reasonably. Of course not all theologians in all religious traditions accept the idea of divine embodiment, and our interreligious study of a Christian and several Hindu theological positions samples only a narrow selection from a broader and more difficult theological scene. But in the traditions where divine embodiment is accepted as possible or as fact, it is dearly held as true. The Christian and Hindu

88. Ibid., 14.31, p. 119.

89. For a comparable Vaiṣṇava downgrading of the importance of Śiva, see Sudarśana Sūri's reading of the *Varāha Purāṇa* in chapter 3.

90. *Tiruvāymoḻi* III.10.6.

theologians considered in this chapter are deeply committed to explaining both the world and divine nature in such a way that makes it at least plausible, to insiders and outsiders, that divine embodiment can occur.

Divine embodiment stands forth as a primary religious belief and has important implications for worship and piety. Believing communities and their theologians cherish symbols that bring home the potent reality of divine embodiment in accessible material forms. The Sacred Heart, Śiva's *liṅga*, and Nārāyaṇa's divine feet are all concrete symbols that express core beliefs in a simple, vivid, and intense manner. They are symbols in Rahner's stronger sense, expressive of the divine reality that they symbolize: God's embodied and accessible presence. Encountering the heart, the *liṅga*, or the feet, devotees begin to apprehend in a tactile and even sensual fashion the material presence and commitment of God to the human race. God is here for us, in this particular form.

Given the intense affective attachment that grows up around these essential symbols of faith, we may wonder whether there is room for conversation about the differences in theoretical and practical conclusions as to when and how God actually becomes embodied. But the power of theological reflection lies in theologians' ability to render particular concrete beliefs and practices intelligible and available for conversation. The Christian, Vaiṣṇava, and Śaiva traditions all develop theologies that ably explain and justify particular ideas about divine embodiment. As a Christian theologian Rahner constructs a theory of symbol that helps him to explain how Jesus of Nazareth can be the unique point where God and humans meet. A Śaiva theologian searches out a language of instrumental bodies and mantra bodies because this language helps him to explain Śiva's real involvement in the world while defending his spiritual perfection. A Vaiṣṇava theologian introduces the aesthetic notion of dramatic gesture in order to emphasize the gracious accessibility of a Lord who is really but uniquely embodied. All these theologies have local and sectarian roots, but as reasonable and intelligently argued they become accessible across religious boundaries. While various theologians may work with varying understandings of human nature and may disagree about the meaning of body and soul and their relationship and about the meaning of birth and embodiment, they all seem comfortable with the paradox of a perfect God who freely chooses to assume a limited material form. So too, they agree on a basic qualified analogy: as humans are embodied, so God becomes embodied, though without the impurities, defects, or deleterious limitations that diminish the human condition. They agree too that the divine body is real, and they reject the theologically unsatisfying alternative of merely apparent birth. They agree that this real embodiment alters the dynamic of human worship. God despises neither the body nor this world; God's involvement uplifts rather than denigrates the human; God's embodiment is real, as is human embodiment.

Some differences regarding divine embodiment are important but not necessarily indications of contradiction. The Śaiva notion that "body" means not only the "material organism" but more important "that which is instrumental to a spiritual being's purposes" interestingly opens up ways of thinking about embodiment that might be ruled out by more literal understandings of body. Likewise, the Vaiṣṇava emphasis on the soteriological value of embodiment—the protection of the good, the defeat of the evil, and the approach of humans to a nearby God—offers a plausible foundation for combining soteriological, incarnational, and sacramental values in a way that the Christian tradition should be able to borrow and use.

It is true that devotion to the Son of God incarnate in Jesus is most often expressed in a totalizing language that excludes the possibility that God might have entered the world in other material forms. But still, many of the supportive Christian theological ideas, such as the openness of the human to the divine, the idea that divine incarnation completes the trajectory of human becoming, and even the idea that incarnation is an unsurpassable act of divine emptying should be recognizable and helpful to Hindu theologians who understand how complete and intense divine love is. While all of the traditions can be exclusive in their devotion and therefore in their theologies, the fact of passionate exclusivity should be no mystery at least to their theologians. It makes theological sense to claim that God is embodied *here* and also that God is not embodied *there*.

Despite the common ground and complementary variations, though, theology remains an argumentative venture. Theologians rank their own beliefs and theologies against those of others, perhaps especially those holding the closest and most similar positions, according to how closely they mirror the views of the theologian's home tradition. Such assessments take shape in further efforts to account for differences in belief. Quite often, theologians such as Rahner establish polar extremes between which the home tradition's theology is comfortably situated: Other theologians exaggerate God's transcendence or God's materiality, while ours represents the prudent mean between those extremes. Or, one may see virtue in extremity: Only our tradition takes embodiment so seriously as to realize the radical paradox of divine action.

Both Śaiva and Vaiṣṇava theologians may find the Christian emphasis on the uniqueness of the Incarnation and the importance of Christ's suffering needlessly literal-minded, perhaps a diminishment of divine dignity and in any case an instrument of polemic. Since our God suffers more than yours, our religion is superior to yours. When Rahner insists on the Incarnation and Christ's subsequent passion and death, he clearly believes that this embodiment, and none other, is the graced, adequate symbolization of God's power, freedom, and compassion. The particularity of the Christian position is clearest at this point, when the reality of embodiment is defined ultimately in terms of God's incarnate suffering.

Both Śaiva and Vaiṣṇava theologians likewise justify the real material presence of the Supreme Lord, even if the Lord's body is extraordinary, unlike other bodies, but they do not give primary significance to the sufferings of an embodied Lord. Rather, God becomes embodied to rectify the human condition, to provide occasions for humans to be taught, and to give opportunities for humans to be near the Lord. But in none of this does God suffer diminishment in precisely the way humans do.

We have seen that Śaiva theologians are wary of any view that suggests that embodiment diminishes the divine. They propose a "disguised presence" of Śiva in teachers who communicate Śiva's mystery and make known the way to him. Their allowance that Śiva has an auspicious body does not translate easily into a notion that Śiva literally walks the earth and enters into relationship with humans, even if traditions report numerous brief encounters. They reject as grossly anthropomorphic the Vaiṣṇava view of divine descents. Christian theologians may worry that "dramatic gesture" makes it sound as if divine embodiment is only apparent and may find the Śaiva understanding of Śiva's presence uncomfortably gnostic. In turn, Vaiṣṇava theologians may find the Śaiva theology rather vague and believe that both the Christian and Śaiva theologians underestimate the Lord's determination to be accessible within the world.

But today no Christian theologian can plausibly use the mystery of divine suffering as a shortcut to a comfortable conclusion that only the Christian understanding of divine embodiment makes sense, as if merely to know in advance of any comparison or dialogue that God does not really suffer in those other incarnations, they are not real. Nor can the graciousness of Śiva's mysterious embodiment in act and word nor the vivid particularity of Nārāyaṇa's multiple embodiments serve as an excuse for ignoring views Christians hold most dear. If I give an account of my beliefs, I then become accountable to a wider theological community that reaches beyond my own tradition. Even the most devout theologians have to defend their beliefs in a way that is at least minimally well informed about what others believe, and they must articulate their beliefs in a way that is at least potentially intelligible to theological peers in other traditions.

Because believers, theologians included, take divine embodiment and its symbols to be core truths in defense of which they can propose reasonable arguments, they must also believe that outsiders should at least be able to recognize their views as reasonable. Admitting the intense particularity of their own beliefs and those central to other traditions, theologians must still learn to offer explanations for their faith that still take seriously and respect the theologies and beliefs of other traditions. Theologians of various traditions can consider together a variety of reasonable theological views regarding divine embodiment and thereafter investigate together whether there are reasons that favor one understanding of that embodiment over other such understandings. In this more concrete interreligious conversation Christian, Śaiva, and Vaiṣṇava theologians can find constructive ways to question one another, to argue intelligently among themselves, and to account for their differing conclusions about how and when divine embodiment has occurred and what it means.

One can think about the options, sort them out, make comparisons, offer criticisms, and then make judgments about what is convincing and what is not. One may decide that Rahner makes more sense than Aruḷ Nandi on this issue, or that Vedānta Deśika explains embodiment more persuasively than

Rahner. But this interreligious theological critique will have to be at least as subtle and complex as the particular theological positions under consideration, as one explores with great respect the web of reasons, practices, beliefs, and pieties that undergird various convictions about God's embodiment.

Where does all this leave us? Here too Roberto de Nobili shows us where a strong emphasis on argument might lead. If I demonstrate the plausibility of my beliefs, this should persuade listeners to change the way they think, and this may lead them to refashion their piety as well. It is reasonable that this should be the case. Although arguments about divine embodiment differ greatly from arguments about whether the world has a maker or not, even at this point de Nobili sees sure and steady reasoning as key, a reliable preparation that better disposes one for the gift of faith. The mysteries specific to the Catholic faith are reasonable, he believes, and reasonable persons will come to respect them as more reasonable than all competing pieties. Mysteries such as the Incarnation and the consequent doctrine of the virginity of Mary are beyond what the mind can discover by itself but are not unintelligible. If learned believers from different religious traditions persevere in discussing the truths of religion with one another, they will eventually admit that the Christian faith is the most plausible. A reasonable person should be able to demonstrate to reasonable Hindus that core Hindu beliefs—for example, belief in Rāma as a divine descent of Nārāyaṇa or in Śiva as embodied and active in the world—simply do not make sense and do not measure up to the standards a reasonable religious person should accept.

In a small work entitled *The Summary of the Catechism*,[91] for example, de Nobili brought together rational principles, critiques of Indian beliefs, and an apologetic agenda, all with the goal of a demonstration of the good sense and holy depth of Christian doctrines. As he saw it, reflection on religious matters would certainly culminate in the acknowledgment that the specific Christian mysteries, including the birth of Jesus from the Virgin Mary, were the most plausible of beliefs. He thought this conclusion was genuinely reasonable, even if faith remained a matter of grace and the great truths were as much first principles as they were conclusions.

Few theologians and observers today share de Nobili's evangelical and optimistic rationalism, but his effort to argue the superior plausibility of Christian piety deserves serious consideration even by those of us who disagree with his reasoning. De Nobili is to be credited for inviting his interlocutors to reflect on specific beliefs and to ask whether they are more or less intelligible than other such beliefs. Honest reasoning and good sense cross religious boundaries. When theologians think about what they believe and find ways to discuss it with theologians of other traditions, this conversation makes very specific beliefs accessible to others.

The Christian can begin to apprehend, learn from, and be changed by Śaiva reflection on God's mysterious presence in the world and by Vaiṣṇava re-

91. In Tamil, the *Ñaṉōpatēca Kuṟippīṭam*.

flection on God's enormous self-humbling. In turn, Śaiva and Vaiṣṇava theologians can learn to think and see God differently after they have meditated on the Sacred Heart and the powerful symbol of the incarnate Son. Thereafter, neither the liṅga nor the cross nor the sacred feet will be thought of in quite the same way. For none of these symbols belongs solely to its original faith community any more, and no one will be easily able to disregard either the good theology or the underlying good faith of believers in other traditions who agree that God is embodied in the world.

There is yet one further step to take in our study. Communities and their theologians often define themselves and others in terms of revelation, which states rather starkly what is true and false, right from the start. It is important for us to consider how appeals to revelation function in relation to whether comparison and dialogue are worthwhile and whether there are still grounds on which theologians of different communities can speak to one another.

5

How Revelation Matters in the Assessment of Religions

Arguments about God's existence, God's identity, and God's manner of involvement in the world have been vigorously pursued and strongly defended in both the Hindu and Christian theological contexts. Distinguishing features notwithstanding, Hindu and Christian versions of the cosmological argument, traditional forms of apologetics, and efforts to explain both divine embodiment and divine transcendence without detriment to either have important common features that cross religious and cultural boundaries. We can conclude that all of these theologians, Christian and Hindu, are engaged in the common work of theology and can be involved in a common conversation through which they can all grow in their knowledge of God's existence, God's identity, and God's activity in the world.

The stubborn differences among traditions reemerge more strongly when we recall how theologians bolster their religious arguments by appealing not only to reasoning and the community's shared understanding of God's identity and activity but also to authoritative (oral or written) texts invested with the authority of revelation. Appeals to revelation encourage and safeguard claims to a special wisdom, which cannot be reduced simply to its rational components. As we shall see, this revelation can be conceived of in several ways: as God's self-communication, as a sacred act of language that transforms those who learn it and either instigates them to right action or enables them to attain higher levels of reality, and as God speaking—to humans and to God—in a beautiful human voice. The tendency to simplify and clarify religious matters by appeals to what is reasonable and common is slowed and constrained by the persistence of revelation as a—or better, *the*—defining measure of truth and identity. It may appear a standard that is unrelentingly severe and perhaps so strict as to be useless in a complex religious environment. Christians hear the Word of God and accept it as such from the start, even if they theologize about it later. Traditional Hindus are born and educated into a world of belief and practice shaped by the Veda, even if they too are able to step back and investigate its rationale at a later stage. Theologians in both traditions defer to the authority of revelation, want to use words and concepts that make that deference clear, and explain the world consonantly with scripture.

Of course, appealing to revelation need not entail abandoning reason. Theologians give reasons even for their appeals to revelation, argue that it is reasonable to give priority to revelation, and strive to have revelation harmoniously guide reasoning in its method and agenda. Such appeals help communities render evident the credibility of the positions they hold due to their adherence to revelation. Not only are certain specific views reasonable, but they are also warranted in the sacred word. So too, what is revealed is not inimical to reason. If a revealed truth does not seem reasonable at first glance, one must keep studying the sacred text until one sees how it shapes a reasonable way of viewing the world.

Prior commitments to revelation afford to a priori evaluations of "the other" a certain respectability and force. Indeed, great deference toward revelation and the judgments consequent upon it may seem to halt or subvert interreligious theological reflection before it gets started. Nothing from outside can ever rival what is learned from inside, from revelation as it illumines the world and uncovers its darkness and wickedness. But when theologians in the various religious traditions not only accept scriptural truths and judgments but also interpret them and then explain their interpretations, show their coherence with other revealed truths, and assess other, possibly competing aspects of reality according to revelation, then we are again presented with the opportunity to bring even the judgment of revelation upon religions into an interreligious, comparative, and dialogical conversation and to do this without diminishing a sense of revelation's power and truth.

To maintain the credibility of theology's interreligious nature, we need to examine more closely how commitments to revelation affect the way Christian and Hindu theologians reason about religions other than their own. What might be learned from reason is from the start constricted by an admission that revelation must remain normative for how the world and even the data of experience are to be understood.

In this chapter I therefore do not intend to survey views of revelation nor to inquire into the criteria (within traditions or across traditions' boundaries) one should use in identifying some utterance as revelatory nor do I exegete specific texts put forward as revelatory. Rather, I push matters forward simply by considering two questions: What is the core of revelation? How is religion (and religions, gods, religious practices and ways of life) to be assessed in light of that core? I focus on several instances where appeals to revelation serve to categorize what is natural, outside of, or opposed to revelation. We shall see that such appeals are used in similar ways in both the Christian and Hindu traditions.

Of course, since we have been reading theological texts in previous chapters, we have already been dealing with issues related to revelation—and with scriptural texts and the scriptural authority that flows from revelation. Most theologians have been formed by scriptural views that are operative even when the theologians appear simply to be presenting reasoned bases for their beliefs. Von Balthasar's understanding of the interpersonal manifestation of God in Jesus Christ is in part a reflection on the specific and historically conditioned contents of the New Testament. The Mīmāṃsā and Vedānta theologians criticized the logicians' induction of God's existence from a perspective of "scripture first," while the Śaivas and Vaiṣṇavas made liberal use of scriptural passages to inform and undergird their reasoned positions about God.

To discern more clearly how theological judgments about religions are made within the confines of a commitment to revelation, we begin by examining how Karl Barth, a Christian theologian, has identified the core of revelation and then used it as the measure for assessing other people's religions. Then we will turn to the Hindu theological traditions for several parallel examples.

Karl Barth: Revelation and the Construction of Religions

Religion in Light of Revelation: A Priori Position

Our inquiry is largely limited to chapter 2 of *Church Dogmatics* I.2, in which Karl Barth explores revelation and religion as related themes.[1] Section 17 is entitled "The Revelation of God as the Abolition of Religion," and in turn it is divided into three subsections. "The Problem of Religion in Theology" (17.1) traces the confusion between revelation and religion and the confusion between Christianity as the religion that is true because it is favored by God and other religions. "Religion as Unbelief" (17.2) explains how religion, in all its various forms, is essentially a human effort to control God, to achieve salvation, and so on, and is therefore entirely different from the only point that matters: the encounter with Jesus Christ as God's revelation. "True Religion" (17.3) assesses Christianity and, by way of two examples, other religions in light of revelation.

Barth insists that prior to any consideration of revelation in relation to a canon of scripture or the content of biblical books, revelation must be understood first of all as an act of God, God's free and gracious self-presentation

1. The general context is as follows: a treatment of the Trinity, as the starting point for understanding the dynamic of revelation, concluded I.1 of *Church Dogmatics*. The sections of I.2 place firmly together the mysteries of the incarnation, the Holy Spirit as the subjective reality of revelation, the relation of revelation and religion, and humans as doers of God's Word (respectively, sections 13–15, 16, 17, and 18 of chapter 2); the character of the Bible itself (chapter 3); and the proclamation of the revealed word in the Church (chapter 4).

to humans. To ponder revelation is first of all to reflect on God in communication with the human race. From the start it is also a question of reflection on that divine speech, the person who is revelation, Jesus Christ, who is revealed, who reveals, and who alone makes God fully present to humans: "According to Holy Scripture God's revelation takes place in the fact that God's Word became a man and that this man has become God's Word. The incarnation of the eternal Word, Jesus Christ, is God's revelation. In the reality of this event God proves that he is free to be our God."[2]

As a matter of general theological principle, Barth's position is of course quite compatible with von Balthasar's and Rahner's reflections on Jesus Christ as the manifestation of God. Revelation is primarily the person of Jesus, not his words nor the scriptural accounts about him. Even the human encounter with Christ and potential reception of revelation must also be primarily about God, because it is the Spirit of God that makes it possible for humans to recognize Jesus and respond to divine revelation.

From the start, the self-authenticating Word of God affords the indisputable, a priori perspective from which everything not the Word, not God's revelation, and secondarily not biblical and ecclesial, is to be judged. Whatever is of human origin and thus not entirely dependent on the divine initiative is best defined by a "not," lest there be some confusion regarding the power of revelation and the human mode of access to it. This applies perhaps particularly to the Christian religion for which more is at stake:

> Revelation singles out the Church as the locus of true religion. But this does not mean that the Christian religion as such is the fulfilled nature of human religion. It does not mean that the Christian religion is the true religion, fundamentally superior to all other religions. We can never stress too much the connection between the truth of the Christian religion and the grace of revelation.[3]

For Barth, revelation alone is the criterion for judgment on what is not revelation. Indeed, that is the judgment: everything else, whatever its value, is not-revelation. Accordingly, his approach to religions is rooted in his insistence that all theological reflection must begin with revelation, God's communication in the incarnate Word, Jesus Christ. It is this first, primal utterance that illuminates and makes clear how things stand between God and humans. In that stark light, one can then see that the whole human situation is spiritually void prior to the enunciation of God's word but also, thereafter, that it is illuminated in Christ's death on the cross.

Barth's assessment of religions is a striking mix of sympathy, Christian self-critique, and great disregard for other religions. But however we evaluate this attitude, it is important to recognize from the start that the contest is not among religions nor between the Bible and the texts of other religions. Rather, Barth is asking his readers to understand the Bible in the context of God's self-manifestation and to give primacy to nothing but that manifesta-

2. *Church Dogmatics* I.2, p. 1.
3. Ibid., p. 298.

tion: God on the one side, everything else on the other, including (of course) religions.

Consequently, the assessment of religions can be undertaken only in accord with an acknowledgment of revelation understood in this fashion. The true study of religions is a secondary function of attention to the Word of God, Jesus Christ, and the Bible. When Barth considers religions he intends to do so strictly in light of the Word of God spoken freely to humans out of sheer grace and without regard for whatever else they may have been doing or trying to do beforehand. Of course, one might begin the other way around. One could begin by studying various human ideas and efforts and then, in light of those, find room for an accommodated version of the Word. But by this method one would be fooling oneself, futilely trying to explain revelation in light of religion.

It is essential to the dynamic of revelation that it drags into clear light both the incapacity of humans to accomplish salvation on their own and their stubborn effort to do so by their religions. However understandable such efforts might be as expressive of a basic human desire for security and contentment, they are essentially worthless when assessed as ways of finding God and salvation. They are doomed to fail and, worse still, they are also evasions of God's Word; they postpone and block the required submission to God, who speaks in Jesus Christ. Because revelation is God's self-offering and self-manifestation, religion—all religions—is actually unbelief, a human substitute for the work of God. Humans try to imagine what God must be like and extrapolate an image of God from within the limits of human experience, but as this act of willful construction "man's religion is simply an assumption and assertion of this kind, and as such it is an activity which contradicts revelation—contradicts it, because it is only through truth that truth comes to man."[4] And, more vividly:

> If man tries to grasp at truth of himself, he tries to grasp at it a priori. But in that case he does not do what he has to do when the truth comes to him. He does not believe. If he did, he would listen; but in religion he talks. If he did, he would accept a gift; but in religion he takes something for himself. If he did, he would let God Himself intercede for God; but in religion he ventures to grasp at God. Because it is a grasping, religion is the contradiction of revelation, the concentrated expression of human unbelief, i.e., an attitude and activity which is directly opposed to faith. It is a feeble but defiant, an arrogant but hopeless, attempt to create something which man could do, but now cannot do, or can do only because and if God Himself creates it for him: the knowledge of the truth, the knowledge of God.[5]

One can only conclude that religion and revelation are irreconcilably at odds with one another. There is no "harmonious co-operating of man with the revelation of God, as though religion were a kind of outstretched hand which is filled by God in His revelation." Revelation does not satisfy the in-

4. Ibid., p. 301.
5. Ibid., pp. 302–303.

herent "religious capacity of man." Rather "we have here an exclusive contradiction. In religion man bolts and bars himself against revelation by providing a substitute, by taking away in advance the very thing which has to be given by God." The clash is stark, since "revelation does not link up with a human religion which is already present and practiced. It contradicts it, just as religion previously contradicted revelation."[6]

The Word of God is not conformed to human expectations as some kind of complement to human striving for the divine. It arrives abruptly, breaks in on the human condition, and shatters the various human projects aimed at acquiring the divine. Therefore, there is no question of valuing religions as preparatory for the Word. Religions are not only judged by revelation but they are also created, named, and given definition in accordance with it: *revelation* is what is "not human striving" but is God's action, while *religion* is human striving, and the world religions are nothing but that striving. Throughout, however, we must remember that if taken as religion and human invention, Christianity is in the same category as the others. Barth emphasizes that Christianity too is under judgment from all angles except that of God's gracious election. The difference, in the end, is that Christianity is chosen by God and is therefore able to adhere strictly to the Word of God and to rise beyond its independent worthlessness and become the locus for the work of God's Word.[7] It is only God's election that makes Christianity the true religion, and we know the fact of this choice from revelation. In theory Barth's position undercuts many of the strategies one might use to assert the superiority of Christianity as morally better, culturally more advanced, theologically smarter, and so on.[8] In practice, though, his Evangelical Protestant rendering of the Gospel remains reliable and relevant as the best available norm by which reliable judgments can be made about every other religion.

Religions Actually Judged: Applying the A Priori

Religions must be judged without compromise and their status as not-revelation clearly uncovered. The Christian religion is graciously allowed by God to be the location of encounter with Jesus Christ; that encounter is a gift that has nothing to do with Christianity as one of the religions. If this assertion seems also to be a dismissal of the theological relevance of anything anyone in any religion might have to say, that too is Barth's intention. The judgment on religions in light of revelation must be a priori; no aspect of the judgment can be affected by actual knowledge of religions. It is not a measured process of weighing evidence, which concludes with the worthlessness of religions; it is a matter of principle, not an induction, and it must be this way. Unless one begins with revelation and judges everything in light of it a priori, one will never gain a proper understanding of revelation at all:

6. Ibid., p. 303.
7. Ibid., p. 298.
8. Ibid., pp. 332, 349.

> Therefore the true and essential distinction of the Christian religion over against the non-Christian, and with its character as the religion of truth over against the religion of error, can be demonstrated only in the fact, or event, that taught by Holy Scripture the Church listens to Jesus Christ and no one else as grace and truth.[9]

Had Barth simply stopped after saying that Christianity—in its evangelical Protestant form—is the one religion that God has justified, his strong faith position might be respected as a spiritual and faith testimony beyond criticism except perhaps by other Evangelical Protestant Christians, who could look at the same Christian sources as Barth and disagree with him about what those sources tell the theologian. But Barth does not adhere exclusively to the a priori; he cannot resist adducing a few examples drawn from particular religious traditions. Similarities are much more troublesome for him than differences, of course, and so it is instructive to notice how he handles similarities on the rare occasion that he does get more specific.

In section 17.3 ("True Religion") of I.2, Barth acknowledges the Yodo Shin and Yodo Shin-shu sects of Japanese Buddhism as seeming to share notions of faith and grace very similar to those articulated in Evangelical Protestantism.[10] He describes briefly the importance of placing trust in Amida, the Compassionate One, and summarizes a kind of Buddhist creed:

> We have to believe in Him, who has compassion on all, even sinners. We have to call on his name, and as we do so all his good works and meritorious acts stream into our mouths and become our own possession, so that our merit is Amida's merit, and there is no difference between him and us.[11]

Barth also asserts that in fact Yodo Shin-shu reduces faith and grace to a kind of mechanism and has no place for the drama of divine intervention for the sake of human redemption. He then entirely deflates the similarity by introducing a key methodological strategy: similarities only help to demonstrate just how specially God has treated his church and how subtle are the human evasions of the fact of this grace. Christians should not be surprised to find a teaching so close to proper Christian teaching even among the Japanese. The similarity is evidence of human ingenuity—humans are very clever in their ideas—but also of divine providence, since the very fact of parallels with Japanese Buddhism reminds Christians that religions and theologies are human products and as such are likely to be found in every place where human invention prevails.[12] That the Japanese think their way to conclusions

9. Ibid., p. 344.

10. "Die Japaner," *Lehrbuch*, 1:252–422. Regarding Barth's knowledge of Buddhism and Hinduism, we note that he mentions several reference works, the most important of which is the 1925 edition of Chantepie de la Saussaye's two-volume *Lehrbuch der Religionsgeschichte*. This is a solid academic collection in which scholars offer learned treatments of modern and ancient religions and offer a summary of secondary sources about each religion. K. Florenz is the author of the description of Japanese religion in the *Lehrbuch*.

11. I.2, p. 340.

12. Ibid., p. 342.

similar to those of Evangelical Protestants should have a chastening, humbling effect on Christians, so they will no longer pride themselves on the uniqueness of Christian ideas. For it is not proper theory that makes Christian faith true, it is rather and only "the name of Jesus Christ."[13] The fact of a Japanese theology of grace shows ultimately that "all this [correct doctrine] the heathen, too, can in their own way teach and even live and represent as a church. Yet that does not mean that they are any the less heathen, poor, and utterly lost."[14] This approach is also rather useful to Barth as a scholar who needs to account for religions rather quickly. No information learned from religious thinkers need ever disturb the theologian except by way of chastening the overconfident. Theological similarities are not really theologically important.

While Barth has some measure of respect for Yodo Shin-shu Buddhism, he more quickly points out negative features of Vaiṣṇavism, particularly the Śrīvaiṣṇava tradition which we have considered a number of times.[15] He dismisses the idea of *bhakti*, devotion toward God:

> *Bhakti* is an act of utter surrender and resignation.[16] In it our own will is placed absolutely at the service of another's. . . . The high or supreme God to whom *Bhakti* is offered can have any name or character. It is the emotion of love itself and as such which redeems man, which enables him to participate in the answering love of God.[17]

Barth notes that there was discussion among the Vaiṣṇavas about the balance between grace and works, as signaled by the famous analogy of the cat and the monkey. The kitten is totally dependent on its mother, who picks it up in her teeth, while the young monkey, also dependent, must nevertheless cling to its mother. For one school of Śrīvaiṣṇavas, humans are like kittens in that they are totally dependent on God.[18]

Barth denies that there is any theological significance to the comparison. For numerous reasons, Vaiṣṇavism's teaching cannot be compared with true

13. Ibid., p. 343.

14. Ibid.

15. Although Barth gives no reference to document the source of his knowledge of Vaiṣṇava theology, he is presumably again relying on the *Lehrbuch*, which, in volume 2, contains a long treatment of religion in India by Sten Kronow ("Die Inder," *Lehrbuch*, 2:1–198). Kronow devotes five sections to the Indian tradition of *bhakti*, which is devotion, love, and participation in God. Kronow's exposition offers fair though brief and rather general descriptions of many important aspects of this devotional tendency in Hinduism, without any explicit Christian theological judgments. He devotes considerable attention to the *bhakti* tradition of Rāmānuja, tradition which Barth mentions in discussing the role of grace and love in Hinduism. Kronow points out that the Śrīvaiṣṇavas, inspired as they were by the non-elitist religion of the Tamil Vaiṣṇava saints—the āḻvārs, including Śaṭakōpaṉ—presented a theology of total surrender, unrestricted by caste considerations, as the superior pathway to God.

16. In discussing "utter surrender," Barth might more correctly have used the term *prapatti* rather than *bhakti*.

17. I.2, pp. 341–342.

18. See Mumme for a theological contextualization of the images of monkey and cat.

Christianity (i.e., Evangelical Protestantism), as we can glean from Barth's further comments on *bhakti*:

> The most uncertain part played by the idea of God, the substitution of surrender and love for faith, and the utter and complete formlessness even of the concept of love, show that we are in a quite different world from that of the Japanese religion of grace, and an absolutely different world from that of Evangelical Christianity. It would be a very degenerate form of Evangelical Christianity which felt that the *Bhakti* religions could claim kinship with it.[19]

A number of criticisms can be gleaned from Barth's brief comments on Vaiṣṇava devotion: devotion (*bhakti*) can be offered to a God of any name or character; the emotion of love, initiated by humans, is what saves and not the gracious love of God; "surrender and love" replace faith; this concept of love is utterly and completely formless; the "idea of God" is uncertain; and finally, the only role *bhakti* religion leaves to God is that he respond to the human decision to love God. On the whole, Barth determines, Vaiṣṇavism is less like Christianity than Yodo Shin-shu Buddhism, although neither is significant in light of revelation.

Of course, Barth's point was never good Buddhology nor respectable Indology but a specifically theological critique. The Christian—Protestant—religion of grace is not the true religion merely because it is a religion of grace nor because it is a better religion of more grace; there may be numerous religions that include notions of grace and that could be included in the category. Rather:

> Only one thing is decisive for the distinction of truth and error, and we call the existence of Yodoism a providential disposition because with what is relatively the greatest possible force it makes it so clear that only one thing is decisive. That one thing is the name of Jesus Christ.[20]

The key to the specificity of the revelation is none of the accompanying theological concepts but only Jesus Christ. There is nothing a Hindu or Buddhist theologian could say that would make a difference. Yet judging solely by "the name of Jesus Christ" still leaves some room for further judgments, such as singling out "Yodoism" and "*Bhakti* religion" for distinct treatments. Barth is also showing that he can be selective in his treatment of the content of religions and briefly at least ventures beyond his simple and pure a priori to make a series of specific complaints about Vaiṣṇavism. "Unbelief" does come in several shades of black.

Barth sets his priorities clearly and within the boundaries of those priorities reasons lucidly about what is humanly and religiously possible outside the community of those who have conformed their lives to revelation. In his own stark way he is an exemplary theologian, reasonable and consistent. As we now turn to the Hindu context we shall see how Barth is not unique in this regard. He shares this approach and attitude with important Hindu theolo-

19. I.2, p. 342.
20. Ibid., p. 343 (slightly modified).

gians as well. That "every religion is to be judged in light of revelation," that there is a true religion, and that religions can be judged are Hindu as well as Christian theological claims.[21]

Reasoning about Religions in Light of Revelation in the Hindu Context

Revelation, the Veda, and the Obligation to Action According to Mīmāṃsā Theology

We saw in chapter 2 that the Mīmāṃsā theologians were skeptical about establishing a completely rational framework for their beliefs about ritual and religious values. In the context of defending verbal knowledge as real knowledge not reducible to a mere expression of experience or reason, they argued that knowledge could not be narrowed exclusively to direct perception, since perception could and should serve as a basis for important inductions (even if not an induction of God's existence). They also believed that in addition to perception and induction verbal knowledge offers a third way of knowing. According to Mīmāṃsā theory, the quest for religious truth begins with submission to the privileged linguistic communication that is the Veda, the canon

21. Some readers will point out that later Barth seems to have softened his position on religions. In *Church Dogmatics* IV.3, for example, his meditations on Jesus Christ as "the light of life" and "the one Word of God" afford him the opportunity to ask how God might be working or speaking outside the explicitly Christian context. He admits that there may be "other lights which are quite clear and other revelations which are quite real. We may think of the prophets of the Old Testament and the apostles in the New. We may think of the genuine prophecy and apostolate of the Church. And why should not the world have its varied prophets and apostles in different degrees?" Indeed, not everything is "valueless, empty, and corrupt," not all the lights are misleading, nor can we conclude that "all the revelations are necessarily untrue" (IV.3.1, p. 97). Rather, Barth says, his point is only to highlight what is first, central, and normative: "Our statement is simply to the effect that Jesus Christ is the one and only Word of God, that He alone is the light of God and the revelation of God. It is in this sense that it delimits all other words, lights, revelations, prophecies and apostolates, whether of the Bible, the Church or the world, by what is declared in and with the existence of Jesus Christ" (IV.3.1, p. 97). But in the end the judgment remains sure, as unrelenting as in the beginning: "But what a mass of rudiments and fragments which in their isolation and absoluteness say something very different from this Word! What strife and contradiction between all these results of one-sided analyses and over-hasty syntheses" (IV.3.1, p. 108). Only a superficial, misplaced comparison—such as would compare the words of the Church or of the Bible with the words of other religious institutions or other scriptures—could succeed in bringing "the Word of Jesus Christ and its claim to validity" down to the level of other such words. But this is impossible, since "we are speaking of the light or Word of the life of Jesus Christ" (IV.3.1, p. 108). Barth opened the door just a crack to a different kind of analysis in which his confession of Christian faith could be explored in a comparative and dialogical context; but then, he shut it rather quickly, lest anyone might actually walk through it. One might also examine Barth's ecclesiology in *Church Dogmatics* IV.3 (second half) and his comments there on the world-Church relationship. See Ward, 2000, pp. 303–311. For perspectives on Barth's assessment of religions that are well-informed both Indologically and theologically, see Carman, 1974, pp. 264–271, and Carman, 1994, pp. 421–429.

of Sanskrit sacred texts for ritual practice, recitation, and meditation. When the Mīmāṃsā (and then Vedānta) theologians criticized the Nyāya induction of God's existence, they contrasted Nyāya's fundamental confidence in the force of reasoning about God with their own insistence that one must learn about ritual performance (or, in Vedānta, Brahman) from revelation, thereafter supporting that knowledge by reasoned arguments. Overconfidence in reason poses a threat to the authority of scripture, and one has to remain skeptical about what can be accomplished by reasoning and even about the plausibility of inductions.

The Mīmāṃsā theologians introduced a series of somewhat peculiar claims in defense of their understanding of Vedic revelation. First, the Veda is eternal. It was not composed or redacted as Veda at some particular time and place but is older than the world. It is beginningless and authorless, always and simply itself. One must therefore reject theories about who authored the Veda, based on what knowledge or for what purpose, and the Veda should not be linked to particular events and people contemporary to a time of actual composition. Obviously then the Veda is quite different from all other texts, purely and simply an act of sacred speech. Moreover, although the Veda is sacred language, it is not a special message from a particular personal speaker. It is not the voice of God nor God's self-communication. Indeed, it is best understood without recourse to the God concept and without dependence on the value of an I-thou relationship. It is effective simply by its linguistic power as it shapes personal and social values. We will see below how Rāmānuja's Vedānta and South Indian devotionalism modify this viewpoint to restore priority to God, but even then revelation appears more as God's verbal embodiment and eternal act of language rather than as divine self-communication. Finally, since the Veda is a beginningless act of language not to be assessed in terms of the particular persons and events nor conceived of as interpersonal communication, it is fundamentally a privileged linguistic event that shapes the cognitive context in which everything else is to be understood. To hear or recite the Veda is to become subject to the revelatory influence of its language and educated by it. One does not reason to the obligatory force of the Veda; it confronts one from the start and molds how one perceives the world and reasons about it.[22]

What does so extraordinary a revelation have to tell us? From the start, it seems, the Mīmāṃsā theologians ruled out linking its significance to the value of any referent mentioned in it. Instead, they focused on its performative power. The early Mīmāṃsā teachers Jaimini and Śabara argued that the meanings of words in the Veda are ordinary and non-esoteric.[23] No particular referent is extraordinary. The things mentioned in the Veda, including the rice

22. See Clooney, 1988c and 1990, particularly pp. 118–125. The overview offered here does not explore all the differences of opinion on how one is obliged by the Veda, e.g., whether this obligation is communicated in terms of self-interest (as in the school of Kumārila) or in terms of a more primordial "ought" (as in the school of Prabhākara). On the differences between the schools, see Clooney, 1990, chap. 7.

23. See *Śabara Bhāṣya*, vol. 1, p. 1, where Śabara elaborates his theory of ordinary language in reference to the *Sūtras* and the Veda; see also Clooney, 1990, pp. 131–137.

and firewood used in rituals and the various gods who are the recipients of offerings, are all knowable in ordinary life by perception, by inference, and by the reliable testimony of trustworthy people. Significance is instead inscribed in the sentences and larger units of Vedic language performance. What one must do in order to fulfill one's ritual obligations cannot be learned from observing the world; it is this path of right action that must be revealed in the Veda, since otherwise it would not be known at all. In turn, the sacred core of that action is the simple injunction to act, the sheer, irreducible force of the imperative itself—Do!—in relation to which the rest of the Veda is to be derived. The core of the Veda's authority and coherence is therefore the sheer obligation that imposes itself on potential ritual performers.

The obligation to action enunciated in the Veda is further specified in two ways. First, although rituals are complex activities defined by numerous features (including special offering materials, certain texts to be recited, gods to whom the offerings are to be made, and particular ways of proceeding), nevertheless the simple essence of the action of sacrifice is the moment at which a sacrificer surrenders some possession to some deity by destroying it in fire. This is the duty enjoined in Vedic obligation in regard to which the rest of the Veda and its rituals are to be measured. Since the Veda intends primarily to instigate ritual practice, its information about ordinary things, such as gods, the performer, and rewards, cannot be allowed to distract from the primary performative intent. Whichever parts of the Veda do not contribute directly to performance (by providing what is to be said or what is to be done) are secondary and must be interpreted in support of the explicitly ritual portions of the Veda.[24] As we shall see below, by Mīmāṃsā standards even the Upaniṣads, which claim to give information about the nature of ultimate reality (*brahman*), the self (*ātman*), and liberation (*mokṣa*), are valuable only if these notions contribute to better ritual performance.

Second, humans too are measured according to this pragmatic revelatory standard and assigned their place in relation to the ritual action. Because revelation is not right knowledge but right action, it comes in user-specific forms. When the Vedic texts announce the obligation to act, the message is not aimed in general at the entire set of conscious beings but only at particular people obliged under particular circumstances. The male brahmin, for instance, has a role as the sacrificer who actualizes the rite by being its patron; and the various priests (ranging from one to sixteen or more) have specific roles to play within the performances of the rites. Some rites are obligatory for all upper-caste males (for example, the daily morning and evening fire oblations); some are obligatory under certain conditions (for instance, at a certain season or at the time of a birth or death); and some oblige only those interested in receiving certain rewards (for example, rites that offer particular benefits, such as the acquisition of more cows or conceiving a new son).

24. As stated by Kumārila in his commentary on Śabara at 1.2.1–18.

As a particular instance of reliable verbal communication, Vedic revelation is distinguished by the deeply embedded religious and ritual values and traditions of the orthodox brahmanical community. Even if the Veda is indisputably true, its location is specific. It was not expressed for everyone all at once, and there was no requirement to present its truth to all nor any reason to expect everyone to be capable of understanding it. The audience capable of recognizing the truth and performing it is small. The Mīmāṃsā theoretical interest in religions is therefore minimal and practical. Revelation is understood as one puts it into practice and is directed and corrected by it. Unprepared—uninterested or illiterate—listeners are not capable of a proper, active response and are not likely to become ready in their current birth. For the most part, nothing much need be said about such persons, provided they do not interfere with the lives of those who are educated in accord with the powerful language of revelation. So too, it should be clear, understanding revelation is not a decipherment of an I-thou, divine–human, encounter. In a sense it is an encounter with language, a prolonged and ever-deepening practice of listening and reading. One is gradually educated according to the standards of the text, an insider gradually enabled to perform properly according to properly understood Vedic texts. That revelation is performative does not close the door to thinking about a wider variety of religious topics, but the wider inquiry has to be mediated through the observation and assessment of behavior rather than ideas. What people think is less important than how they act.

Mīmāṃsā's Grammar of Religious Plurality: Stretching the Boundaries of Orthodoxy

This strict Mīmāṃsā position, a reading of the world focused entirely on the commitment to right performance by the right people, exemplifies a severe commitment to an a priori revelation. In effect, it is positively Barthian. Nonetheless, because they are theologians, the Mīmāṃsā theorists still have to account for the world, the seemingly non-Vedic reality that is not ordered to Vedic performance and is even dismissive of Vedic values. After establishing the authority of the Veda, the Mīmāṃsā theologians still have to assess the status of whatever might seem to lie beyond the boundaries of Vedic revelation without merely claiming that what is Vedic is revealed and what is not Vedic is not revealed. We now examine how the narrow reading of Vedic and non-Vedic is widened in a shift as the single criterion—the Do! of ritual obligation—is broadened into a standard of moral rectitude and thereafter (in Vedānta) into a new appreciation of knowledge.

The problem of religions is taken up when the Mīmāṃsā theologians turn their attention to the wide array of practices and texts counted in the category of looser textual authorities described as "what is remembered" (*smṛti*). These are traditions and traditional texts, oral and written, which record moral and ritual activities that, even if not entirely documented in the Veda, are practiced and promoted by respectable people who otherwise observe the Veda.

Such traditions lack the authoritative weight of the Veda but cannot be simply dismissed. The Mīmāṃsā solution is to stretch the boundaries of the Veda to include a much wider range of materials and to account for the new in such a way as to respect the already settled authority of the old.

The criteria for this expanded inclusion are stated and applied in sections I.2 and I.3 of the *Mīmāṃsā Sūtras* of Jaimini and elaborated by his commentator Śabara and particularly by Kumārila Bhaṭṭa in his commentary on Śabara. The key rules can be summarized in accord with Kumārila's comments in *Tantravārtika* I.3:[25]

> Traditional texts, and the practices they prescribe, must be disregarded when they truly conflict with the Veda, since the Veda always takes precedence.[26]
>
> But the presumption is that there is no conflict; properly interpreted, traditional texts and practices will be seen to conform to the Veda; one can assume that these traditions can be traced back to either extant or lost Vedic texts.[27]
>
> Traditional texts and practices can be rejected if it is clear that they are prompted by base motives or malicious intent.[28]
>
> If the performers of traditional practices are of good character and reputation, this can be accepted as grounds for determining that the practices have some Vedic connection.[29]
>
> If words have Vedic and non-Vedic meanings that appear contradictory, Vedic meanings take precedence.[30]
>
> Words and customs of foreign origins are to be interpreted as having the same meanings as their counterparts in the Veda; they are not to be excluded merely because they are not found in the Veda.[31]
>
> Other traditional texts with practical value, such as accessory ritual texts, popular customs, and grammatical treatises, are likewise to be respected as authoritative insofar as they are compatible with the Veda and have some clear use.[32]

Although Kumārila insists on defining reality within the limits of revelation, his definition is somewhat generous as he rules in favor of connections and even indirect legitimacy. This scheme relies on more elastic factors, such

25. The *Tantravārtika* is Kumārila's commentary on Śabara's commentary (*bhāṣya*) on the *Sūtras* of Jaimini, I.2–III.8. The *Ślokavārtika* is a commentary on just the first part (I.1) of Śabara's commentary on Jaimini, but in it Kumārila also elaborates amply the philosophical bases of the Mīmāṃsā positions.

26. I.3.1–2.

27. I.3.3.

28. I.3.4.

29. I.3.5–7.

30. I.3.8–9 (according to one of several interpretations of the topic offered by Kumārila).

31. I.3.10. Kumārila explains that words such as *pika* (cuckoo) and *nema* (half) are used in the Veda but are not Sanskrit words. It only makes sense to interpret such words as they are understood by the people who use them so long as no conclusions contrary to the Veda would have to be drawn.

32. Accessory ritual texts (1.3.11–14, seventh topic), popular customs (1.3.15–23, eighth topic), grammatical treatises (1.3.24–29, ninth topic). Under the seventh topic Kumārila raises the question of the Buddhists, and rejects Buddhist positions as incompatible with the Veda.

as possible Vedic connections, evidence of good behavior, and the lack of apparent contradiction to the Veda. Any small indication of a Vedic resemblance counts a great deal. The instinct, it seems, is to include as much as possible in the Vedic fold even if the first reason for this inclusion may be an instinct for self-preservation in the face of the new. It remains elitist because it appeals to the example of the "right" people, who serve as models for right behavior because, somewhat circularly, they are already known to be respectable and reliable. Observe what honorable people do, and search out reasons for their behavior that are at least indirectly connected to the Veda. By contrast, the illiterate, those who misbehave, and mere outsiders matter less, and their behavior has no deep religious significance.[33]

We can better understand the elasticity that Kumārila pragmatically introduces into the Vedic calculus if we note where this elasticity stops and where the limits are firmly drawn. This we can do by examining an important case, the exclusion of the Buddhists and their religion. As we saw in chapter 2, Kumārila and the Buddhists agree on the defectiveness of the induction of a God who is both the maker of the world and author of the Veda. But Kumārila broke with the Buddhists because of his views of language and objective reality. In explicating *Pūrva Mīmāṃsā Sūtras* I.3.3–4 and I.3.11–14 in the *Tantravārtika* Kumārila denies orthodox standing to the Buddhist writings on moral rather than philosophical grounds.[34]

33. Jayanta Bhaṭṭa's elaborate defense of the Veda in the fourth part of the *Nyāya Mañjarī* proceeds along much the same lines as that of Kumārila, to whom Jayanta seems indebted. Jayanta insists that reliable scriptures, both primary and secondary, need to be internally coherent. He likewise recognizes that their significance has much to do with right ritual and moral practice. As for deciding which traditions are authentic, he too suggests standards that are not severely restrictive. Even inferior traditions can be respected provided they do not contradict the Veda explicitly nor promote unacceptable morality. The various schools of the Veda, which differ among themselves regarding the details of text and practice, should all be recognized as harmonious except if some clear reason compels one to judge otherwise. One can similarly judge local traditions. Some texts and practices must be rejected because they do not live up to settled criteria. They are not accepted by respected persons; they were only recently composed; they introduce unprecedented conduct; greed may be a motive for their composition; and they preach doctrines that cause good people to be anxious. Jayanta likewise defends the authority of *dharmaśāstra*, the texts that describe and order the life of orthodox people, as well as the authority of the traditional texts of the Śaivas and Vaiṣṇavas. He observes that there is nothing about such texts that inherently contradicts the Veda, since whatever differences they may contain are optional and do not directly contradict the obligations imposed by the Veda. That a different God is worshiped in each context is not treated as problematic. See *Nyāya Mañjarī*, pp. 544–563.

34. In elucidating Śabara's commentary on *Mīmāṃsā Sūtras* I.1.5 in his *Ślokavārtika*, Kumārila engages various philosophical positions, including perhaps most prominently several Buddhist philosophical positions that threaten the Mīmāṃsā understanding of linguistic reference and the nature of reality (the referent). He explores a number of topics that pertain in part to Buddhist objections and refutes them in detail and quite vigorously. In the *Ślokavārtika* the attack on Buddhism is not simply a condemnation of heterodox beliefs; philosophical criteria come into play. Kumārila believes that right religion and right thinking go together, and both cohere with the right teaching of Vedic revelation. Wrong ideas are contrary to the Veda, and it can also be demonstrated reasonably that they are wrong.

In interpreting I.3.3–4 Kumārila indicates that a wide range of heterodox positions (including Sāṁkhya, Yoga, the Vaiṣṇava Pañcarātra, and the Śaiva Pāśupata) is to be rejected because proponents often deceitfully cover personal ambition with a thin veil of orthodoxy. These practitioners pretend virtue but in fact are only pandering to popular opinion and enriching themselves. Some religious practices are no better than magic, even if they are mixed with a bit of Vedic orthodoxy so as to appear reputable. And then there are the extreme practices of foreigners, who engage in odd customs (for example, having everyone sit down and eat together). But the Buddhists merit particular criticism because their views are so contrary to the Veda.

At I.3.4, three criticisms are highlighted. First, on many practical points such as gift giving, sacrifices, caste restrictions, and acts of worship, the Buddha's teachings actually contradict the Veda:

> In the case of the traditional texts of the Buddha, barring a few stray declarations of such virtues as self-control, charity, and the like, all that they have to say is contrary to the approved conclusions of all the fourteen subsidiary sciences. They are spread by the Buddha and others whose behavior is divergent from and contrary to the way of the three Vedas.[35]

Second, the Buddha violated the rules of caste. Although he belonged to the second, *kṣatriya* caste, he presumed to teach; he did not show proper deference to the brahmins and their values, and even took for himself honors due to them; he taught everyone, indiscriminately:

> Moreover, [these spurious Buddhist texts] were taught to deluded men outside the three castes, to those outside all four castes, and to confused people. As such, such texts can never even be thought of as based upon the Veda. He transgressed his own *kṣatriya* dharma in taking upon himself the works of teaching and receiving gifts. How can we believe that true dharma would be taught by one who has transgressed his own dharma?[36]

Kumārila adds that even Buddhists praise the Buddha in a way that actually condemns him and themselves as well:

> Thus [the Buddha] is praised: "For the sake of the well-being of humanity, he transgressed his own duties as a *kṣatriya*, and having taken up the teaching role appropriate to brahmins, he taught in [a] way not followed by brahmins, who are not able to transgress the prohibition [of teaching outsiders]. Prompted by his mercy toward others, he even went to the length of afflicting the good dharma which is not to be taught to outsiders!" Those who live according to his teaching all act in a manner entirely at variance with the dharma ordained in the Veda and tradition, and thus are known for their contradictory behavior.[37]

If the Buddha does not follow the rules of correct teaching and the transmission of knowledge, why should anyone respect his teaching?

35. I.3.4, p. 167.
36. Ibid.
37. Ibid., pp. 167–168.

Third, the Buddhist (Śākya) teachings are suspect because they have no basis in any Vedic tradition and can be explained for other, ignoble reasons: "We find that they are largely due to avarice and other such causes. Since such motives are clear, there can be no inference of any other basis."

It is quite remarkable that Kumārila interprets the Buddha's appeals to ordinary experience and reasoning, but not to the Veda, as proof that the Buddha has already conceded that there is no special authority behind his positions:

> In the course of their teaching of Dharma, the Śākyas and others never make any assertions that are not supported by arguments based upon actual experience, nor do they imitate Gautama and others who assert their teachings to be based on the Veda. They merely put forward many arguments of the sort that are very far removed from true Dharma.

The consequence is clear:

> Such persons should not be respected even by polite words, and they have been denounced as heretics, violaters, and mere reasoners. It is the compilations of these people that *Manu* and others have declared fit only to be avoided: "Those traditions that are outside the Veda and those that promote wicked views are entirely without benefit, and are described as based in dark lethargy."[38] It is certain that, with respect to dharma, such traditions are outside the pale of the three Vedas and should be disregarded when authoritativeness is at issue.[39]

In section I.3.11–14 Kumārila then attacks the Buddhist positions again, and I will summarize his judgments briefly.[40] This time he rejects the idea that they may be at least of practical value, analogous to grammatical texts or ritual rubrics. Although some marginal texts and practices can be taken seriously and judged compatible with the Veda, the Buddhist views cannot be accepted since they contradict the Veda. They are also internally incoherent, since they argue against the eternity of the Veda while proposing eternal status for the teachings of the Buddha himself. Their texts are not written in proper Sanskrit but are spoiled with popular usages and vernacular terms. Although one might counter that the Veda too was surely composed by fallible human beings, this is not the case. Close observation shows us that no one could ever invent what the Veda says by drawing merely on human experience. Even the idea of gods is beyond human experience, since we never see gods in ordinary life and would never have thought of them had not the Veda informed us about them. The sole purpose of Mīmāṃsā theology, then, is to make clear and certain just how remarkable the Veda is. By contrast, the implication is, it is rather easy to trace and predict what the Buddhists say and the circumstances that prompted them to speak as they do.

38. *Laws of Manu* 12.95.

39. I.3.4, p. 168.

40. In the following section, I cover his position in I.3.11–14, pp. 232–237.

By his severe judgments Kumārila divides his world into the Vedic and the non-Vedic realms, even if he can stretch the boundary between the two when he wants to make room for the customs of men he respects. His assessment of the morals of Buddhists would hardly be convincing to a Buddhist and indeed would be offensive. Nonetheless, his selective theological assessment is worth noting since it affords us another case, different from Barth's, where an orthodox theologian draws the line and limits what can be included within the boundaries of the revealed word.

While we certainly cannot claim that the theologies of Kumārila and Barth are identical, they do share a readiness to draw their theologies of revelation in order to make judgments, benign or harsh, about competing religious communities. Their grounds for dismissing other religious traditions and revelations differ—faith takes the lead for Barth, right practice is primary for Kumārila—but they share the conviction that dismissal is legitimate and warranted by revelation. Kumārila engages in a kind of empirical study in order to estimate the limits of the Vedic connection, while Barth extrapolates from his sense of Christian revelation what must be true about other religions. Each finds a few examples by which to illustrate and confirm his established views. Although they are diametrically opposed thinkers, who share little regarding the specifics of right religion, even their opposition depends on a shared sense of the necessity of religious exclusivity.[41]

Kumārila's strict standards notwithstanding, it is also evident that his defense of the Vedic tradition did not succeed in ending debate over what was orthodox and what was not. From within the fold, so to speak, the Vedānta traditions refused to accept entirely the Mīmāṃsā definition of revelation in terms of right action and the accompanying obligations and instead insisted on the informative function and power of revelation. For Vedānta, this insistence changed the way in which the boundaries of orthodoxy and heterodoxy were to be sorted out. From yet another angle, the vernacular Śaiva and Vaiṣṇava traditions introduce non-Vedic materials that reflect other, more popular theistic pieties, such as the Āgamas (Śaiva Traditional Texts) and Vaiṣṇava vernacular poetry. The Śaiva and Vaiṣṇava theologians argue not only that such pieties are peripherally legitimated by the Veda but also that they are of equal status and perhaps even superior. God, and not the text,

41. Here too, a brief comparison with Jayanta's position is illuminating. Like Kumārila, Jayanta excludes the Buddhists not because their rational arguments are defective but on practical ritual and moral grounds:

> No worthy person approves of the authenticity of the scriptures of the Buddhist schools, since these scriptures which [seemingly] teach the means of final emancipation really teach misconduct. It is a plain fact that the Buddhist scriptures are outside the Vedas, since we learn that they abandon all manners and customs arising from duties prescribed for the different castes. Although they are [seemingly] liberative from worldly suffering, they are sinful and intent upon harming living beings. They are composed due to confusion. For these reasons these scriptures cannot be taken as authoritative. (*Nyāya Mañjarī*, p. 551)

becomes the guarantor of revelation and right religion. Let us consider these Vedānta and devotional theistic positions in turn.

Is Revelation Informative? A Mīmāṃsā-Vedānta Debate

As we have seen in the previous chapters, in most respects Vedānta adheres to the Mīmāṃsā views regarding Veda and revelation. Major features of the Mīmāṃsā world view carry over, including reliance on the same criteria in establishing minimal sufficient Vedic connections as prerequisite for the authority of texts. They too ruled out some of the same opponents, such as the Buddhists. Vedānta uses the methods of Mīmāṃsā exegesis even to establish the unanimity of the disparate Upaniṣadic texts as pointing to the unity or even identity of Brahman and self (*ātman*). In practice, learning Vedānta relies on the Mīmāṃsā way of doing things, as the competent reader is educated by immersion in the sacred word and disabused of the obstacles that make a proper apprehension of Brahman impossible. A complete education in the language, culture, and practice of revelation is required of those who would learn from the Upaniṣads. By some reckonings, everyone is in the long run eligible for this knowledge, but no one is ready without education.

The notable exception is that the Vedic canon is extended to include the Upaniṣads. Since the Upaniṣads stress meditation and the quest to know ultimate reality, Vedānta nurtures an epistemological dynamic that in the long run makes it diverge sharply from Mīmāṃsā's performative program. Brahman and the eternal self replace ritual practice as the primary objects of knowledge and the measure by which everything else is to be judged. Although one must be cautious in speaking of Brahman as an object of knowledge, in some sense at least it is an objective and knowable referent. Since Brahman exists outside the Veda, one cannot stipulate that it is knowable only through texts in the way rituals are known through texts. Knowledge of Brahman cannot be caused even by meditation. The meditator still has to realize Brahman in a moment of awareness.

Although the emerging differences between Mīmāṃsā and Vedānta are significant, for the most part the Mīmāṃsā theologians exhibit less urgency in attacking or criticizing other world views and do not even bother to argue against the Upaniṣadic claims regarding the self or Brahman. As long as the adherents of Vedānta and other systems live up to the standards of orthodox behavior and do not abandon right practice, there is no urgency to attack their peculiar views of the Veda. By contrast, Vedānta theologians formulate judgments about the intellectual content and deficiencies of many other traditions with respect to their ideas about ultimate reality and the nature of the self,[42] and in polemical contexts brand the Mīmāṃsā system as mere ritualism or simply a preparation for Vedānta.

42. This is most strikingly pursued in *Uttara Mīmāṃsā Sūtras* II.2, where (as we saw in chapter 3) the ideas of Yoga, Sāṃkhya, Buddhism, Jainism, the Pāśupata Śaiva and Pañcarātra Vaiṣṇava religious systems are lined up in a series of decreasing levels of error and critiqued accordingly.

Let us examine just one example of an actual Mīmāṃsā-Vedānta debate over whether the Veda only gives privileged directions on how to act or whether it also and primarily reveals privileged knowledge. Let us begin with the restrictive Mīmāṃsā position, which is aimed at denigrating the importance of a discourse about Brahman and self. In the "Śāstraparicheda" (Definition of the Instructive Texts) section of his *Prakaraṇa Pañcikā*, the eighth-century Mīmāṃsā theologian Śalika Nātha discusses the nature and authority of verbal knowledge, and explains the standard Mīmāṃsā view that the Veda is revelatory particularly in its instigation and enablement of ritual action.[43] In the course of this explanation he takes up the Vedānta view that Upaniṣadic texts such as "Knowledge, Bliss, Brahman" (*Bṛhadāraṇyaka Upaniṣad* 3.9.28) are informative claims, which complete Vedic revelation and are essential to salvific knowledge. He rejects this view and argues that even the meanings of these Upaniṣadic words—*knowledge*, *bliss*, Brahman—can be determined by an analysis of common usage and reference and need not be thought of as special knowledge that has to be revealed. As noted above, things talked about in the Veda, including religious realities such as these, are denoted by words whose meanings are ordinary and can be ascertained in non-Vedic contexts. Children learn from their parents and elders and do not need scripture to know the meanings of such words. Therefore, the authority of the Veda should not be aligned too closely with communicating the meaning or reference of such words. In any case, knowledge of such words does not make any particularly significant contribution to one's obedience to the revealed ritual commands.

Śalika Nātha then acknowledges another version of the Vedānta argument.[44] Upaniṣadic statements are effective simply because they give information; even performative texts, such as Vedic ritual instructions, must be informative in order to fulfill their function. For example, a simple declaration such as "a son is born to you" brings great joy to the recipient since the sentence conveys powerful information not reducible to the meanings of the individual words in the sentence, "son," "born," "you." So too, "he lights a fire with wood" informs us that wood can be used in building a fire; by using the words together, the sentence tells us more than we are told by the words *fire* and *wood*. From this Vedānta perspective, one need not sharply separate the understanding of words from the acknowledgment of commands, as if the informative and the performative were conflicting alternatives. It is simpler to claim that the Veda and particularly the Upaniṣads contain some sentences that instruct listeners as to the performance of right actions and others that are revelatory simply in terms of the information they communicate.

43. Śālika Nātha is a key thinker in the Mīmāṃsā school founded by Prabhākara Miśra. The "Śāstraparicheda" is itself a subsection of Śālika Nātha's overall study of the means of right knowledge, the *Pramāṇa Pārāyaṇa* section of the *Prakaraṇa Pañcikā*, pp. 229–266. The following comments on his view of Vedānta draw on pp. 239–242.

44. A position attributed to the ninth-century Vedānta theologian, Maṇḍana Miśra.

Śalika Nātha rejects this reasoning. One can never establish an exact correspondence between declarative statements and affective responses such as joy or fear. There are numerous reasons why "a son is born to you" might produce joy. Perhaps the cause is simply the idea that a child has been born. It may also be the more specific idea of the birth of a son or of just one child and not several. It could even be the simple fact that there was no added announcement that one's wife had died in childbirth. Only if we observe the joyful person in some particular context can we decide why some particular statement is joy producing and in what way. Thus the information still has to be assessed in a wider, largely performative context. Even statements that are apparently not connected to action must have some implicit or indirect relation to action if they are to be significant.

As for the Upaniṣadic claim that the self is a required object of knowledge—for example, as stated in the Upaniṣadic command "the self must be known"—Śālika Nātha argues that the Veda is only stating the obligation to undertake the act of meditating on the self. That meditation on the self is obligatory need not entail any specific view of the self's nature or why it should be an object of meditation. Whatever one wishes to know about the self can be learned by other, ordinary, and extra-Vedic means. In fact, Vedānta has it wrong anyway. There is no evidence to support the Vedānta view that the self is blissful nor that it is "deeply" blissful but somehow covered with suffering. Reasoning leads us to conclude that the self is not a unique, perfect reality. If the Upaniṣads are telling us that the self is blissful, they may well be wrong.

Śālika Nātha's position cleverly undercuts the Vedānta viewpoint. The Vedānta theologians are wrong about the self, but even were they right, their views would change nothing, since theories about entities like the self do not have primary religious import. The authority of the Veda is not directed to such teachings and is better preserved if we leave such teachings in the realm of opinion. The Veda's power is closely connected to its primary focus—ritual performance—and that connection remains stable whatever Brahman and self turn out to be.

For a Vedānta rejoinder we turn to a section of Rāmānuja's extensive *Śrī Bhāṣya* comment on *sūtra* I.1.1 of the *Uttara Mīmāṃsā Sūtras*.[45] Rāmānuja summarizes Śālika Nātha's position fairly closely and quotes it several times. He then proceeds to reassert the authority of the Upaniṣads in three ways. First, it is not true that words' meanings are known simply from ordinary usage and then introduced where relevant into Vedic contexts. Words have multiple meanings and only in context can one determine which meaning is pertinent. But it is the Veda that specifies the context that enables us to understand properly the words relevant to liberating knowledge. Moreover, even

45. Pp. 148–151. For a clear statement of the Nondualist Vedānta view of revelation, see Murty; on the Mīmāṃsā concept of revelation, see D'Sa; Bilimoria. For another ancient Hindu theology of revelation, see Carpenter's exposition of Bhartṛhari, the fifth-century grammarian and theologian.

when the Veda clearly imposes an obligation, it is also communicating meanings appropriate to the particular actions in question. Second, even if the authority of scripture is related to ritual performance, there are ample instances in the Upaniṣads where knowledge of Brahman is announced as obligatory, to be pursued in meditation practices. But there is no justification for reducing this knowledge to an accessory of ritual practice nor to a meditation practice in which actual knowledge is only secondary. Real knowledge of Brahman, not the practice of meditation, is primary in the Upaniṣads. Third, as was already stated in one of the objections entertained by Śālika Nātha, the alleged disjunction between information and performance is not as clear-cut as the Mīmāṃsā theologians claim. Even an obligation to act involves some understanding of the goal of that action and what is to be achieved by it. The Veda informs us about the goal as well as instructing us about the path for reaching it. Performative language indicates obligatory actions, which lead to particular ends presented as objects worth knowing and achieving. Discussions of performance can also be informative in important ways. In ordinary experience we often learn the meanings of words and their referents from the observation of actions, as when, for example, someone hears and obeys a command, and a child observes what the person does in this regard. So too, when the Upaniṣad commands "the self is to be known," the point is also to inform us that the object of meditation—the supreme object—is known only by coming to understand informative Upaniṣadic texts. The value of meditation is communicated but also the supreme importance of the object to be known in meditation. The Veda, in its last and most important section, the Upaniṣads, must be interpreted as informative about Brahman.

When the Vedānta theologians insist that the canon be extended to include the Upaniṣads and knowledge of Brahman, they also have to explain why the settled Vedic canon proposed by the Mīmāṃsā scholars, made up entirely of texts related to the rituals, is inadequate to the full meaning of human nature. It is characterized, for example, by consciousness and bliss and cannot be reduced to agency, action, and reward. Knowledge about Brahman demands a different understanding of human knowers, their capacities, and their destinies, and the Upaniṣads provide this information.

This Vedānta theological view maintains the authority of the Veda as a whole and does not deny the obligation invested in Vedic ritual injunctions by the Mīmāṃsā theologians. It is a form of inclusivism that maintains the Mīmāṃsā ordering of Vedic values while effectively reversing them. Activities are obligatory accessories to knowledge of Brahman, which is the supreme object of knowledge; the ritual portion of the Veda is subordinated to its knowledge portion, the Upaniṣads. By this reordering of priorities, the canon of revelation is expanded to make room for newer religious values.[46]

46. See also *Uttara Mīmāṃsā Sūtras* III.4.1–17, where the perspectives on action (*kratu-artha*) and the performer (*puruṣa-artha*) are similarly reversed in the Vedānta calculus. See Clooney, 1990, chap. 3.

God Speaks Tamil Too: Śaiva and Vaiṣṇava Perspectives

A second example of how the margins of an orthodoxy defined by revelation are widened and the criteria for right religion adjusted returns us to the South Indian tradition, where one finds a debate over whether revelation can occur outside the Sanskrit Vedic tradition and in other languages. In a way, the challenge is greater than that posed by Vedānta to Mīmāṃsā, since texts composed in Tamil could not be easily governed by the linguistic and social rules for Vedic affiliation, which Kumārila proposed. Since Tamil belongs to the Dravidian family of languages, it could not even be ranked as a decadent form of Sanskrit.

A basic fear was loss of control. Were the vernaculars to gain religious prominence and the high standards regarding proper Sanskrit expression diminished, "unlicensed" non-brahmins too could become religious authors, and then anyone could say anything and call it religious. While traditionalists feared this development, other theologians, particularly in the growing devotional movements dedicated to Śiva and Viṣṇu, welcomed the widening of the possibilities of religious authorship and authority.

Here we consider two examples from the South Indian context. The first is from Aruḷ Nandi's *Śiva Jñāna Siddhiyār* and the Tamil Śaiva Siddhānta tradition, and the second is from the Vaiṣṇava tradition of the Tamil saints known as the *āḻvārs*, which lay behind Rāmānuja's Vedānta. In both cases, an appeal to the intention and authority of God expands and realigns the order of religious truths and values. It overcomes possible splits in the canon by giving the divine author priority over language, knowledge, and performance.

Śiva Jñāna Siddhiyār gives us a sense of how scripture is framed and how it functions in the Śaiva tradition. In VIII.2 Aruḷ Nandi is concerned with defending the authority of the Vedic scriptures and the texts specific to the tradition written either in Sanskrit or Tamil, the Śaiva Traditional Texts (*āgamas*). The problem is similar to that taken up by Kumārila, though with two distinctions. First, some of the Śaiva Traditional Texts are not in Sanskrit and so lack the clear and evident affiliation to the Sanskrit Veda, its language, learning, and way of life. As Tamil vernacular texts, they are beyond the strictures and disciplines that control proper Sanskrit learning and are therefore open, in theory at least, to the possibility that people will say genuinely different things in different ways. Second, in order to defend their authority Aruḷ Nandi appeals to theistic arguments, particularly the fact that Śiva is the author of these texts.

Section VIII.2 of *Śiva Jñāna Siddhiyār* is concerned with assessing different religious paths and highlighting different nuances regarding the Śaiva path itself. Several introductory verses, which we noted in chapter 3, affirm that those wishing to advance spiritually must step skillfully among the possible paths in order to come to that right doctrine and right practice that is embodied in both the Tamil and Sanskrit traditions:[47]

47. See also my comments in chapter 3 on the following two verses.

> They leave the outer systems, enter the orthodox fold, and move through the paths of the traditional texts, the various stages of life and their duties. They practice hard asceticism, learn many difficult sciences, master the Vedas and reflect on the Purāṇas. Thus they come to understand very clearly the truth of the Veda, and attain the Śaiva way. After practicing right behavior, right action, and right integration, by means of knowledge they reach the feet of Śiva.[48]

The true and defining religion is the religion of Śiva (Hara), a religion that is both coherent and comprehensive:

> The systems put forward along with their doctrines and doctrinal books are many, but they conflict with one another. One may ask which is the true system, which the true doctrine, and which the true book. The true system, doctrine and book is the one about which one does not argue, "This part is true, that part is not," and which includes everything within itself in right order. Hence, all these [systems, doctrines, books] are accounted for [in] the rare Vedas and Śaiva Traditional Texts, and these two are placed beneath the sacred feet of Hara.[49]

Like Kumārila, Aruḷ Nandi works out a way of ranking systems in relation to one another, but he relies on a theistic calculus rather than on an appeal to linguistic, social, and cultural values. Whatever is connected with God is good. He goes on to characterize and rank the kinds of sacred texts that are available and ends with a strikingly abrupt assessment of what can be said to those who do not accept scripture:

> The rare Vedas and Śaiva Traditional Texts are called the "First Book," and Hara graciously taught all this immeasurable truth. Then other beings tried to interpret it according to their own reasoning, and so founded other schools. Traditions, mythological texts, and disciplinary manuals, etc., are "guidebooks." Supporting disciplines are the "assisting books." But there is not anything there that has not been said in Revelation and the Śaiva Traditional Texts, and we cannot find anything to say to those who think otherwise.[50]

The next verses reaffirm this view. Both the Veda and the Śaiva Traditional Texts are important though distinguished by different scope:

> The only two books are the Vedas and Śaiva Traditional Texts. All other books are offshoots of these. This first book was given by the pure one who has no beginning, and it is two. Of the two, the Vedas are general, and the Śaiva Traditional Texts are rare and specific, the former for all good people, the latter for the spiritually advanced. Beyond what the broad Veda says, the Śaiva book contains the flawless truths of the Vedānta. Other books present preliminary views, but the Śaiva Traditional Texts alone propose the correct view.[51]

Ultimately, the Lord's grace is the source of all scriptural authority:

48. VIII.2.11, p. 227.
49. VIII.2.13, p. 229.
50. VIII.2.14, pp. 229–230.
51. VIII.2.15, p. 230.

> He is the supreme lord, in whom all intelligence, all primacy, and all beneficence are inherent. His intelligence is manifest by the works he has made manifest, the Vedas and Śaiva Traditional Texts. His primacy is known when he grants pleasure and pain in turn to those who follow the ancient way and those who do not. When he removes their deeds by making them consume their double [good and bad] fruits, he is beneficent. We behold all this in Śiva.[52]

Because Śiva is the subject and source of true revelation, it is no longer crucial to ask whether such revelations are in Sanskrit or Tamil. God speaks both languages. Nor can Vedic standards be the sole criteria for the evaluation of behavior. Candidates for the title "scripture" are to be judged according to whether they originate in the divine author's grace, what they tell us about God and love of God and how they contribute toward a salvific knowledge and love of God, and not by linguistic and social considerations. Śiva alone is the source for the authority of scripture; in a real sense he is the author of the Veda and of the Śaiva Traditional Texts: "The Śaiva Traditional Texts are the book of the wise one who is pure and beginningless."[53] Śiva gives the Veda and Traditional Texts and is known through them. This introductory verse nicely captures the subtlety of the position:

> By his grace we can know Śiva in the Traditional Texts, by proper argumentation we can understand clearly, and by the act of knowledge we dispel the darkness within our minds and attain life. Birth, Māyā, and darkness are removed, and we can dwell in the company of the devout.[54]

The challenge of defending the authority of Tamil-language texts is taken up explicitly in the Śaiva tradition. Śivāgra Yogin, an important commentator on *Śiva Jñāna Siddhiyār*, pushes the matter further by calling into question the independence and eternity of the Veda and by arguing that it is actually dependent on Śiva. Both the Vedas and the Śaiva Traditional Texts are to be judged in terms of their relation to Śiva. To forestall expected opposition, Śivāgra Yogin addresses a series of objections, which would relegate the Śaiva Traditional Texts to inferior status:[55]

> *Objection*: the Śaiva Traditional Texts have an author and are neither eternal nor free from potential faults. *Response*: it is true that neither the Vedas nor the Śaiva Traditional Texts are eternal. Both rely for validity on Śiva's grace; they are authoritative because they are his utterances.
>
> *Objection*: the Śaiva Traditional Texts are not based on the Vedas and are not accepted by proper, respected people. *Response*: Śiva is the most proper and most respected person, and clearly he accepts the Śaiva Traditional Texts which he has promulgated.

52. VIII.2.17, p. 230.

53. The introduction to the *Parapakkam*, verse 13, p. 8. (In the Tamil edition, this verse is found as verse 19 in the introduction to the *Supakkam*.)

54. Introduction to *Supakkam*, p. 115, n. 10.

55. Since I have not been able to obtain Śivāgra Yogin's commentary on *Śiva Jñāna Siddhiyār*, I have had to rely on the summary of his position given by Devasenapati in *Śaiva Siddhānta*, pp. 37–47.

Objection: the Śaiva Traditional Texts point to a highest human goal, union with Śiva, which [is] not authorized in the Veda. *Response*: the Veda is not contradictory to this goal, and supportive texts can be found.
Objection: the Śaiva Traditional Texts are self-contradictory. *Response*: they are not self-contradictory, but teach different paths for different people with different capacities.
Objection: the Śaiva Traditional Texts teach and encourage improper religious practices. *Response*: these practices are suited to the capacities of different kinds of people and are appropriate for those people.

At a general level the challenge is the same as that which faces the Mīmāṃsā theologians: a right judgment on religion based on a right understanding of revelation. But the actual calculus has changed from that proposed by Kumārila. Not only are the Śaiva Traditional Texts placed on an equal level with the Veda, but the older criteria of correct language and social propriety are subordinated to affiliation with Śiva, now the sole, primary, and sufficient criterion. While the Śaiva theologians are disinclined actually to dismiss the Veda and its obligations, they have nevertheless opened the doorway for an account of revelation and a justification of religious ideas and practices that is based simply on relationship to Śiva, whether or not proper according to older Vedic standards. The excellence of the divine author and benefits for the widest possible audience become the key criteria and displace the older notion that a specific scriptural language itself, enjoyed by a smaller group of experts, might set the standard for excellence. As we saw in the previous chapter, though, Aruḷ Nandi does not extend his generosity toward religions other than those warranted by the Vedic and Śaiva Traditional Texts. Vaiṣṇavism, for example, is relegated to a low position in his calculus of true religion.

The Tamil Vaiṣṇava tradition itself gives evidence of similar efforts to balance respect for the Veda with the need to extend its boundaries in order to honor new vernacular scriptures. The eighth–ninth-century Vaiṣṇava saints known as the *āḻvārs* frequently mention the Veda in their songs; they affirm its enduring value while at the same time downgrading it. A few citations from the *Tiruvāymoḻi* of Śaṭakōpaṉ, introduced in the previous chapter, will suffice to indicate the primary attitude of these saints. The Lord is the author of the Veda: "For the highest one who produced the excellent Vedas" (VI.6.5); "He is the Beginning of the ancient Veda " (I.6.2); "The first one, source of the Vedas" (III.5.5); and "The temple enjoyed by the One who once spread forth the Vedas" (II.10.10). The Lord is the key meaning of the Veda: "He likewise dwells in the Veda, a lotus light dwelling in the four fine mysterious Vedas" (III.1.10). Brahmins well versed in the Veda are often described as devoted to praising the Lord: "those learned in the four Vedas, gods on this rich earth, join their hands and offer praise in all directions."[56]

56. *Tiruvāymoḻi* VIII.4.8.

The Vaiṣṇava theologians argue persuasively for the value of the Tamil-language revelations while yet not entirely relegating the Sanskrit tradition to the sidelines. While the relationship of the Tamil and Sanskrit traditions could have been portrayed antagonistically so as to sever the connection between the language traditions, in Vaiṣṇavism the desired outcome was rather a deeper and more complex interaction between the two. Yet even here, more radical possibilities appeared. While the northern school of Tamil Śrīvaiṣṇavism maintained a serious interest in Sanskrit language materials, it appears that in the southern school interest in Sanskrit waned considerably, even if the connection with the Vedic tradition was never ruptured.

Most important for its theology of revelation, the perfection of a text like *Tiruvāymoḻi* is made to depend on the perfection of its divine author and the gracious transformation of its human author. The primary author is God, but by extension Śaṭakōpaṉ the human author is portrayed as the perfectly cooperative partner in the enunciation of a message that is both divine and human.[57] The decisive element is Śaṭakōpaṉ's own struggle to praise God adequately, something he cannot do simply by reciting the Veda. He has to compose and sing in his mother tongue and praise God in words that are his own, rooted in his own experience of God. His extraordinary, immediate experience of God becomes the defining criterion for revelation. This tendency climaxes when Śaṭakōpaṉ claims that he himself has become God's voice, since God chooses to speak through him, in his human voice:

> He has exalted me for all time, day after day he has made me himself,
> and by me he now sings himself in sweet Tamil,
> my Lord, my first one, my abiding light—how can I sing of him?
> How can I sing of him? He has become one with my sweet life,
> he makes me sing sweet songs which I sing by my own words,
> by his own words my marvelous one now praises himself,
> the first of the three forms who sang before me. (VII.9.1–2)

Deeper than the issue of language—this language or that language—is this claim that God chooses a human voice and chooses to speak in one human person's own words. More important than either the Sanskrit or Tamil languages is that Nārāyaṇa speaks in Śaṭakōpaṉ's human words. A person desiring to grow spiritually need only turn to the Lord and not to that ancillary Veda that speaks about him: "Without relying on the thread of the four Vedas as refuge, we have destroyed the great three, birth, death, and disease."[58] In theory respected, the Veda is in practice displaced due to a shift in the standards as to what counts as revelation.

Above we saw how Śivāgra Yogin defended Tamil-language scriptures, and a similar engagement of the objections is found in the tradition of Vaiṣṇava commentaries on the *Tiruvāymoḻi*. Since this was the most important of the Tamil Vaiṣṇava works, it occasioned the clearest and sharp-

57. See Clooney, 1985.
58. *Tiruvāymoḻi* VIII.3.2

est battles about whether scriptural authority could extend beyond Vedic and Sanskrits boundaries. Nañjīyar, who wrote the first introduction to the *Tiruvāymoḻi* in the twelfth century CE, directly raises the question of the authority of the Tamil hymns with respect to the Sanskrit tradition. He admits a similar series of objections against a vernacular scriptural tradition. For example, Śaṭakōpāṉ's songs are written in Tamil, which is unsuitable for sacred purposes; Śaṭakōpaṉ was a low-caste man; women, low-caste men, and people from outside the Vedic tradition have access to his songs and know them well; his songs give prominence to sexual imagery; and they downplay the value of goals highly prized in the Veda, such as total solitude and lordly power. Nañjīyar rejects each vigorously, mainly by turning it into an advantage. For example, Tamil is the Lord's favored language, and the Lord has graciously favored a low-caste man to sing in God's name. It is all the more amazing and glorious that the songs are for everyone and that women, the low caste, and outsiders should appreciate them. The songs affirm older Vedic categories but more brilliantly teach passion for God, daring to use even a sexual language to communicate the intensity of this love.[59]

Nañjīyar adds other arguments that affirm that these songs are orthodox and cannot be excluded from the canon: they proclaim the Lord's glorious nature clearly; they inspire and increase devotion; they cause unsurpassable joy in those who hear them; they are doctrinally sound because they attest that Brahman is the efficient and material cause of the world; they properly state that liberation comes from knowledge of Brahman; and the Veda itself confirms what the songs say.[60]

Here again, as in the Vedānta and Śaiva traditions, we see theologians retain but expand older evaluations of revelation by revising the standard for what is at revelation's core. God's initiative is primary, and the saint's experience of God's gracious intervention in his life becomes the source of new revelation as God speaks in words available to all. While the Śrīvaiṣṇava theologians of 700 years ago do not offer a more general theory of multiple and universal revelations, they have nonetheless paved the way for such possibilities. When God speaks and humans hear, revelation is possible.

Differences aside, the Śaiva and Vaiṣṇava affirmations of vernacular traditions agree in opening up yet another way of interpreting religions in light of revelation. Although neither embraces a notion of universal salvation, the shift from text and language to the gracious will of God (Śiva or Nārāyaṇa) subordinates the old social and religious values of performance and self-realization to a different recognition, powerfully revealed, that it is God alone who makes religion salvific.

59. Nañjīyar's introduction (which has not been translated) can be found in volume 1 of the *Tiruvāymoḻi* with commentaries (known as the *Bhagavat Viṣayam*) published by Krishnasami Ayyangar (Tiruchi: Books Propagation Society, 1975; pp. 55–70). On the main features of Nañjīyar's exposition, see Thiruvengadathan; Clooney, 1992.

60. P. 63.

Revelation as Limit and Bridge in Interreligious Theology

We began this chapter by examining a strong, exclusive version of the Christian claim about revelation and the world "outside revelation," as articulated by Karl Barth. God's gracious word is uttered through and as Jesus Christ, who is the single definitive Word of God to the human race. Religion is not revelation, and it has nothing to offer the believer. While the Christian Church faces in both directions—toward God's revelation and toward becoming a religion—other religions are turned the wrong way and may even be in flight from the clear light of God's Word. We resisted the temptation to read this theology either as a self-evident and decisive judgment on religions or as a dead end precluding comparative and dialogical reflection. We respected Barth's endeavor, in part because it is precisely what one might expect a certain kind of theologian, Christian or Hindu, to pursue. It is articulate theology, it tells us something about how theologians—Christian or Hindu—think, and it invites us to think about what and how we believe. We then examined one strand of Hindu theologizing about revelation, the firm Mīmāṃsā position regarding the Veda. Whatever else the Veda says and tells us, its core is the sheer *ought*, which impels the capable person to perform the Vedic rites. Although Mīmāṃsā is thoroughly pragmatic in its systematization of its views, here too religions are judged in light of revelation, and Kumārila Bhaṭṭa's standards are as severe and resistant to change as Barth's.

We did not explore Christian theologies alternative to Barth's, but figures such as Dupuis, Heim, and Ward (in chapter 1) and even Rahner (in chapter 4) indicate for us at least some of the available options. As we noted too, Swinburne's rational Christian theology opens up some very promising avenues for conversation across religious boundaries. We did examine in some detail further developments in the Hindu tradition as the Mīmāṃsā boundaries are stretched by the Vedānta theologians in their reflection on the Upaniṣads (where knowledge of Brahman became more important than instruction on Vedic ritual performance) and by theologians in the Tamil vernacular traditions (where the initiative of the divine author and the value of the divine–human encounter became more important than ideals of sacred language).

Reading Barth along with Kumārila, Śālika Nātha, Rāmānuja, Nañjīyar, Aruḷ Nandi, and others has been a particularly challenging task insofar as we have had to take several theological positions that seem to lead to mutual exclusion. If one adheres to Barth's theology, it may be hard to take Mīmāṃsā Vedānta or Śaivism seriously; if one follows Kumārila or Rāmānuja, Barth's theology will seem misguided. Yet it has been possible to think about all these theologians together because Barth does have much in common with such theological colleagues from the Mīmāṃsā and Vedānta traditions; he and they both are concerned to defend the absolute priority of revelation and accordingly develop consistent theories about how the core of revelation is located in a simple, even primal revelatory power, which is not the product of human ingenuity or spirituality nor identical with the words that make up the texts popularly identified with revelation. On this basis these theologians work out more extended theologies of revelation, which afford multiple strategies for assessing and locating outsiders. They decide what conforms to revelation and what does not, and this theologizing about the other opens them to dialogue with the other. The world is divided into two groups: those who have accepted the obligation imposed by revelation and those who have not.

Barth sees revelation as God's sheer gift, his Word from outside the natural sphere where religions flourish. For Kumārila, revelation was distinguished by a sheer, original obligation to perform rituals. Both thereafter elaborated ways of sorting and ranking religions in relation to revelation. For theologians like Rāmānuja, revelation had to do primarily with a transformation of consciousness; though never divorced from considerations of orthopraxis, it was nevertheless a wisdom about Reality that was irreducible to Vedic commands. For Aruḷ Nandi, revelation was assessed in terms of devotion to the divine author, who was the source of these life-giving texts. But in all these cases the world is transformed and assessed according to scriptural values.

Like Barth, the Vaiṣṇava and Śaiva theologians root their theories of revelation in a theistic world view. The sacred word is given legitimacy in relation to God's intent. But they do not develop a rhetoric of revelation as "encounter with God," nor do we find in their writing so stark a tendency as Barth's toward an understanding of revelation as a personal divine initiative that must stand over against anything humans might attempt on their own. Instead, the divine speech that is sacred language—and not just its content—plays a more central role in instilling cultural and religious values. Formation according to the key values encoded in language remains central. One must be educated and reeducated to hear the beautiful and captivating word that speaks of God, that leads one to discover God within one's life, and that enables one to become the kind of person who can encounter God.

Kumārila, his Mīmāṃsā colleagues, and most Vedānta theologians are Barth's kindred spirits. While Barth was firmly exclusive regarding the distinction between revelation and everything else, he did not want to exclude any person from a possible encounter with God, which could succeed where religions would always fail. While the Mīmāṃsā theologians did not refrain from acid attacks on the Buddhists and others who promoted wrong practice, they adjusted their theory of revelation to make room for some seemingly novel religious practices and beliefs, which they did not wish to exclude entirely. Vedānta theologians then stretched the core Mīmāṃsā strictures on revelation in order to highlight more emphatically a revealed content, revelation's power to tell us about the world as it really is. The Śaiva and Vaiṣṇava theologians expanded the Vedānta categories in order to say a great deal more about the divine author (as in Śaiva Siddhānta) and the value of the vernacular tongue (as in Śivāgra Yogin's defense of popular Śaiva songs and Nañjīyar's defense of the *Tiruvāymoḻi*). In all these instances, strict boundaries are set as a measure by which to rule out unacceptable values and practices; yet those same boundaries are in fact continually adjusted to include new religious resources and even new canons in new languages.

Numerous secondary theological claims, smaller similarities and differences, can be analyzed and reassessed in relation to other traditions' theological self-understanding. We can all ask whether Barth is right in insisting that religions are "unbelief" in light of revelation, whether Kumārila is correct in distilling the essence of the Veda to the Do! of ritual performance, and whether Aruḷ Nandi clarifies or confuses issues by incorporating deities into his overall genetic description of reality. We all need to ask ourselves whether our positions make sense even to those who do not already believe as we do and whether there are ways we can better explain our positions and their implications for other people's faiths.

The methodological similarities that appear will not be of the sort that makes substantive agreement likely, even in the long run. Because these Hindu and Christian positions are similar in their judgments on self and other in light of revelation, the most striking similarities—there is a transcendent divine utterance, the word is the measure by which all is judged, and even, God speaks perfectly in these words and need not speak in other words—may actually instigate conflicts that are all the more direct. The positions of Barth and Kumārila, for instance, are close enough that they may be seen as bringing the interreligious conversation about revelation to a complete halt, a dead-end.

But even here the fact that religious reasoning is under way prevents a halting of the conversation. If theologians remain committed to reasoning about what they believe, then larger differences, difficult similarities, and exclusionary judgments are never the end of the matter. Although claims about the meaning and power of revelation are deeply intertwined with issues specific to a particular faith in a particular community, theologians in both the Hindu and Christian traditions still attempt to clarify the issues involved in a reasonable and intellectually accessible manner so as to win a favorable hearing from outsiders who are open to reasoning about religious matters. As theologians who judge religions by revelation these thinkers also attempt to explain their judgments and render them more plausible and intelligible. Barth distinguishes revelation from religion and religions, Kumārila sorts out the performative and informative components of scripture, and Aruḷ Nandi and Naññjīyar subordinate languages and texts to the divine person who speaks them.

Although the efforts of these theologians to identify the core of revelation are restrictive and at a first level exclusive, they are determined to account for a wider variety of human activities. Inevitably they have something to say about others and even about one another, actually, as when Barth comments on the Śrīvaiṣṇava understanding of devotion, or potentially, as when Kumārila surveys the wider array of those who do not live according to the Veda because they have not been educated by it. Barth could not bring himself to stop after a page or two of *Church Dogmatics* with an abrupt assertion of the truth of Christian revelation, a truly simple and spare a priori, much as that stance would have been supportive of his real point. Instead, he applied his theory of religions to Japanese Buddhism and South Indian Vaiṣṇavism and sought to explain to fellow Christians why theological similarities could not be allowed to be positively significant. Likewise, Kumārila felt compelled to explain what was wrong with the seemingly edifying ethic of the Buddha, while Aruḷ Nandi had to point out the absurdity of the Vaiṣṇava concept of divine descent. Nañjīyar criticized the narrowness of the old Vedic orthodoxy once it was reviewed in light of Nārāyaṇa's overwhelming grace.

Today we form our opinions about what others believe in a world where there is available to us a vast array of published and translated texts from other theological traditions, where travel is easy, and where living representatives of those other traditions are nearby. As we read Karl Barth and Kumārila Bhaṭṭa, Aruḷ Nandi and Nañjīyar, along with the scriptures to which they are committed and in fidelity to which they theologize about the wider world, we are creating an interreligious theological opportunity unlike any available to any of them. More than ever, ideas fly back and forth across traditional boundaries, and modes of interpretation are shared and altered by attention to how other theologians have been interpreting their sacred texts and reading the world in light of them. Accountability becomes all the more inevitable and reasonable, comparison a standard dimension of professional theology, and mutual dialogical accountability a normal aspect of any theological writing.

Accordingly, judgments on religions actually help to foster ongoing theological exchange instead of bringing it to a sudden end; if I make a claim about other traditions, I am then reasonably obliged to speak with articulate believers in those traditions. If a disciple of Barth today dismisses the Śrīvaiṣṇava understanding of grace, Hindu theologians who know that theology well can dispute the point and argue against it persuasively if they also know Barth's theology. If a disciple of Kumārila were to undercut the authenticity of Buddhist teachings, today he or she might soon find a Buddhist response that challenges the portrayal of Buddhism that had been constructed to fit the Mīmāṃsā world view. Heirs of Kumārila Bhaṭṭa and Barth who wish to be theologians and not simply custodians of other people's ideas cannot escape this dialogical responsibility with its comparative and apologetic context.

When the comparative and dialogical processes are seriously underway and the interreligious nature of theology is securely fixed in everyone's consciousness, theologians can still go on to restate, in a better-informed and potentially more persuasive manner, the fundamental doctrines of their particular traditions, such as are based in revelation and extended from understandings of revelation. For there is no good reason why doctrines drawn from revelation after a comparative and dialogical process need be necessarily more uncertain or tentative than they might have been when enunciated first and in ignorance of other traditions' theologies. A Christian, Mīmāṃsā, or Śaiva theology can still be argued forcefully, even in an apologetic mode that does not hesitate to offer reasons in support of the truth of what scripture says. Theologians can still draw on revelation to make and express judgments about the wider world, including what is outside the community shaped by revelation, other people, and their religions. But if theologians make their criticisms in an informed and professional manner and are knowledgeable about the theological understandings of revelation and religion held by the traditions they criticize, any ensuing arguments will surely be richer, more intelligent, and more helpful to all involved. Arguments fueled by ignorance are the ones that harm us.

Attention to Roberto de Nobili again clarifies some of the available options as to where a measuring of religions according to revelation might lead. As we have seen, he sought to overcome the apparent gap between reason and revelation by emphasizing the matters that are conformable to revelation, including basic principles of reasoning, natural moral imperatives, and even the evident limitations to what humans can know. After all, the God who speaks in revelation is a reasonable God and a God who made humans to be reasonable. De Nobili believed that all reasonable people should be able to agree at least on the minimal set of moral and religious truths confirmed in revelation. Faithful to the principles of Thomas Aquinas, de Nobili finds reason to be a true friend to revelation and authentic religion. While he did not believe that faith is reducible to the reasonable, he believed that proper reasoning could open one to the truths of revelation. The paths toward an apprehension of the truth and toward a surrender to revelation are, if not identical, at least journeys in the same direction.

De Nobili expected sincere and honest Hindus to become open to the deeper truths of revelation, which tell us what can be known about who God is, who we are, and how we should live our lives. He thought that this meant that Hindus could be persuaded to become better disposed to Christian revelation, which, though a higher mystery, is still a truth toward which the human mind tends. It is difficult to share de Nobili's confidence that he could thus narrow the gap between reason and revelation and demonstrate to Hindus that the reasonability of his version of revelation was superior to theirs. We know too much about traditions other than our own, and we know too much about how minds, even the minds of theologians, may be tempted to shut down in the face of what seems new and different.

But de Nobili's intuition that correct religious reasoning can render people open to revelation is worthy of respect even today. It is theologically reasonable to think that attention to revelation is reasonable, and theologians in both the Hindu and Christian traditions affirm this. When theologians claim that revelation (as their community recognizes it) is *the* unique source of knowledge and privileged articulate word that illumines reality, they usually go on to assert that this revelation is (to some extent) linguistically and rationally accessible. If so, the revelation becomes a potential object of scrutiny, no longer immune to interreligious, comparative, and dialogical investigation. If revelation is not inimical to whatever is properly intelligible and verbal, then beginning to understand opens a path toward revelation and toward vulnerability to its claims. Revelation, however severely its demands may be construed, also enables interreligious conversation as theologians learn from theologians in other traditions regarding how they read revelation and form theological positions in keeping with what they read.

It is important to keep before us the new location of confessional theology. Revelation may be a starting point for theologians, but later on it is more importantly a concluding section of a theological project that is already interreligious, comparative, and dialogical. We return to revelation and listen to it again in light of everything we have heard, read, and learned in the interreligious conversation. The best confessional theologians will be those who inquire intelligently into their faith and the faith of others, who make skilled comparisons and contrasts, and who admit that there is necessarily a bit of a leap involved in moving from an understanding of revelation to a judgment on the theological positions developed in another religious tradition. Theology, even though rooted in revelation and aimed at constructing world views that fit revelation, is a shared enterprise involving some theologians who are Christian and some who are Hindu—and then too Jewish and Muslim theologians and others. Claims about revelation do not stifle comparison and dialogue but infuse and inspire them.

6

Faithful and Reasonable Theology in a Pluralistic World

Reviewing the Practice of Theology Based on Our Hindu and Christian Examples

Religious traditions differ in many ways, but theology is a human and religious activity common to those many traditions. Religions are unique, and truths are revealed, while theology remains in large part a more mundane, complex, and interreligious activity in which there is no substitute for comparative and dialogical practice. Such is the working thesis underlying *Hindu God, Christian God*. While individual theologians might be excused due to their narrower specializations, on the whole no theologian today can intelligently avoid theology's interreligious implications. Consequently, good theologians are inevitably involved in reconstructing theology as a comparative and dialogical project that thereafter can be seen again as confessional, attentive to specific traditions' views, and confident in asserting arguable religious truths.

This volume has also made a second claim, which moderates the grand sweep of the preceding one: the opportunities present in the interreligious situation are most fruitfully appropriated slowly and by way of small and specific examples taken seriously and argued through in their details. As admitted in chapter 1, *Hindu God, Christian God* has been based on just a few Hindu and Christian examples. It makes no comprehensive claim; it is a kind of induction and suggests a certain transformation of theology based on that induction. We also should study other examples from other traditions in other pairings, including, Christian-Buddhist, Buddhist-Muslim, and Jewish-Confucian. Once introduced and studied, such examples may serve as the basis for further theological claims.

Interreligious theology is not the domain of generalists but rather of those willing to engage in detailed study, tentatively and over time. Gradually, these examples can be woven together in the larger framework of a more richly multidimensional interreligious theology. Since the larger project is barely under way, the reflections that follow can only be tentative and should not be taken as precluding what will be learned in further experiments.

If the theological debates explored in the preceding chapters are good examples, reflection on them will contribute to reshaping how we understand and practice theology as a discipline that is interreligious, comparative, dialogical, and yet still confessional. We know a little more now, and so can and must think about theology just a bit differently. Theologians like von Balthasar, Barth, Kumārila, and Aruḷ Nandi are not easily coopted for an easy theory of religious similarities. They are articulate and opinionated thinkers, who demand our attention for a long time, even after we may have hoped to have left them behind. Even if we are happy to think along the same lines as Richard Swinburne or Jayanta Bhaṭṭa, thinking through their positions together gives us much more to ponder. *Hindu God, Christian God* depends on such examples, for it is a comparative induction that aims at moving forward incrementally our knowledge about theology and its methods.

As theological boundaries are crossed and new collegial partnerships forged, theologians can learn to think through and express their most compelling beliefs in a conversation that is no longer coextensive with the boundaries of their own tradition. Pondering God's existence, making a case for the one true God, exploring God's work in the world generally and in the particular case of divine embodiment, and explaining how revelation guides us in thinking about religions are all key theological tasks, which remain in place just as they were before theology was understood to be interreligious, comparative, and dialogical. But because theological reflection now regularly crosses religious boundaries, it is no longer interesting nor fruitful for the community of scholars to engage in the task of theology entirely within the framework of just one tradition's history, technical vocabulary, and creeds to the exclusion of a broader interreligious theological exchange with regard to all these issues. To consolidate my case for this broadened and renewed theology, in this chapter I return to the portrayal of theology initially offered in chapter 1, where I highlighted its interreligious, comparative, dialogical, and confessional characteristics. Thereafter I conclude by sketching a bit more fully what we might learn about God in all of this.

Theology as Interreligious

Richard Swinburne, Jayanta Bhaṭṭa, Hans von Balthasar, Śaṃkara, Rāmānuja, Sudarśana Sūri, Śrīpati Paṇḍita Ācārya, Karl Rahner, Vedānta Deśika, Aruḷ Nandi, Karl Barth, and Kumārila Bhaṭṭa are some of the theologians whose writings have provided the substance of the chapters of *Hindu God, Christian God*. In chapters 2 and 3, our primary interest was to highlight resemblances between the Hindu and Christian ways of reasoning about God's existence and God's identity. My emphasis was therefore on continuity among traditions, differences notwithstanding. In chapters 4 and 5 our primary focus was the choices that theologians make in adjudicating the tension between what they believe and hold as intelligible and the evidence for competing faith positions, which all claim authority and intelligibility. In those two chapters, we were interested particularly in the reasoned but also rather intuitive process by which traditions privilege their own beliefs while holding other traditions to stricter, less accommodating standards. Although in important ways these theologians differ—the Christians among themselves, the Hindus among themselves, and the Hindus and Christians compared—I have argued that there is sufficient common ground in terms of themes and methods to warrant concluding that they are all fellow intellectuals engaged in the discipline that Christians have called theology.

The four chapters thus offer examples in support of the thesis that there is no good reason today to keep theological traditions separate from one another as if Christian theology is something entirely separate from Hindu theology or vice versa. While there may be some beliefs, practices, and credal formulations justly recognized as unique to particular traditions, almost all of what counts as theological thinking is shared across religious boundaries.

It makes sense therefore to minimize the number of theological claims possibly unique to traditions by a Comparativist's Razor: theological ways of understanding faith, reading, conceptualizing, and arguing are presumed not to be tradition-specific unless a case for this specificity is put forward and argued plausibly in the broader interreligious context. While we can and should respect the tendency of theologians to distinguish themselves from others and to discover special and attractive qualities in their own theology, there is no value in respecting this tendency to the point where it blocks thinking across religious boundaries.

If Hindu and Christian theologies do share common features, this in turn enables us to uncover additional possibilities, which raise more questions than have already been answered, as the common features are problematized, differentiated, and refined. To say that theology is interreligious is not a conclusion but a starting point for a more serious conversation among interested theologians from all traditions. The rhetoric of uniqueness can subsequently be taken seriously again, after re-examination in light of how traditions make their claims and try, as best they can, to show that their claims are reasonable as well as faithful. But none of this amounts to much unless theologians in various traditions actually take up the challenge posed by *Hindu God, Christian God*. I hope readers will review their own theologies in this interreligious context and feel free either to agree or disagree with my induction about the common ground shared among different religious traditions.

Theology as Comparative

Once theologians recognize the common ground shared across religious boundaries, regular comparative practice becomes necessary. Even prior to arguments about disputed issues, one must theologize in a way that includes vigorous and vital interchange with theologians of other traditions. How irenic or combative one is likely to become in this situation will depend on what one is willing to do with what one acknowledges to be the case. Barth was correct when (as we saw in chapter 5) he realized that much of his own doctrine of grace could be found in Japanese Buddhist theologizing and possibly in the Śrīvaiṣṇava theological context as well. But his response to this situation was more homiletic than theological. He treated the similarity as a rebuke aimed at Christians tempted to prize fine theologizing, but he did not seem to allow the Buddhist and Hindu theological positions to affect his theology in the thousands of pages of *Church Dogmatics* that followed. Having noted similarities and disposed of them, he left Buddhists and Hindus behind and returned to a more pristine Christian project. But it now makes no sense to theologize that way; comparison must be conceded its theological significance.

Progress must be inductive and based on experiments. Instead of broad comparisons of the Hindu and Christian religions, smaller comparisons such as have been offered in the preceding chapters are more useful and appropriate. Each carefully established similarity or difference gives us something about which to think. Christian theologians, for example, now have various options to consider as they react to these particular Hindu materials read along with these particular twentieth-century Christian theologians. Some will recognize their own attitudes in the logicians' argument that it is reasonable to affirm a God who is maker of the world. Others will find their views echoed in the Mīmāṃsā, Vedānta, or Buddhist judgment, which argues that God's existence must be inconclusive. When God's identity is the issue, some will be inclined to agree with Śrīpati Paṇḍita Ācārya and Aruḷ Nandi, who hold that a creator God who graciously draws humans along a path of spiritual advancement is a God who makes most sense in terms of what "God" must mean. Others may find more convincing Vedānta Deśika's mix of arguments drawn from reason and exegesis, although they may also find too specific and demanding his insistence on Upaniṣadic revelation and the Vaiṣṇava corollary that Brahman is Nārāyaṇa. Some Christian theologians will likewise agree with the Vaiṣṇava theologians that God can take on a particular human form and freely choose to share the human drama, even if some are then disturbed by the Vaiṣṇava theory that God's embodied activity is no more nor less than dramatic performance (*abhinaya*). Others may be inclined to agree with the Śaivas who find the Vaiṣṇava view of divine embodiment (human and animal) too physical, demeaning the dignity of God and violating the standards for proper divine and human behavior. Similar decisions will have to be made from the Hindu side too, as Hindu theologians begin to make sense of the wide variety of Christian positions on issues of common interest and discern and assess similarities and differences. Some will find Swinburne's combination of several arguments in favor of God's existence the way to make the case for God's existence finally more plausible, while others will join Barth in moving more quickly to the starker challenge of revelation first. Many Hindu theologians will welcome Rahner's generous insight that everything human already points to the mystery of God become human, while a few may find themselves in agreement with von Balthasar in discovering how the miracle of one divine self-manifestation rules out every other.

To say that theology involves multiple comparative judgments is not an obvious nor insignificant point that can be acknowledged passively before one moves on to some other interesting topic. Once we constitute comparison as a proper theological exercise—neither pretheological nor a substitute for theology—then all of theology is affected. Every theological position can be brought into the comparative framework by rereading it in light of relevant positions taken by other theologians from the various traditions involved in the conversation. I have focused on God's existence, apologetics, embodiment, and revelation's judgment on religions, but I might just as well have focused on other topics, such as the unity of God, sin, ignorance, the formation of religious communities, issues of gender and sexuality, or concern for social justice.

One also has to know what to do with these similarities and differences once they are identified, how to decide which ones matter more, and how to determine which are the significant questions raised by them. Making sense of similarities and differences is not a pretheological sorting of details but a theological enterprise that must be undertaken meticulously and with respect for the complexities of theological judgments. What is most interesting and important eludes a reductive approach that appreciates only one's own theology and respects no other views as true theology.

Good comparative theology is a discipline to be practiced and a skill to be learned. Comparing is a particular activity that theologians can undertake in this new situation, where theology's common, interreligious features are recognized. One has to know which theological ideas, questions, and claims related to which texts (or practices or images) one should compare, and one has to decide how to speak of them in a way that highlights the interesting similarities and differences involved without allowing extraneous features to confuse the comparisons. One must be able to use the comparisons, with theological good sense, in order to draw conclusions that illuminate the traditions and the theological issues at stake. Ideally, *Hindu God, Christian God* has enabled readers to think differently and more clearly about God's existence, the question of naming God properly, divine embodiment, and the power of revelation as the norm for understanding religions. Much of the challenge facing me in writing this volume has been to present interesting and fruitful comparisons in each chapter and then to venture judgments about how important these comparisons are. Much of the reader's work will be to decide whether I have succeeded or whether other examples and judgments might have served better the purpose of showing why theology is interreligious.

That all theology is comparative does not enable us to predict theological conclusions. Theologians in two traditions may theologize in similar ways, yet because of the different starting points and different dynamics of their whole projects they may in the end come to diametrically opposed conclusions. Indeed, even the similarities may make sharper differences possible. We notice obvious similarities between the positions of Sudarśana Sūri and von Balthasar, for instance, in their understanding of the true religious apprehension of God and the need to account for other religious paths as bereft of independent religious significance. Though God is a mystery, God can to some extent be known, right views about God can be defended, and wrong views can be corrected. But in the end they still differ regarding God's name and what God says. Karl Barth and Kumārila Bhaṭṭa agree that the world is to be assessed by strict standards of revelation and that all kinds of religious efforts are misguided, but they certainly disagree on what actually counts religiously and how the Vedic and Biblical religions are actually to be evaluated theologically. They agree on much, but each marginalizes the other. If the heirs of both theologians notice this, they can begin to discuss their respective theological strategies of marginalization. Since comparison is not reducible to an appreciation of similarities, noticing important differences—for example, different theologies of creation or of embodiment—need not indicate a break or end to theological conversation.

Theology as Dialogical

Achieving a heightened awareness of the interreligious and comparative dynamics of theology is not enough. Such awareness is a beginning that opens the way to dialogical accountability, most often on a textual level first but certainly also by way of other personal, individual, and social connections with theologians in other traditions. If theology is interreligious and comparative, the circle of theologians keeps widening. We must be ready to practice a dialogical theology where theologians in other traditions are our colleagues on the whole range of theological issues, which have been only touched upon in this book.

This dialogical moment in theology is characterized by the emerging need and capacity to account for one's positions in a way that is as accessible and intelligible as possible to theologians in other religious traditions. The slender and strong thread of shared theological reasoning makes us accountable to one another; interreligious accountability leads interlocutors into a real, shared consideration of important theological issues where no faith position remains inaccessible to theological conversation. While distinctions must be made between insider and outsider discourse, theologians cannot neatly separate a more minimal rational or apologetic account of religious truths aimed at outsiders from a full theology for the members of the community, as if outsiders are merely unprepared for deeper and more properly theological conversations. While distinctions in audience are appropriate, they do not hold up in any fixed and entirely predictable pattern; one's audience is composed of those who understand, whoever they may be.

Theologians who are able to give an account of their communities' beliefs also become accountable in a second sense. They are responsible to the theologians of other religious traditions, and they learn to receive honestly and with an open mind the questions and criticisms those theologians put forward. One learns to listen and to take seriously these differing views and anticipated objections even when formulating one's own theology. What is interreligiously intelligible and inherently comparable is also dialogically accountable.

I now wish to suggest two ways in which this accountability can be defined in two kinds of comprehensive account, which I will frame with the order of the preceding four chapters in mind. A first account begins in the most intimate particulars of one's faith tradition and moves toward a broad rational conversation; a second account begins with a common realm of observation and reasoning and moves to reflections increasingly interior to the traditions' deepest faith positions.

According to the first account, this process might be seen as an outward-reaching effort to explain core scriptural and religious beliefs to a wider audience by offering increasingly accessible reasons for what is believed. From this perspective, one seeks to render at least partially intelligible what one already and intensely believes by giving reasons in support of it, moving from specific beliefs, which are not easily accessible to those outside the community, toward general positions more broadly accessible to reasoning religious persons. The expectation is that core truths, even though communicated in revelation and ultimately demanding religious surrender, can be talked about and to some extent explained, even persuasively. From a theistic perspective we may legitimately presume that the God who speaks in revelation is a God already involved in the world and to some extent already familiar to all people. According to this view, it is not surprising that God's existence should be recognized by everyone who is willing to reason clearly. On an intermediate ground, familiarity with God's action and identity is to some extent to be expected. Once we assert that God exists, we can also achieve a reasonable consensus on the approximate list of perfections indicated by the name "God" and can even begin to sketch a likely profile of divine behavior, God's likely speech and action.

By the first account, such considerations—revelation, divine involvement in the world, God's identity, and God's existence as explanatory of the world—can thus be retraced along a trajectory from particular communal beliefs to broader claims, as if one is moving from chapter 5 back toward chapter 2:

a. There is privileged divine communication, sacred speech, unlike any other source of knowledge. It should command human attention and shape human responses and behavior. God speaks to humans in specific words, which eventually become recorded in a canon of scripture, which theologians will identify as the Bible, the Veda, or as some other sacred speech (chapter 5).
b. This privileged sacred speech is intelligible because it is consistent with the wider activity of God in the world even (as in chapter 4) a divine choice to become embodied. This wider activity informs us more widely about the God who illumines, guides, and uplifts humans in deed as well in speech (moving from chapter 5 to chapter 4).
c. Faith in the active, embodied presence of God in the community, even in human form, is consonant with God's nature and character. We can recog-

nize God as likely to act graciously in expected ways; to some extent we know who God is (moving from chapter 4 to chapter 3).

d. That there is a God who acts in these ways is supported by the more widely compelling proposition that there must be an intelligent and reliable God who is the maker of this world. All reasonable persons should be able to understand what "God" means and at least to admit that it is plausible that there is a God (moving from chapter 3 to chapter 2).

By this account, the primary trajectory of theology is not a journey toward the exclusive, increasingly specific beliefs internal to a community. Rather, one proceeds from the community's core convictions as the starting point toward an ever more broadly accessible conversation about God in relation to life in the world and views of the world. At any stage, although perhaps more easily later on, new theological interlocutors can join this conversation. The conversation's original energy lies in specific religious beliefs, which may be presupposed to be unique but which are nonetheless made available to a much wider audience. Throughout, though, the goal remains to render intelligible what one already knows and believes on a sufficiently broad common ground that one can begin a conversation with some theologians from some other traditions. Whether the conversation partners must proceed all the way to the final point and discuss whether it is reasonable at all to speak of "God" depends on the prior beliefs of one's interlocutors. One would not have to argue about God's existence or the unity of God with a Nyāya logician or a Vedānta theologian, but one would have to raise the matter with a Buddhist.

According to the logic of my second account, one would instead see the theological program as a series of answers to further questions, answers that in effect point with increasing specificity toward claims characteristic of a religious community's internal sense of its own faith. Now the movement is inward rather than outward as reasonable persons are drawn step by step into a conversation of more specific beliefs. The starting point may be presented as a truth that, though not uncontroversial, any reasonable person should be able to grasp—the world requires explanation. The further questions asked and reasons given gradually demand more of the interlocutors, and demand that judgments be made about the implications of ideas to which the participants have already agreed. The reasonable person is gradually drawn into a consideration of truths which command more and more attention, commitment, and love. This, as we saw in chapter 1, was the agenda and confidence that de Nobili brought to his dialogue with Hindus: if you are willing to ponder the mystery of the order of nature, you should also become open to increasingly more specific and religiously important truths. The ordering of topics suggested earlier might then be transposed as in this book:

d. "How should we explain what we know about the world's origins by empirical observation?" There must be a God who is the maker/cause of the world (chapter 2).

c. "Can anything more be known about this God who is the maker of the world?" One can speak about the character and behavior of God and buttress one's opinions by rational arguments, appeals to common moral values, and even attention to scriptural resources that offer plausible insights into the divine nature (chapter 3).

b. "Does this God become involved in the world, and can this involvement include even a divine decision to become embodied?" One can give reasons that it is plausible to think that God can choose to become embodied, and one can explain embodiment in terms that show this embodiment to be real (chapter 4).

a. "Is there privileged divine speech that informs us of this God's intentions and guides judgments about humans who live seemingly beyond the scope of revelation and practice other religions?" One can respond that it is reasonable to conclude that the God who makes the world and is continually involved in it also speaks specifically to humans (chapter 5).

By this second account, the theological conversation traces a certain reasonable progression into increasingly intense and demanding intellectual and religious commitments. One question opens the way for another, in a series of choices that are increasingly more challenging and less accessible to reason. At issue, gradually, is not only a maker but also the God of a particular tradition and then a God who intervenes in the world in certain embodied forms and speaks in certain ways. Each chapter thus also marks the gradual tightening of the circle of theologians who can comfortably converse about God's character, identity, embodiment, and speech. Each answer to each further question involves small leaps in logic buttressed by plausibility not by necessity. God can reasonably be called by a particular name, but the determination that one name and not others is the right name is always going to be less compelling rationally than the assertion that God, maker of the world, exists. God can become embodied, and God can teach through a particular revelation, but it is still less reasonably compelling to argue that God has chosen only *this* body or spoken only in these sacred words. Theologians in various traditions can become involved slowly by discussing whether the world around us can be explained, but they may find it difficult to stop with that question, and eventually they will be drawn into a deeper and more particular conversation about who God is, and what God says. Eventually it may appear reasonable to surrender and worship.

By the first account, one begins an interreligious conversation with reasoned testimony about one's deepest beliefs; by the second, one begins with more easily accessible opinions regarding how the world is to be explained. Decisions about which path to follow are likely to depend as much on personal preferences as on theological reasons one might offer in support of one or the other. Some may prefer to begin by considering the positions of Swinburne and Jayanta Bhaṭṭa, while others will begin by worshipping the *liṅga* or sitting quietly in a church sanctuary. But in both cases faith and reason are important and complementary resources. Whether theologians conceive of their theology as moving from or toward their most specific beliefs, they are in any case venturing to reason about what they believe, to search for words to express their thoughts, and to speak in a way that ostensibly makes some sense to those who do not share their faith fully or at all. They are engaged in the effort to render faith intelligible and articulate, and they move back and forth along the spectrum of faith positions expressed in intelligible, arguable discourse. As theologians learn from one another, they can also make better, informed choices about the concepts and words they use in composing a theology that is infused with faith, which opens into worship. At every stage, however, they can be open to the comparisons, questions, and arguments posed by reason.

Both the inward- and outward-reaching scenarios make possible a theological dialogue that crosses the boundaries of faith, tradition, and community. Both enable theologians of diverse traditions to converse about beliefs that are presented in terms at least partially accessible to reasonable scrutiny. We can talk about whether the world requires a cause, who is God, and we can also discuss the meaning of embodiment and whether God's body must be like a human body in all or just in some respects. When theologians dialogue with their counterparts in other traditions, they are inevitably given new options regarding the words and concepts available for presenting their beliefs. Theologians appreciative of the interreligious context will begin to take into account the responses they receive from the theologians who comprehend their views to some extent and yet in part also misunderstand or disagree. This mutually corrective conversation further enlarges the shared theological ground. The more such accounts are offered and accepted, the more evident and fruitful the common theological ground becomes.

As I have already suggested, however, *Hindu God, Christian God* can at best be only partially successful in making the case for theology as dialogical. It involves a great deal of textual dialogue and mutual accountability, and I have to some extent tested its ideas in moments of actual dialogue with Hindu theologians. But additional examples are required, and my claims must be tested more broadly. This book is just one comparative theological project carried forward by one Christian theologian seeking to take seriously theology's interreligious, comparative, and dialogical dimensions. It is an invitation to dialogue and therefore is necessarily incomplete until other Christian theologians and theologians from other religious traditions respond by interpreting the examples differently or introducing other, more difficult examples. Until then, the claim that theology is dialogical remains a hypothesis.

Theology as Confessional, Again

The preceding reflections on theology as interreligious, comparative, and dialogical, understood in light of the examples detailed in the preceding chapters, are meant also to render more plausible the capacity of theologians to articulate their traditions' confessional claims even in a decidedly pluralistic world where theology itself is henceforth dramatically changed. Even in this new context theological truths can be put forward, argued, and affirmed. Although theological truths must be mediated and restated in accord with the complexities and new possibilities of the wider theological context, they can remain justly and vigorously confessional, as theologians make efforts in actual well-informed conversations with other theologians to convince their colleagues even in other religious traditions of the truth of what they believe and think. Faith remains specific and definitive in its claims, but now the accompanying theologies can claim a respectable confessional character only by taking seriously the new context in which theology has to find and defend its intelligibility.

Nothing much would be gained theologically were *Hindu God, Christian God* merely to foster a learned and complicated relativism. Dialogue must permanently shape the whole theological environment, but dialogue is not the primary goal of theology, which still has to do with the articulation of the truths one believes and the realization of a fuller knowledge of God (insofar as that is possible by way of theology). Both within traditions and across religious boundaries, truth does matter, conflicts among claims about reality remain significant possibilities, and making a case for the truth remains a key part of the theologian's task. There is no reason to settle for a situation where theologians can no longer argue the truth of their community's faith claims or of particular theological positions.

But now the price is higher; theology is an interreligious, comparative, and dialogical discipline, and theologians ought not equate illiteracy with faith nor confuse loyalty to their religious tradition with all that is theologically necessary. At least by way of judiciously chosen examples, theologians must become well versed in the basic features of other theological traditions, whether they are remarkably similar, in part significantly different, or completely different from their own. A Hindu theologian is a better theologian if he or she is well informed about theologians like Swinburne, von Balthasar, Rahner, and Barth (and their classical predecessors) or equivalent figures from some other tradition. A Christian theologian is a better theologian if he or she is well informed about Jayanta, Kumārila, Rāmānuja, and Aruḷ Nandi (and their contemporary heirs) or equivalent figures from some other tradition. If a theologian is well informed and faithful, if he or she manages to adhere to the faith while yet listening and learning intelligently from theologians in other traditions, then we have a theologian who can still argue convincingly even after theology has been recognized as interreligious and a much wider conversation has been convened.

We need not pretend that Hindu and Christian theologians all believe the same things nor hold the same positions, even if their theological arguments are similar in important ways. Differences have been quite clear throughout this book, and it is likely that theologians who have studied other traditions will continue to disagree on specific issues. One may understand the Nyāya induction and the Buddhist critique of it and still disagree with one or both positions. One may understand why Rahner and von Balthasar see in Jesus God's complete and unique revelation and still find their theological arguments and conclusions weak.

Throughout this book I have stressed both the importance of faith and the power of reasoning in the project of theology. Once faith positions and claims are discussed within a faith community in a way that is supposed to make sense to its members, they also become accessible to a wider public. Then the community is no longer in the position to decide solely on its own whether its self-presentation and its judgments about other theologies are plausible or not. If theologians reconsider their positions in light of what other theologians in other religions think and offer as alternative explanations, thereafter they must also review their hitherto a priori evaluations of those other religions and theologies. The heirs of Barth and Kumārila are not excused from the wider interreligious conversation, if they still want to be listened to even within their own communities. Theological credibility may be rooted in one's home soil, but it flourishes abroad.

Even after theologians admit similarities and differences in faith, we will still be obliged to examine theological differences in detail, one by one, in collaboration with colleagues even from other religious traditions. One can ponder for example whether an evangelical Christian's critique of rational theology is a plausible critique or whether Dharmakīrti has it right when he dismisses the Nyāya induction of God's existence. One can ask whether von Balthasar's theology of Christ as the form is intelligently and convincingly connected to his opinions about the founders of other religious traditions or whether Aruḷ Nandi's genetic theology with its prediction of pure-being, passionate, and lethargic gods and religions is at all fair to other Hindu views of God. Is Rahner right in seeing the Incarnation as a fulfillment of both the divine and human realities? Is the Vaiṣṇava notion of dramatic gesture a plausible way of explaining real divine embodiment? Did Barth have more insight into Japanese Buddhism than Kumārila had into Indian Buddhism? Once one formulates plausible answers to questions such as these—and to all the related questions—one is beginning to make progress toward more plausible representations of the traditions in question.

On some points of theological difference one's allies may be theologians in one's own tradition. On some, one may find closer allies among theologians who belong to other traditions. Christian theologians who agree with the Nyāya logicians on the cogency of the cosmological argument thereby also disagree with many Christian theologians, with Mīmāṃsā and Buddhist theologians who do not believe there is a God, and with Vedānta theologians who are skeptical about whether inductions of God's existence can ever be cogent. Similarly, differing views about the meanings of embodiment and divine embodiment will lead some Christian theologians to side with the Śaivas, who reject more material notions of divine body, and others to ally with the Vaiṣṇavas, who favor a more literal understanding of embodiment. Some Hindu theologians will agree with von Balthasar and Vedānta Deśika on the special nature of divine communication, while others will view a Nondualist assessment of religious differences as popular, confused, or simply inadequate constructions imposed on a fundamentally ineffable reality.

Interreligious theological conversations need not be any more quickly conclusive than other theological conversations. Faith can be clear and certain without waiting upon the decisions of theologians; the cry of the poor will be heard, or not, whether or not a theologian has decided what to make of the differences between Rahner's and Sudarśana Sūri's assessments of divine embodiment. A Christian does not affirm that Jesus is Lord simply because he or she first decided that it is theologically implausible to think that Nārāyaṇa is the material and spiritual cause of the world. A Śaiva theologian does not hold back from surrender to the mystery of Śiva's presence in the teacher simply because he or she has not yet decided whether von Balthasar's theory of form is convincing or not. Neither faith nor theology has to suffer merely because the other proceeds differently. Theology is not obliged to avoid interreligious complications, which faith may at first find unsettling or distasteful. Faith can be simple and stark, but theology must be patient, tentative, and willing to endure complication.

Complicated enough in this limited case of Hindu and Christian theologies considered together, this interreligious theological task will be made even more complex by attention to still other traditions—Islamic, Buddhist, Chinese, indigenous oral traditions, and so on. Theologians who consider all these factors may balk at the enormity of the project. After all, were this obligation to an interreligious, comparative, and dialogical theology taken seriously as a necessary complement to faith, then few successful theological claims about the truth of Christianity or of some particular Hindu tradition could ever be made, and it would become almost impossible to dismiss other traditions' theologies as inferior, flawed, or irrelevant. True. Nevertheless, there seems to be no good alternative for theologians who are serious about their work and respectful of their colleagues in all religious traditions.

In the short run, we can at least reflect more closely on the persuasive force that is supposed to underlie theological argumentation within communities and across religious boundaries. The goal of theological conversation is in part to persuade others that one's own positions are plausible, that they are more reasonable than alternative views, and that it makes sense to affirm even the most specific beliefs of a reasonable tradition. Theological explanations must aim also at persuading theologians not familiar with nor sympathetic to everything the theologian takes for granted within his or her own tradition. It makes sense to affirm the Christian account of the world's creation and to affirm that the Bible is inspired by the same God who makes the world; in light of those affirmations it will also make sense for Christian theologians to affirm that Jesus is Lord. But it also makes sense to affirm that Brahman is both the material and efficient cause of the world and so too that the Upaniṣads are the eternal verbal manifestation of Brahman; in light of those affirmations it will also make sense for a Vaiṣṇava theologian to affirm that Brahman is most fully known when invoked as Nārāyaṇa and for a Śaiva theologian to affirm that Śiva is the mysterious reality revealed in the Upaniṣads.

If the theologian is a worshiper of Nārāyaṇa, he or she may question the meaning of "Śiva" and what kind of God Śiva could be. A theologian who worships Śiva may wish to improvise secondary roles for deities determined to be real but less important, short of simply denying their existence. A Christian theologian may simply deny that Hindu deities exist but then go on to assert that Hindu theology is a real testament to human ingenuity, to natural striving, and even to the action of a gracious God. In all these Hindu and Christian theologies faith and reason appear harmonious though never identical in their methods or conclusions. None of the Hindu or Christian positions considered in this book can be merely discarded, so it is up to theologians to learn, teach, and inquire across religious boundaries as to why any one of these views is more plausible than another.

Some may undertake this debate in the spirit of Roberto de Nobili, who thought that reasonable religious people of any tradition, if willing to reason honestly and courageously, would eventually agree with his Christian theological affirmations. Even today, a theologian can argue inspired by this hope. But Christian and Hindu theologians disagree among themselves on the matters taken up in these chapters, and not all theologians in either tradition will sympathize with de Nobili's approach. Theological consensus in an interreligious context is not likely to be achieved quickly, and whatever consensus does emerge will cross boundaries and unite and divide theologians of the same and different communities. If there is a theological argument across religious boundaries, it will have to be a long-term project in which the arguments are actually pursued among theologians of various traditions who respect one another as colleagues, and not in the abstract.

Even if a theologian wants to make a judgment about the overall truth of one tradition compared with another—my religion is true, theirs is not—aiming at this large judgment will not justify ignoring entirely the tradition one has judged. It is not true that all the theological concepts and methods of one tradition are superior to all the concepts and methods articulated in another theological tradition. There can be no single judgment by which one theology is entirely affirmed and other theologies entirely negated. If a theologian merely ignores other theologians or merely talks about them rather than to them, those other theologians will not be persuaded, and one's own theology will appear even weaker than before.

Making theological judgments and taking sides is rarely going to be a clear-cut practice that upholds "the Christian position" and rejects "the Hindu position" or that defends Vaiṣṇava theology and relegates Catholic theology to an inferior level and so on. Rarely will there be a full theological consensus, even within one tradition, on theological issues as complex as those considered in the preceding chapters. In any case, *Hindu God, Christian God* (and books like it) should help change theologians' attitudes toward positions with which they disagree, particularly those enunciated in other religious traditions. One Hindu theologian puts forward the view that the world has no maker; another holds that Śiva is God while other gods are natural but secondary features of an evolving world; a third may argue that Nārāyaṇa's incarnations are real—dramatic—gestures; and someone may suggest that revelation is deeply inscribed in nature and in the syntax of the Sanskrit language. A Christian theologian will have to understand each view, assess what significance it might have for Christian theology, and then decide how to respond to it. But he or she should be able to think through these Hindu views with a recognition that these Hindu views are no less complex, sophisticated, or intelligent than the Christian alternatives. Similarly, a Hindu theologian should at least be able to recognize the rich and persuasive theologies underlying Christian claims about Jesus as the unique embodiment and form of God's presence in the world and to see the sources of such a position in a faith that makes reasonable and persuasive claims, in response to which a Hindu theologian can and should make some intelligent decisions.

Knowing God More Fully

As admitted in chapter 1, *Hindu God, Christian God* has focused rather narrowly on theological reasoning about God in order to highlight and emphasize this crucial interreligious tool. Once we agree that reasoning is invaluable in the interreligious theological context, we can of course again view theology's scope more widely. Considerations of God's existence can open into a deeper wonder at the world around us; arguments about God's true name and identity can be restored to a context of remembering how God has worked in our Christian and Hindu traditions; explications of how the Lord of the universe can become embodied can give way to more intense love for God's nearby presence in our lives; and receiving revelation as the rule by which to understand religion and religions can be considerably deepened by allowing ourselves to be educated in authentically Hindu or Christian ways. But such richer projects, within each tradition and across the boundaries, constitute several more books.

In any case, better theology is not the primary goal of theology. Rather, the faithful theologian seeks to know God more fully, at least insofar as this can be achieved by theologizing. What then have we learned of God from this volume?

To answer this question I return for a final time to the four positions proposed in chapter 1, reviewed earlier in this chapter, and studied in terms of detailed instances in the four intervening chapters. This time I assert them as theological claims that, in my view, are plausible and supported by many theistic theologians from the Hindu and Christian traditions:

a. There is a world that is a complex and coherent whole, and it can best be explained by affirming that there is a God who is its maker (chapter 2).
b. God's identity can be further specified according to expectations fostered by traditions and as portrayed in scriptures. Theologians are correct in identifying God and in ruling out incompatible portrayals of God (chapter 3).
c. God can choose to become more specifically involved in human affairs, even by embodiment in a specific human form (chapter 4).
d. There is divine revelation, which confirms but also constrains and guides human reasoning, informs humans about how to think and act properly, and reliably guides believers in their judgments about people in other religious traditions not formed according to revelation (chapter 5).

None of these claims is uncontroversial, and none is immune to objections. Each might be phrased differently and possibly better. But each claim is plausible and can hold its ground in debate and commands support among a sizable proportion of Christian and Hindu thinkers. The theological effort to explain who God is has much to do with balancing a rationally articulate definition of God with ever more specific accounts of who God is and what God says and does, and we must acknowledge that there has been more than one intelligent explanation. Nor is there any reason to separate four "Christian claims" from four "Hindu claims." As we saw above, the lines of agreement and disagreement on such issues cut across expected religious boundaries. Numerous Hindu and Christian theologians have formed successful and coherent accounts of God.

As theological positions and not simply faith assertions, all four claims need to be examined along the lines taken up in the respective chapters and understood to be informing us not only about theological arguments but also about God. God is the source of the world, God is not a total mystery but can in some real though limited way be known and named, God can become embodied, and God speaks in revelation. Despite my respect for Buddhists, Mīmāṃsā theologians, and Nondualist Vedānta theologians, I am a Christian theologian who sides with Hindu theistic theologians and, among those Hindu theologians, with Hindu monotheists, Śaiva and Vaiṣṇava. I favor not only the minimalist position about God's existence proposed in the context of the cosmological argument by Jayanta Bhaṭṭa and Richard Swinburne but also the stronger positions of theologians who believe that God can be further identified as a certain kind of person, who is likely to have acted and to act in certain ways and not other ways. I side with Rāmānuja and von Balthasar, both of whom think it reasonable and worthwhile to speak more amply about God. While I respect the Śaiva view of Śiva's mysterious and indirect embodiments, I prefer the stronger, more vivid Vaiṣṇava claim that God can assume a specific human body. I find this claim closer, in theory and sentiment, to the Christian theological position with which I grew up and which I have found reasonable and satisfying over the years. In agreeing that God can become embodied in a real physical body without yet compromising divine perfection, I am also willing to defend specific theological views about divine embodiment, such as are intelligently explained by theologians Karl Rahner and Vedānta Deśika. I appreciate Kumārila's and Barth's strict interpretation of revelation and revelation's judgment on religions but find the more expansive boundaries proposed by the Śrīvaiṣṇava and Śaiva theologians more convincing and consonant with what I know about God.

Such are some of my theological judgments. Although these four positions are closely aligned with the faith positions of my own religious tradition, the Roman Catholic, I have also examined closely Hindu reasons given for such positions as well as the arguments against them. As positions that find support in both the Christian and Hindu traditions, they are shared by theologians in different religious traditions who differ otherwise in many important respects. These positions are not merely peculiarities that happened to have evolved for various historical reasons in just one tradition where certain people argued for certain reasons. Moreover, although proposed in a comparative context, these positions are admittedly reassertions of traditional and even premodern positions. Yet the power of the interreligious, comparative, and dialogical moment also demands for them renewed consideration even by theologians who may have previously discounted them within their own tradition. Crossing the distances of cultures and religions may help us to cross distances of time as well. Nonetheless, since these theological positions are a kind of induction based on the examples adduced in this book, they also remain open to argument and correction.

In stating these claims and arguing as I have, I may well disturb some theologians in the Hindu and Christian traditions. I am asserting that whether they are liberal or conservative, they should stop pursuing their theologies as if no other plausible theology exists. They should get specific about others' faith and not just about their own. Even on the most basic issues of theological method and theological truth, they should enter into an interreligious conversation. I may also disappoint those more determined readers who find that I did not in the end actually decide which God, religion, or theology is the right one. I did not even say that Rahner's theology of divine embodiment is superior to Aruḷ Nandi's or Vedānta Deśika's. I did not conclude that Jesus is God and Śiva is not God. With annoyance they may point out that all I said was that theological decisions of that sort can in principle be made—and made persuasively—if someone is willing to do the work involved. I may therefore also disturb skeptics who believe that theological positions cannot be argued nor taken seriously as rational claims that might survive as true and applicable across linguistic, cultural, and religious boundaries.

Such complaints are legitimate in their own way. But if someone wishes to argue against the methods and conclusions put forward in *Hindu God, Christian God*, this too can be done plausibly only in a comparative context, either by intelligent alternate readings of the examples I have given or by more telling counterexamples from Christian, Hindu, and other traditions. One may wish to consider, for example, other Christian theologians who think differently than those introduced in these chapters. One may also wish to suggest attention to other Hindu theologians who, for example, write about goddesses or who write from outside the dominant brahmanical traditions and in the vernacular. In any case, arguments accompanied by good examples are those which will be able to go beyond the claims made in *Hindu God, Christian God*. Those that draw simply on one tradition's resources to dispose of other theological positions are not likely to be persuasive in a theological conversation that is intentionally interreligious.

But one may still wish to push things further and ask for more decisive conclusions. Is God "the God of our Lord Jesus Christ" or "Nārāyaṇa, whose spouse is Lakṣmī" or "Śiva, Lord of the Pāśupatas"? Is it a fact that God has become embodied in Jesus Christ but not in Rāma and Kṛṣṇa? Is the Word of God expressed in the words of the Veda and the Śaiva Traditional Texts but not in the Bible? Does it matter whether I gaze upon a *liṅga* or a Sacred Heart image in my home? Though rhetorically impressive and in some ways logically urgent, such disjunctions, baldly stated, are not likely to be fruitful in an interreligious, comparative, and dialogical context. Again, even if such dichotomies and the choices they compel upon us originate in confessional theology, persuasive responses today still have to wait upon the hard work of a fully interreligious, comparative, dialogical, and (then) confessional theology. Resolving this dichotomy by proffering a firm choice is a fruitful though only initial step in this richer theology, which is Hindu, Christian, and more. Once it is made, one must still talk about it with fellow theologians who are members of other religious traditions.

Even so, some readers may wish to ask me in particular: "You, after all, have supposedly been engaged in this complex theology, and you seem to know something about Christian and Hindu theologies, so tell us then: Is God the God of our Lord Jesus Christ, or Nārāyaṇa, whose spouse is Lakṣmī, or Śiva, Lord of the Pāśupatas? Is it a fact that God has become embodied in Jesus Christ but not in Rāma and Kṛṣṇa? Is the Word of God expressed fully in the Bible but only in some vaguer fashion in the words of the Veda and the Śaiva Traditional Texts? And do you not know God well enough by now and the theologies involved to decide whether it is 'Christian God' *or* 'Hindu God'?" Good questions, to which the answer is simple but also, unfortunately, still complicated.

As a Christian believer—who also happens to be a theologian—I willingly profess my faith in the God of our Lord Jesus Christ, who was born as the child of Mary, who died on the cross for our sins, rose into glory, and sent forth the Spirit upon us. By direct implication this faith claim, which is not intended to be true just for some people, excludes other such faith claims. But this admission, in itself rather obvious, leaves us exactly where we started. If I wish to speak of my faith as a theologian and make considered and intelligible judgments as a theologian, then I still have to make a case that is plausible and persuasive in an interreligious theological conversation. As I have stated previously more than once, truth is not exempt from the interreligious, comparative, and dialogical process. I still need to be able to explain why I find the Christian and Roman Catholic theology that follows from my faith to be more convincing than that which follows from the faith of a Śālika Nātha Miśra or a Śrīpati Paṇḍita Ācārya. Otherwise, my faith claim—uninformed, vague, and unpersuasive at least in the public and interreligious conversation—will, though admirable as faith, fail to win over anyone who might be listening. So the requirements of an interreligious, comparative, and dialogical practice still pertain.

In the long run, then, the questions about God's existence, presence and activity in the world, embodiment, and sacred word are questions that will entail great theological labor before they can be plausibly answered. In the short run, faith and reason must both do their work. On the one hand, I can assert the truths of the Christian faith without compromise; on the other, until the theological work is done, I can still state that these truths need to be tested in a comparative and dialogical conversation. On the one hand, I agree (in various ways, with certain accommodations) with Swinburne, von Balthasar, Rahner, and Barth; on the other, for now (in various ways, with certain accommodations), I agree with Jayanta Bhaṭṭa, and I cannot disagree with Aruḷ Nandi, Vedānta Deśika, or Nañjīyar. I confess that Jesus is Lord, but I cannot now assert that Śiva is not Lord nor that Nārāyaṇa did not graciously undergo embodiment in order to enable humans to encounter their God. The work of the theologian is a work of faith and reason, and it is not complete until both have done the best they can.

Beyond This Book

In the preceding chapters I have posed as our task the composition of a broader conversation in which we articulate our faith—whether we are Christian, Hindu, or of another faith tradition—and make the case as to why it is plausible to believe "as we do and not as you do." For this reason I have written *Hindu God, Christian God*, hoping to contribute to a wider conversation wherein we might make compelling sense of our faith in our time as innumerable theologians have likewise attempted in their particular circumstances.

It should be clear by now that I readily concede that my exposition of an interreligious theology is still largely a Christian's project. Not only have I begun my chapters with Christian theologians, but I frame the questions and discover answers that fit nicely into the categories and expectations of the Christian theological tradition. Although I hope not to have presented Swinburne, von Balthasar, Rahner, and Barth in a purely Christian way, it is still just to assert that had I started with Indian materials and Hindu categories articulated in Sanskrit or perhaps Tamil technical vocabulary, many things in the individual chapters and the overall structure of this work would be different. Even words such as *theology*, *religion*, *comparison*, and *dialogue* are used here in ways that remain predominantly indebted to the Christian tradition.

Were a book like this to be written from a more Indian perspective and perhaps in Sanskrit or Tamil, it would certainly be a different book. Some differences would be smaller matters of nuance and emphasis; others would be more important and more elusive. A Hindu theologian might be inclined to give even more consideration to religious systems, such as Mīmāṃsā, which do not require the notion of "God," and might more expertly explore the subtleties of thinking in Sanskrit. Hindu theologians might likewise want to distinguish Christian monotheism of the kind von Balthasar has in mind from the assertions that Nārāyaṇa or Śiva is Lord, which more easily and significantly remain compatible with the existence of other gods. While I did compare and contrast revelation as language, as in the case of the Mīmāṃsā theory of the Veda, with "revelation as personal encounter with God" as in the case of many Christian theories of revelation, a Hindu theologian might make more of this point. A conservative Hindu theologian, writing in Sanskrit, might be inclined to see the whole English-language discussion that occupies chapter 5 as somewhat pointless. I can also imagine that some Hindu thinkers would not write a book like this at all, and some might say that this entire discourse, with its terms like *interreligious*, *comparative*, and *dialogical*, is the product of a

Western and Christian world view. While this version of resistance to comparative study will have its own Hindu contours, in practice the end result is much like the resistance put forward by Christian theologians similarly inclined to avoid theology's interreligious dimensions. Since theology today is interreligious, comparative, dialogical, and again confessional, I can venture to argue that the hesitant Hindu theologians too will do a favor to the rest of us and to themselves if they enter this larger conversation.

Although it is not for me to say what these Hindu rewritings of my book would look like, I can imagine several possible versions. First, a scholar committed to the Veda or one whose reading of Hindu vernacular literature is influenced by the Vedic concern for language might begin with issues of language, text, commentary, and the educational and aesthetic refinements and requirements considered requisite for theological learning. This in turn would open up issues of pedagogy and how one learns and thus becomes the kind of person who can read a theological text adequately. Then one could turn to a particular text that is dominant in the Hindu tradition and spell out a world view in terms of its categories. Then, in that context, one could begin to look for interreligious, comparative, and dialogical parallels in some Christian theological tradition—perhaps monastic?—in which similar aesthetic, pedagogical, and commentarial instincts predominate. Second, one might follow the lead of the Vaiśeṣika and Nyāya thinkers introduced in chapter 2 and develop much more thoroughly an adequate, scientifically plausible description of the world and its sources. From a Nyāya perspective this would open the way for an empirical, realistic, and modest argument in favor of God's existence, rationally forceful even prior to any particular understanding of who God is or how God acts. Modern Western thinkers, such as Richard Swinburne might be drawn into this conversation in order to make clearer still the force of reasoning about God's existence and nature. A Nyāya author might then make an entire book out of this book's chapter 2. Third, some Śaiva and Vaiṣṇava theologians might write a book rather similar to *Hindu God, Christian God,* reviewing all of theology from the stance of faithful reflection on what God, Lord Śiva, or Lord Nārāyaṇa has done in the world. Fourth, one might also take seriously either the Mīmāṃsā or Nondualist Vedānta versions of a nontheistic religious discourse, and reconsider from a radically different perspective both Christian and Hindu views of God's existence, identity, embodiment, and speech. I certainly have no objection to alternative versions of this project. It would be interesting indeed to see another book like this *Hindu God, Christian God*, written entirely by a Hindu theologian and from a primarily Hindu perspective—perhaps inversely entitled "Christian God, Hindu God."

Hindu God, Christian God has no pretense of being a complete and thorough theology of theology. It will survive only in the way that good theology ever survives, as considered, critiqued, emended, and supplemented by further theological contributions—this time not just in one theological tradition but also in the writings of theologians in numerous religious traditions. For now, this has simply been a set of examples proposed and thought through by one Christian theologian who has studied some Hindu texts and thought about them in light of what he knows of Christian theology. Every aspect of the project is specific, limited, and in need of contestation. I certainly welcome the contributions of other theologians, from Hindu and other backgrounds, who wish to demonstrate by better examples how this book is nothing more than a few examples with which one might begin but not end.

In any case, the inquiry and conversation must eventually be broadened well beyond the boundaries established in this book. While a consideration of Hindu and Christian materials is a particularly appropriate and rich source for this new understanding of theology and its parameters, in the long run there is no reason to restrict the reconstruction of theology to Hindu and Christian sources, taken separately or together. Without undue difficulty, other traditions can be brought into the conversation with the same attention to similarities and differences as marked the particular comparisons undertaken in this volume. We have already touched on Buddhist materials in the preceding chapters, since Buddhist positions were much on the minds of Hindu theologians. There is much more to say on the topics with respect to the Buddhist positions and, by extension, the often similar (and similarly critical) Jaina positions.

I would also be happy to read "Muslim God, Christian God" or an interreligious theology written entirely differently from an African or East Asian or Native American perspective. As for the Christian positions, these can be enriched by greater attention to other Christian theologians, many of whom are quite different from Swinburne, von Balthasar, Rahner, and Barth. One can certainly explore far more deeply than I have here the Jewish roots of Christian identity and Christian theology.[1]

Later and after numerous interreligious, comparative, and dialogical projects that cross many religious boundaries and draw faithful theologians from diverse traditions into numerous conversations, perhaps someone will be able to write a simpler book, simply entitled "God." That such a book cannot be written now but may be written in the future if we all do our work is something about which theologians everywhere should think.

Sometimes the mind does enable faith to go where it could not have imagined traveling on its own.

1. Fruitful work in regard to some of these further possibilities has already been done by some of the authors listed in the bibliography. See for example Burrell, Cabezon, Carman, Henderson, Kaltner, Makransky, and Neville.

A Hindu Theologian's Response: A Prolegomenon to "Christian God, Hindu God"

Parimal G. Patil, Emory University

There are significant asymmetries in the project of "comparative theology" that reflect and reveal the complex historical, intellectual, and political realities of Christianity's encounter with "others." The invitation by academic theologians to Hindu intellectuals to now participate in such projects is welcomed, long overdue, and must be accepted. Such participation, however, must be prefaced by an acknowledgment of these asymmetries and their effect on the interreligious, comparative, dialogical, and confessional dimensions of the rejuvenated theology called for in *Hindu God, Christian God*. Attention also must be paid to the two separable senses of "theology" made use of in this work: theology as an intellectual practice that has been shared by people belonging to numerous traditions of religious reflection, and theology as an academic discipline that is located in Euro-American style academies throughout the world. *Hindu God, Christian God* is important, in part, because it makes significant demands of both. In what follows it must be recognized that in both senses of the term *Hindu God, Christian God* restricts "theology" to its more "scholastic" interpretations. Of the innumerable points of possible theological contact between Hinduism and Christianity, it is with a particular form of religious reasoning that *Hindu God, Christian God* chooses to begin. This form of religious reasoning results from years of academic training in institutional contexts in which highly abstract thinking is valued and often privileged. It is not for everyone, and, as Clooney has noted, it is certainly not the only way to theologize. For those of us who are Hindu and interested in practicing theology, however, such a beginning must be celebrated, since for too long now the Hindu counterparts to Swinburne, von Balthasar, Rahner, and Barth have not received the attention that they so richly deserve.

I intend this chapter as a prolegomenon to a work that is imagined in *Hindu God, Christian God*, a work in which a Hindu theologian takes up the interreligious, comparative, dialogical, and confessional theology articulated here. I will begin by pointing out the important, but underappreciated, asymmetries between Christian and potential Hindu versions of the project and then will consider how they could affect an imagined "Christian God, Hindu God."

Asymmetrical Demands

It must be recognized that as a form of intellectual practice, theology has been shared by intellectuals belonging to Christian and Hindu traditions throughout their diverse histories. The textual history of both traditions makes this impossible to deny. This history also makes clear that there are numerous areas of shared concern as well as those that are tradition specific. As Clooney's examples have demonstrated, theological topics, methods, and even conclusions have been shared across these diverse traditions. This fact must, as Clooney has argued, be conceded its theological significance. What is not shared, however, are the institutional contexts in which Christian theology is currently practiced. Due to the complex history of premodern South Asia, the effects of colonialism, and the decisions made by South Asian social and political leaders in conceptualizing modern nation states, there are very few Hindu institutions that correspond to the diverse academic and nonacademic institutions in which Christian theology is practiced today. This is especially so for the philosophical forms of theology considered here. It is, for example, unlikely that many of the Hindu theologians to whom Clooney refers would have the institutional (and therefore intellectual) support necessary for producing their work today. The interreligious space about which Clooney writes is, therefore, defined by shared concerns and, for the most part, asymmetric contexts.

This incredible asymmetry must also be conceded its significance. Whether theology as interpreted and practiced by the intellectuals to whom Clooney refers is to be a part of Hinduism's future is for Hindus to decide. Whether the intellectual concerns described by Clooney will be shared in the future will also depend on whether Hindus and Christians continue to recognize their importance. If the academic discipline currently (mis)labeled "theology" is meaningfully to be anything other than Christian theology, however, it must create institutional space for non-Christian theologians and the study of non-Christian theology. Without the presence of professional Hindu theologians in the academy, for example, the interreligious project of *Hindu God, Chris-*

tian God will remain an entirely Christian enterprise. It will represent just another subdiscipline of Christian theology and will radically alter the comparative and dialogical dimensions of the project. It is also likely that in such an environment Hindu theology will only be used in service of Christian theology and will not be given an opportunity to respond. Without institutional space for Hindu theologians and the study of Hindu theology, moreover, it is difficult to imagine that Hindu traditions would not be more easily misused. Theology must, therefore, either accept its interreligious dimensions through sustained engagement with the voices and texts of others who share this intellectual (and not yet institutional) space or provide principled reasons why this space must be redescribed to exclude, for example, the intellectuals to whom Clooney refers. Responsible use of the term "theology" demands at least this much.

Hindu God, Christian God demands much more, however, by arguing that an awareness of this shared space should result in the detailed examination of specific interreligious examples and that this examination must take place with mutual or "dialogical" accountability. These are the comparative and dialogical demands that are placed on theologians and theology by Clooney's work. Clooney acknowledges and repeatedly comments on the high cost of these demands for contemporary Christian intellectuals: they must learn new theological languages, vocabularies, doctrines, and styles and welcome new conversation partners and create institutional space for them. The costs for Hindu intellectuals are significantly different and, in many ways, even higher.

For Hindu intellectuals, Clooney's comparative and dialogical demands are historically familiar and therefore, in principle, easily accepted. In the past, theologians from various Hindu traditions produced theological work in which they articulated and defended their beliefs through explicit consideration and criticism of the views of their Hindu, Buddhist, and Jaina rivals. Although areas of theological difference were generally highlighted in these works, their commitment to comparison was based upon deeper similarities in language, vocabulary, intellectual context, and style. And while these texts were primarily directed to members of the tradition in which they were produced, they were clearly read and responded to by those against whom they were arguing. They were, therefore, "overheard" and, in my opinion, were often designed to be so. Rejuvenating and expanding these conversations to include Christian theologians is, in an important sense, demanded by and a proper part of Hindu tradition. As aspects of theological method, therefore, these demands should not be resisted. The textual traditions referred to previously were, after all, very nearly comparative and dialogical in Clooney's sense. The costs for Hindu intellectuals, which are both practical and theological, lie elsewhere.

Including Christian interlocutors in these already interreligious, comparative, and dialogical conversations will, for example, require redescribing Christian examples within the technical vocabulary and genre conventions of these texts. Even if composed in English, however, such work will be unintelligible to most academic theologians and is unlikely, therefore, to find an audience in the contemporary academy. What this means is that in order to "account for one's position in a way that is as accessible and intelligible as possible to theologians in other religious traditions," Hindu intellectuals will be forced, at least for the present, to conform to the vocabulary and genre conventions of contemporary philosophical theology. Although the invitation to participate in the project of "comparative theology" is issued to all Hindu intellectuals, it is, in reality, directed toward those already capable of writing in the languages and style of the Euro-American academy. And since there are, in effect, no professional Hindu theologians, the invitation is directed more narrowly still to Hindu intellectuals in disciplines such as Anthropology, Areas Studies, Indology, or History of Religions. In such disciplinary contexts, however, constructive and normative work is rarely respected and, in fact, is generally believed to reveal that those who produce it lack the "scholarly" distance that is necessary for rigorous and responsible work in these disciplines. The participation of Hindu intellectuals in the project described in this work may come, therefore, at a very high professional price.

In addition, many of the most important Hindu theological texts are unedited, untranslated, and only rarely studied in the academy. For example, not one of the texts together with the commentaries discussed by Clooney has been completely translated into English, French, or German. This is, in part, because Indian theological traditions have been rarely discussed by historians, philosophers, philosophers of religion, or religious ethicists. The secondary resources upon which Christian theologians rely for their own theological work are, therefore, not available for potential Hindu theologians. For Hindus, properly theological work must be preceded by a great deal of work in religious history, philology, and philosophy. This is, of course, also the case for Christians. The difference, however, is that Hindu intellectuals will be required to pursue this work by themselves, in relative isolation, and without the breadth and depth of conversation partners so helpful for sustained theological reflection. For Hindu participants in the project of comparative theology, therefore, a significant amount of work will not be explicitly theological. This fact radically alters the dialogical demand described by Clooney. Not only will Hindu theologians be responsible to those with whom they are in critical theological conversation, but they will also be responsible to the demands of each of the disciplines upon which their theological work is based.

Related to this dialogical demand are questions about how Christian and Hindu theologies and theologians should relate to one another in the interreligious space that they share. Such questions are also theological questions and must be considered by Hindu intellectuals interested in practicing theology. *Hindu God, Christian God* is, for example, a work of theology that is clearly interreligious, comparative, dialogical, and (yet still) confessional. It is self-consciously a work of Christian theology: its selection of topics is governed by interest in specific Christian doctrines, it is written by a Christian theologian, and it is intended primarily for a Christian audience. It is, then, a work from within a tradition, by a member of that tradition, and for that tradition and its members. It is, however, not just a work of Christian theology but, more important, also a work of theology. While it is a work from within a tradition, it also is a work from within an academic discipline; while it is written by a member of a particular tradition, it is also written by a professor who self-consciously locates himself in that discipline; and while it is primarily intended for members of a particular tradition, it is also explicit in its hope that it will be read and responded to by those who are not. It is in the interreligious space defined by shared concerns, methods, and conclusions that the discipline of theology is located. This is, at least, how I read *Hindu God, Christian God*. In this space, a Christian theologian may produce a work of Christian theology that is also (and non-trivially) a work of theology. What distinguishes Clooney's vision of this project is his attention to specific examples and his insistence on mutual, intellectual accountability. His work is not just a Christian theology of religions to which a Hindu theologian may respond by offering only a few corrective remarks or producing her own Hindu theology of religions. Clooney's project is different. Its attention to specific theological examples requires that Christian theologians engage with their Hindu counterparts in a way that makes quick generalizations impossible. Such an approach is sure to generate deep (and even difficult) questions for the Hindu material and is similar, therefore, to how Christians currently engage theologians from their own tradition. The dialogical demand of Clooney's work further deepens this engagement by requiring that theologians not only learn from other traditions but also that they be accountable to them. It is in being accountable to other theologians in the manner described by Clooney that necessitates meeting in the virtual space of the discipline of theology. It is here that theologians from diverse traditions can become genuine colleagues (and not just theological rivals). And it is here that Hindu theology can be responsibly and rigorously recontextualized by (among others) those of us who are Hindu and interested in the practice of theology. What Hindus must carefully consider, however, is whether *Hindu God, Christian God* provides a proper model for practicing Hindu theology and introducing it to the academy.

The challenge for potential Hindu theologians is to maintain the integrity of tradition while attempting to recontextualize it in a context that is, in many ways, intellectually familiar but institutionally new. It is the challenge of forming tradition while continuing to be genuinely formed by it. Such work must have an authentic voice from Hindu tradition and also be a part of the discipline of theology; it must be the work of a Hindu scholar who is also a theologian; and it must serve both the interests of tradition and the needs of the discipline. As suggested earlier, the general method described in *Hindu God, Christian God* is already a proper part of some Hindu theological traditions. The theological examples that Clooney has chosen to discuss, however, represent a wide variety of disparate Hindu theological subtraditions. And as Clooney himself notes, he has only considered those aspects of the examples that are most relevant for his theological purposes. Given that his primary purpose is to convince Christian theologians that theology is deeply interreligious, his approach is proper. The picture of Hindu theology that emerges from his work, however, is not the theology of any particular Hindu theologian or theological tradition. It does not seem, therefore, to itself provide a proper model for Hindu theology. For Hindu theologians, an interreligious, comparative, dialogical, and (yet still) confessional theology must look somewhat different. This is due, in large part, to the asymmetries referred to previously.

"Christian God, Hindu God"

In what follows, I want to outline how I believe those of us who are Hindu and interested in theology should interpret Clooney's invitation to participate in the project of comparative theology. In imagining my version of "Christian God, Hindu God," I will focus on the theological example discussed by Clooney in chapter 2 and his expressed hope, in chapter 6, that a work based on it may be written.

Interreligious

In my view, as Hindu theologians, we should begin our work as Clooney does, by defining the interreligious space within which we could locate our theological projects. Furthermore, three general principles should govern how we choose this space. In my view, for example, it is important that we focus on just one theologian or theological subtradition; in choosing to be formed by Hindu tradition, we must allow ourselves to be guided by genuine instances of it. Attention to a particular theologian or theological text and its commentarial traditions should provide the necessary guidance. In addition, given the lack of attention to Hindu theology in the academy, there is a desperate need for systematic work that considers individual theologians and traditionally defined subtraditions of Hindu theology. Such work would also be of great theological significance since it would help us to recover specific theological resources with which to interpret and shape Hindu tradition in a new institutional context. Secondly, I think it is important that Hindu theologians focus on (or at least include some) "classical" material in their work. For the past few centuries, Hindu theological texts have, for the most part, not been produced. It is almost necessary, therefore, that we consider "pre-modern" theological traditions. These traditions also represent the very best of Hindu philosophical theology and, in my opinion, provide the only real parallels to the sort of Christian theology considered by Clooney. In drawing our attention to theological topics, methods, and conclusions that are not only shared with other theologians but are also a proper part of Hindu tradition, these first two principles should enable us to create the interreligious space for our projects. Finally, it is important that in conceiving of this space we identify where we differ with contemporary theologians. While Clooney has chosen to focus on similarities, we must also highlight differences. One of the lessons to be learned from Hindu traditions of philosophical theology is that attention to differences often leads to a deeper understanding of one's own position. Given the asymmetries discussed earlier, it is essential that Christian theologians not just think of Hindu theology as Christian thinking differently arranged. There is much that is shared, but there is also much that is new. It is in drawing attention to what is new and different that Hindu theologians may best be able to serve our own interests and those we share with our Christian colleagues. Both interests must be balanced if the interreligious space is to be properly Hindu and meaningfully theological.

The interreligious space for my imagined version of "Christian God, Hindu God" would also be defined in terms of these three principles. My work, for example, would focus on the work of one Hindu intellectual, the Nyāya philosopher and Hindu theologian Udayana. Udayana is, most famously, the author of a work devoted exclusively to Nyāya theism. In addition, he composed introductory manuals to the Nyāya and Vaiśeṣika systems of philosophy; commentaries or subcommentaries on the foundational texts of each system; and a very important work of apologetics. Guided by Udayana's work, my own theological interests, and those of Christian philosophers and theologians such as Alston, Plantinga, and Swinburne, I would define the interreligious space for my project in terms of a shared theological interest in cosmological and inferential arguments for the nature and existence of God, in the theories of religious reasoning in which such arguments are presented, defended, and critically assessed, and in the role of such arguments in religious life. In my work, I would also pay close attention to where Udayana disagrees, for example, with Christian versions of the cosmological argument and Alston, Plantinga, or Swinburne's theories of religious epistemology.

Comparative and Dialogical

Once the interreligious space has been defined, Hindu theologians should explore it with full awareness of the other scholars who have occupied this space in the past, of the philosophers and theologians who are present in it today, and of those who may wander in it in the future. Creating a productive conversation among this diverse group of scholars is, in my view, one of the important challenges posed to us by Clooney's work. I think that there is one methodological principle that could govern the comparative and dialogical dimensions of our Hindu theological projects. This principle, which may be called "multiple contextualization," describes how Hindu textual material could be understood and interpreted given the diverse set of conversational contexts to which our work will be held accountable. There are at least three contexts in which I believe such work should be interpreted.

The first context to which the work of a Hindu theologian should be comparatively and dialogically responsible is, in my opinion, the intellectual world of the theologian or theological subtradition upon which she or he has chosen to focus. Since very little is known in the academy about Hindu traditions of theology, it is essential that we make a commitment to first understanding them as they were understood by traditional theologians. This requires thinking along with these theologians in the technical vocabulary and style of Sanskrit philosophy, in understanding the interreligious space in which they practiced comparative theology, and in trying to discover their own theological concerns. In order to be comparatively and dialogically accountable to these theologians and their traditions of theology, a primarily historical and exegetical mode of inquiry must accompany all other theological work. The first context to which my imagined work would be responsible, therefore, is the intellectual world of Udayana and his Buddhist, Mīmāṃsā, Nyāya, and Vedānta interlocutors.

The second context is the academic discipline of theology. This is the primary context for Clooney's work. Unlike Clooney's approach, however, in which both Hindu and Christian examples are discussed explicitly (and side by side), I believe that we should devote most of our attention to presenting Hindu theological examples in, as Clooney suggests, an explicitly comparative and dialogically accountable manner. This is not inconsistent with Clooney's approach, but another instance of it. Explaining, in English, theological arguments formulated in technical philosophical Sanskrit (or Tamil and others) is already a deeply interreligious, comparative, and dialogical task. As with English descriptions of medieval Christian theology, the semantic range of existing English terms will need to be extended and new technical terms will need to be proposed. The work of specific Christian philosophers and theologians will also need to be carefully interpreted in order to properly characterize Hindu theories in contemporary philosophical and theological vocabulary. It is not possible, in my opinion, to accurately describe Hindu arguments and theories in English without a deep familiarity with philosophical and Christian theological writing in English. Thus, any discussion of Hindu material that is authentic to tradition and intelligible to contemporary theologians will already have to be comparative and dialogically responsible to Christian traditions of theology. This is, of course, a contingent feature of the contemporary academy. As theologians from other traditions are allowed to contribute to the conceptual resources of the discipline, the vocabulary and style of English language theology should, as Clooney too hopes, become properly interreligious. In addition, since Christian theological material is relatively well known in the academy and there are numerous secondary sources in which much of it is discussed, Hindu theologians may not need to devote the same attention to Christian examples that Clooney devotes to Hindu examples.

In my imagined work, for example, I would devote most of my attention to carefully presenting Udayana's version of the cosmological argument and the Nyāya epistemological theory within which it is formulated and defended. In order to accurately describe Udayana's views in a manner that is fully intelligible to my Christian colleagues, however, my discussion of Udayana would have to be in critical conversation with Christian examples of the cosmological argument and Christian theories of religious epistemology. Hindu theologians cannot, in my opinion, ignore Clooney's insight that "the opportunities present in the interreligious situation are most fruitfully appropriated slowly and by way of small and specific examples taken seriously and argued in their details." What I am suggesting here is simply that given the asymmetries in the project of comparative theology, we may be able to treat Christian examples differently than Clooney has treated Hindu ones.

Hindu theology, as an intellectual practice that is located both within and without the academic discipline of theology, is the third context to which, I believe, Hindu theologians should be comparatively and dialogically accountable. While the work of the authors discussed by Clooney may be of only historical interest to many, it was certainly not of just historical interest to the theologians themselves. As Clooney's discussion makes clear, these theologians considered themselves to be arguing for philosophical and theological positions that could be supported by persuasive, if not demonstrative, arguments. And as with most constructive work in theology, their work was also part of a much broader intellectual context in which their arguments and ideas mattered to a variety of different people and for a variety of different reasons. If their arguments and theories are not considered with the same philosophical and theological seriousness with which they were offered, the traditions of which their arguments are a part will be done a great disservice. Hindu traditions of theology require, therefore, that in addition to explaining traditional arguments and theories, we (all) try to assess their claims to validity and truth. Interpreting theological work in multiple contexts is helpful for such an inquiry. It becomes possible in this broader intellectual context to develop new perspectives on the arguments, to discover hidden premises, to see more clearly the consequences of the positions, and to make, therefore, more informed evaluations. This level of engagement is, as Clooney recognizes, necessary for developing an accurate and rich understanding of tradition and its constructive aspirations and possibilities.

To satisfy the comparative and dialogical demands of Hindu theology in my imagined work, I would, for example, attempt to critically evaluate the success (or failure) of Udayana's arguments and epistemological theory in light of what I learned from interpreting his work in the two contexts described above. Equally important to my work, however, would be to consider the role that such arguments and theories could have in religious life; perhaps by taking seriously and further exploring an idea taken from one of Udayana's commentators that philosophical theology could itself be a form of religious practice. In my view, interpreting Udayana's work in this way takes him seriously as a philosopher and theologian and thus begins to satisfy the comparative and dialogical demands of Hindu tradition.

Confessional

Hindu theologians should also follow Clooney, in my view, in moving through the interreligious, comparative, and dialogical dimensions of our projects in order to take seriously the role that our theological work could have in constructive Hindu thinking and confessional theology more generally. Such an interpretation modifies, though only slightly, the confessional character of Clooney's project by recognizing that due to the long absence of significant new work in many Hindu traditions of theology we will often have to rejuvenate theological traditions as we seek "to convince (our) colleagues, even in other religious traditions, of the truth of what (we) believe and think." We will, in other words, often have to reconstruct the very philosophical and theological platforms from which we will develop and then argue for our own theological views. In my opinion, therefore, Hindu theologians should interpret the confessional character of Clooney's theological project more generally, as a call to think interreligiously about what Hindu traditions have been for the explicit purpose of articulating what (why and for whom) they should now be. One way for us to satisfy this confessional desiderata may be to return to each of the three contexts discussed above, but this time for the explicit purpose of developing further (and arguing in favor of) our own theological positions by engaging our theological colleagues, both Hindu and Christian, as Clooney suggests. To develop one's own position in this way is, in my view, to allow critical interreligious, comparative, and dialogical reflection on the work of a Hindu theologian or theological subtradition to lead to new and perhaps more sophisticated theological claims that can then be tested against the claims of tradition, the claims of academic theology, and those of contemporary Hinduism. What is most central to the confessional dimension of theology for Hindu theologians is, in my opinion, the recognition that we will need to responsibly reconstruct tradition and have the courage to be evaluated by it and our (new) theological colleagues as we argue on its behalf. Such recognition and courage could, in my view, help to rejuvenate the study of Hindu traditions in the academy, the discipline of theology, and contemporary Hinduism by strongly supporting Clooney's position that even the confessional dimension of theology does not need to remain an entirely tradition specific enterprise.

The confessional character of my imagined project would depend, therefore, on a constructive position that is based upon Udayana's views. As an example, suppose that this constructive position supports Udayana's version of the cosmological argument and the religious epistemology within which it is presented, defended, and discussed. In this case, the confessional dimension of my project would be to argue, as Clooney might also suggest, in favor of Udayaṇa's views. I might begin, for example, by arguing in support of Udyana's epistemological theory in the context of Swinburne's work or Plantinga's theory of warrant. I might also choose to argue in support of Udayana's inferential argument for the nature and existence of *īśvara* (God) by responding, perhaps, to more recent criticism of Christian versions of the cosmological argument or the so called "design inference." In my work, however, I would also choose to argue for how Udayana's arguments and conception of *īśvara* challenge, and therefore affect, contemporary forms of Hinduism. As Hindu theologians, such constructive concerns must also shape the confessional and apologetic character of our work.

Accepting Clooney's invitation to participate in theological work that is properly interreligious, comparative, dialogical, and (yet still) confessional is, in my opinion, an important way in which Hindu intellectuals can begin to address the significant asymmetries in the project of comparative theology. *Hindu God, Christian God* is especially important since, in my opinion, when interpreted in light of these asymmetries it provides a framework within which potential Hindu theologians can remain genuinely formed by tradition even as we work in service of it and the academic discipline that we may someday share with our Christian (and hopefully other) theological colleagues. While the narrow thread of religious reasoning with which Clooney constructs his work may not run through every Christian or Hindu tradition of theology, its strength resides in the undeniable reality that it is present, at least partially, in many of them. As a bridge between Christian traditions of philosophical theology and Hindu tradition, moreover, religious reasoning joins academic theology to what are, in my opinion, some the most difficult, neglected, and yet powerful traditions of Hindu theology. It is, as Clooney recognizes, in being brought face to face with theologians from other religious traditions that Christian theologians may finally be persuaded of the extent to which "theological connections and commitments cross religious boundaries." It is Clooney's insistence, furthermore, that comparative theological work should proceed slowly, with detailed attention to specific examples and dialogical accountability that, I think, ensures that such meetings will remain respectful of Hindu and Christian tradition and still be theologically productive for both. As Clooney has emphasized, however, this too, is only a beginning. From this focused meeting point it will be necessary, as Clooney reminds us, to open up to the (wonderfully) diverse set of Hindu theological traditions, many of which do not have obvious Christian counterparts, and to an ever widening circle of theological colleagues. As a place to begin, however, *Hindu God, Christian God* must be celebrated since, as I mentioned earlier, for too long now the Hindu counterparts to Swinburne, von Balthasar, Rahner, and Barth have not received the attention that they so richly deserve. To learn from others is, as both Clooney and Indian tradition remind us, to raise ourselves up so we may better see and realize the Truth.

> prajñaṃ vivekaṃ labhate bhinnair āgamadarśanaiḥ |
> kiyad vā śakyam unnetuṃ svatarkam anudhāvatā ||[1]

1. A proverb shared with me by my teacher, perhaps rendered in English as follows: "The intellect becomes properly discriminating through different scriptures and systems of philosophy. To what extent could it be possible to rise up just by following one's own reasoning?"

Appendix I: List of Theologians

Christian

Roberto de Nobili (1577–1656)
Richard Swinburne (1934–)
Karl Barth (1886–1968)
Karl Rahner (1904–1984)
Hans Urs von Balthasar (1905–1988)

Hindu

Nyāya (Logic)

Jayanta Bhaṭṭa (Ninth century)
Annaṃbhaṭṭa (Seventeenth century)

Mīmāṃsā (Ritual)

Jaimini (c. Second century BCE)
Śabaraswāmin (First–Second century)
Prabhākara Miśra (Seventh century)
Śālika Nātha (Eighth century)
Kumārila Bhaṭṭa (Eighth century)

Vedānta (based on Upaniṣads)

Bādārayaṇa (Fifth century)
Śaṃkara (Eighth century), Nondualist
Nṛsiṃhāśramin (Sixteenth century), Nondualist

Vaiṣṇava (and Vedānta)

Rāmānuja (Eleventh century), moderate Nondualist, Vaiṣṇava
Sudarśana Sūri (Twelfth century), moderate Nondualist, Vaiṣṇava
Vedānta Deśika (Fourteenth century), moderate Nondualist, Vaiṣṇava

Śaiva (and Vedānta) Theology

Śrīpati Paṇḍita Ācārya (Thirteenth century), moderate Nondualist, Śaiva
Aruḷ Nandi (Fourteenth century), Śaiva Siddhānta, Tamil vernacular

Appendix II: Note on the Translations and Pronunciation

Translations

I have used available translations from the German for the works of Hans Urs von Balthasar, Karl Barth, and Karl Rahner. For materials composed in the Sanskrit and Tamil languages, I have consulted translations where available and used them when possible, though in many cases I have made small adjustments and clarifications. In all cases, page references refer to the available translations and to the Sanskrit or Tamil versions only when there are no translations.

Pronunciation

For approximate pronunciation of letters with diacritical marks, several rules will be helpful. A long mark over a letter—ā, ī, etc.—indicates a lengthened sound. Other vowels are brief, unextended, and unaccented. A dot under a letter—ṛ, ṭ, and so on—indicates a retroflex movement of the tongue as part of pronunciation. Ś is pronounced somewhat like *sh*, perhaps a bit less aspirated. Other sounds—for example, ḻ, ṉ, ṟ—indicate Tamil letters that appear rarely in this book and need not vex the reader, who may pronounce them as l, n, and r.

Bibliography

Amaladass, Anand, and Clooney, Francis X. *Preaching Wisdom to the Wise: Three Treatises by Roberto de Nobili, S.J., Missionary and Scholar in Seventeenth-Century India.* St. Louis: The Institute of Jesuit Sources, 2000.

Annaṃbhaṭṭa. *Tarkasaṃgraha with the Dīpikā.* Translated and annotated by Swami Virupaksananda. Madras: Sri Ramakrishna Math, 1994.

———. *The Tarkasaṃgraha and Dīpikā with the Nṛsiṃhaprakāśikā of Raya Narasiṃha.* Edited by Satkari Sarma Vangiya. Varanasi: Chaukhambha Sanskrit Sansthan, 1997.

Āśramin, Nṛsiṃha. *Advaita Dīpikā with the Advaita Dīpikā Vivaraṇa of Śrī Nārāyanāśrama*, 3 vols. Varanasi: Sampurnanand Sanskrit Vishvavidyalaya, 1984.

Ayyangar, Krishnasami. *Cātimatam*, vol. 2. Tirucci: Sri Vaisnava Sudarsanam Press, 1993.

Barth, Karl. *Church Dogmatics.* I.2: *The Doctrine of the Word of God.* Translated by G. T. Thomson and Harold Knight. Edinburgh: T. & T. Clark, 1956. IV.3.1: *The Doctrine of Reconciliation.* Translated by G. W. Bromiley. Edinburgh: T. & T. Clark, 1961.

Bertrand, J., S.J., *La Mission du Maduré d'après des Documents Inédits*, 4 vols. Paris: Librairie de Poussielgue-Rusand, 1847, 1848, 1850, 1854.

Bhaṭṭa, Jayanta. *Nyāyamañjarī.* 2 vols. Edited with notes by Surya Narayana Sukla. Kashi Sanskrit Series 106. Varanasi: Chowkhamba Sanskrit Series Office, 1971.

———. *Nyāyamañjarī* (The Compendium of Indian Speculative Logic). Translated by Janaki Vallabha Bhattacharyya. Delhi: Motilal Banarsidass, 1978.

Bhaṭṭa, Kumārila. *Ślokavārtika*, 2 vols. Translated by Ganganatha Jha. Delhi: Sri Garib Das Oriental Series, 1983.

———. *The Tantravārtika*, 2 vols. Translated by Ganganatha Jha. Delhi: Sri Garib Das Oriental Series, 1983.

Biardeau, Madeleine. *Théorie de la Connaissance et Philosophie de la Parole*. Paris: Mouton, 1964.

Bilimoria, Purusottama. *Śabdapramāṇa, Word and Knowledge: A Doctrine in Mīmāṃsā-Nyāya Philosophy*. Boston: Kluwer, 1988.

Bronkhorst, Johannes. "God's Arrival in the Vaiśeṣika System," *Journal of Indian Philosophy* 24 (1996): 281–394.

Burrell, David. *Knowing the Unknowable God: Ibn-Sina, Maimonides, Aquinas*. Notre Dame, Ind.: University of Notre Dame Press, 1986.

———. *Freedom and Creation in Three Traditions*. Notre Dame, Ind.: University of Notre Dame Press, 1993.

Cabezon, Jose, ed. *Scholasticism*. Albany: State University of New York Press, 1998.

Carman, John. *The Theology of Rāmānuja: An Essay in Interreligious Understanding*. New Haven, Conn.: Yale University Press, 1974.

———. *Majesty and Meekness: A Comparative Study of Contrast and Harmony in the Concept of God*. Grand Rapids, Mich.: William B. Eerdmans, 1994.

Carpenter, David. *Revelation, History, and the Dialogue of Religions: a study of Bhartrhari and Bonaventure*. Maryknoll, N.Y.: Orbis Books, 1995.

Charumathy, V. "Brahmavidyāvijaya of Mahācārya. Unpublished Ph.D. dissertation. Chennai: University of Madras, 2000.

Chemparathy, George. *An Indian Rational Theology: Introduction to Udayana's Nyāyakusumañjali*. Vol. 1, De Nobili Research Series, edited by G. Oberhammer. Vienna: Indological Institute of the University of Vienna, 1972.

Clooney, Francis X. "Divine Word, Human Word in Nammāḻvār," *In Spirit and in Truth*, edited by Ignatius Viyagappa, S.J., pp. 155–168. Madras: Aikiya Alayam, 1985.

———. "*Devatādhikaraṇa*: A Theological Debate in the Mīmāṃsā and Vedānta Traditions," *Journal of Indian Philosophy* 16 (1988a): 277–298.

———. "I Created Land and Sea: A Tamil Case of God-Consciousness and its Śrīvaiṣṇava Interpretation," *Numen* 35 (1988b): 138–159.

———. "Why the Veda Has No Author: Some Contributions of the Early Mīmāṃsā to Religious and Ritual Studies," *Journal of the American Academy of Religion* 55 (1988c): 659–684.

———. "Evil, Divine Omnipotence and Human Freedom: Vedānta's Theology of Karma," *Journal of Religion* 69 (1989): 530–548.

———. *Thinking Ritually: Rediscovering the Pūrva Mīmāṃsā of Jaimini*. Vol. 17, De Nobili Research Series, edited by G. Oberhammer. Vienna: Indological Institute of the University of Vienna, 1990.

———. "Extending the Canon: Some Implications of a Hindu Argument about Scripture," *Harvard Theological Review* 85 no. 2 (1992): 197–215.

———. "The Task of Philosophy at the Meeting Points of Cultures," in *The Role of the Philosopher Today*, edited by Anand Amaladass, S.J. pp. 120–138. Chennai: T. R. Publications for Satya Nilayam Publications, 1993a.

———. *Theology after Vedānta*. Albany: State University of New York Press, 1993b.

———. "The Emerging Field of Comparative Theology: A Bibliographical Review (1989–95)," *Theological Studies* 56, no. 3, (1995): 521–550.

———. *Seeing through Texts: Doing Theology among the Śrīvaiṣṇavas of South India*. Albany: State University of New York Press, 1996.

———. "Roberto de Nobili's *Dialogue on Eternal Life* and an Early Jesuit Evaluation of Religion in South India," in *The Jesuits: Cultures, the Sciences, and the Arts 1540–1773*, edited by John W. O'Malley, S.J., and T. Frank Kennedy, S.J., pp. 402–417. Toronto: University of Toronto Press, 1999a.

———. "The Existence of God, Reason, and Revelation in Two Classical Hindu Theologies," *Faith and Philosophy* 16, no. 4 (1999b): 523–543.

———. "The Interreligious Dimension of Reasoning about God's Existence," *International Journal of the Philosophy of Religion* 46, no. 1 (1999c): 1–16.

———. "Śaṃkara's Theological Realism: The Meaning and Usefulness of Gods (*Devatā*) in the *Uttara Mīmāṃsā Sūtras Bhāṣya*," in *New Perspectives on Advaita Vedānta: Essays in commemoration of Professor Richard DeSmet, S.J.*, edited by Bradley J. Malkovsky, pp. 30–50. Leiden: Brill, 2000a.

———. "Vedānta Deśika's 'Definition of the Lord' (*Īśvaraparicheda*) and the Hindu Argument about Ultimate Reality," in *Ultimate Realities*, edited by Robert Neville, pp. 95–123. Albany: State University of New York Press, 2000b.

———. "From Truth to Religious Truth in Hindu Philosophical Theology," in *Religious Truth*, edited by Robert Neville, pp. 43–63. Albany: State University of New York Press, 2000c.

Cuttat, Jacques-Albert. *The Encounter of Religions: A Dialogue between the West and the Orient, with an Essay on the Prayer of Jesus*. Translated by Pierre de Fontnouvelle with Evis McGrew. New York: Desclee, 1960.

Davis, Richard. *Ritual in an Oscillating Universe*. Princeton, N.J.: Princeton University Press, 1991.

Deśika, Vedānta. *Adhikaraṇasarāvaḷi with the Adhikaraṇacintāmaṇi of Vaiśvamitraśrīvaradaguru and the Sārārtharatnaprabhā of Uttamur T. Viraraghavacarya*. Chennai: Ubhaya Vedānta Granthamala, 1974.

———. *Nyāyasiddhāñjana with the Saralaviśada of Śrī Raṅgarāmānuja and the Ratnapeṭikā of Sri Kṛṣṇatātayārya*. Chennai: Ubhaya Vedānta Granthamala, 1976.

———. *Nyāyapariśuddhi with the Nyāyatattvaprakāśikā of Śrī Vātsyavīrarāghavācārya*. Chennai: Ubhaya Vedānta Granthamala, 1978.

———. *Śrīmadrahasyatrayasāra*. Translated by M. R. Rajagopala Ayyangar. Salem, India: Literary Press, n.d.

Devasenapathi, V. A. *Śaiva Siddhānta as Expounded in the Śivajñāna-Siddiyār and Its Six Commentaries*. Chennai: University of Madras, 1974.

Dharmakīrti. *Pramāṇavārtika with the Vṛtti of Manorathanandin*. Dharmakīrtinibandhavali, vol. 1. Edited by Dwarikadass Shastri. Varanasi: Bauddha Bharati Press, 1961.

D'Sa, Francis X. *Śābdaprāmaṇyam in Śabara and Kumārila: Towards a Study of the Mīmāṃsā Experience of Language*. Vienna: Indological Institute of the University of Vienna, 1980.

Dupuis, Jacques. *Toward a Christian Theology of Religious Pluralism*. Maryknoll, N.Y.: Orbis Books, 1998.

Fiorenza, Francis S., and John P. Galvin, *Systematic Theology: Roman Catholic Perspectives*. Minneapolis: Fortress Press, 1991.

Ford, David F. *The Modern Theologians: An Introduction to Christian Theology in the 20th Century,* 2 vols. New York: B. Blackwell, 1989.

Gautama. *The Nyāya Sūtras of Gautama with the Bhāṣya of Vātsyayana and the Vārtika of Udyotakara*. Translated by Ganganatha Jha. Delhi: Motilal Banarsidass, 1984.

Gawronski, Raymond. *Word and Silence: Hans Urs von Balthasar and the Spiritual Encounter between East and West*. Grand Rapids, Mich.: William B. Eerdmans, 1995.

Gopalakrishnan, R. *A Study of Śivajñāna Siddhiyār Parapakkam*. Chennai: University of Madras Philosophical Series, 1987.

Griffiths, Paul. *An Apology for Apologetics*. Maryknoll, N.Y.: Orbis Books, 1991.

Heim, S. Mark. *Salvations*. Maryknoll, N.Y.: Orbis Books, 1995.
———. *The Depth of the Riches: A Trinitarian Theology of Religious Ends*. Grand Rapids, Mich.: William B. Eerdmans, 2000.
Henderson, John. *Scripture, Canon, and Commentary: A Comparison of Confucian and Western Exegesis*. Princeton, N.J.: Princeton University Press, 1991.
———. *The Construction of Orthodoxy and Heresy: Neo-Confucian, Islamic, Jewish, and Early Christian Patterns*. Albany: State University of New York Press, 1998.
Hiriyanna, M. *Outlines of Indian Philosophy*. London: George Allen and Unwin, 1951.
Jackson, Roger, "Dharmakīrti's Refutation of Theism," *Philosophy East and West* 36, no. 4 (1985): 315–348.
Kaltner, John. *Ishmael Instructs Isaac: An Introduction to the Qur'an for Bible Readers*. Collegeville, Minn.: Liturgical Press, 1999.
Keenan, John. *The Meaning of Christ: A Mahayana Christology*. Maryknoll, N.Y.: Orbis Books, 1989.
———. *The Gospel of Mark: A Mahayana Reading*. Maryknoll, N.Y.: Orbis Books, 1995.
Lakshmithathachar, M. A. *Viśiṣṭādvaita Kośa*, vol. 1. Melkote, Karnataka: Academy of Sanskrit Research, 1983.
The Laws of Manu, translated by Wendy Doniger and Brian K. Smith. New York: Penguin Books, 1991.
Makransky, John. *Buddhist Theology: Critical Reflections by Contemporary Buddhist Scholars*. Edited by Roger Jackson and John Makransky. Richmond, UK: Curzon Press, 2000.
Messer, Richard. *Does God's Existence Need Proof?* Oxford: Clarendon, 1997.
Mṛgendrāgama: Kriyāpāda et Caryapāda avec le commentaire de Bhaṭṭanārāyaṇakaṇṭha. Edited by N. R. Bhatt. Publications de L'Institut Français d'Indologie No. 23. Pondichery: Institut Français d'Indologie, 1962.
Mṛgendrāgama: Sections de la Doctrine et du Yoga avec la Vṛtti de Bhaṭṭanārāyaṇakaṇṭha et la Dīpikā d'Aghoraśivācārya. Translated into French by Michel Hulin. Publications de L'Institut Français d'Indologie No. 63. Pondichery: Institut Français d'Indologie, 1980.
Mṛgendrāgama: Vidyāpāda et Yogapāda with the Commentary of Nārāyaṇakaṇṭha. Edited by Madhusudan Kaul Shastri. New Delhi: Panini, 1982.
Mṛgendrāgama: Section des Rites et Section du Comportement avec la Vṛtti de Bhaṭṭanārāyaṇakaṇṭha. Translated into French by Hélène Brunner-Lachaux. Publications de L'Institut Français d'Indologie No. 69. Pondichery: Institut Français d'Indologie, 1985.
Mumme, Patricia Y. *The Śrīvaiṣṇava Theological Dispute: Maṇavāḷamāmuni and Vedānta Deśika*. Chennai: New Era Publications, 1988.
Murty, Sacchidananda. *Revelation and Reason in Advaita Vedānta*. Delhi: Motilal Banarsidass, 1974.
Nagatomi, Masatoshi. "The Framework of the Pramāṇavārtika, Book I," *Journal of the American Oriental Society* 79 (1959): 263–266.
Nandi Aruḷ. *Śivajñāna Siddhiyār*. Translated by J. M. Nallaswami Pillai. Chennai: Meykandan Press, 1913.
———. *Civañānacittiyār: Parapakkamum Supakkamum*. Edited by C. C. Mani. Tirunelveli: Arul Nanti Civam Arulpani Manram, 1995.
Narayanan, Vasudha. *The Vernacular Veda: Revelation, Recitation, and Ritual*. Columbia: University of South Carolina Press, 1994.

Neville, Robert C., ed. *The Human Condition*. Albany: State University of New York Press, 2000.

———. *Ultimate Realities*. Albany: State University of New York Press, 2000.

———. *Religious Truth*. Albany: State University of New York Press, 2000.

Nobili, Roberto, de. *Ñāṉōpatēca Kurippīṭam*. Tuticorin: Tamil Ilakkiya Kaḻakam, 1965.

Oberhammer, Gerhard. "Der Gottesbeweis in der Indische Philosophie," *Numen* 12, no. 1 (1965), 1–34.

Rahner, Karl. "Anonymous Christians," *Theological Investigations*, vol. 6. Translated by Karl-H. and Boniface Kruger, pp. 390–398. New York: Crossroad, 1982.

———. "On the Theology of the Incarnation," *Theological Investigations*, vol. 4. Translated by Kevin Smyth, pp. 105–120. New York: Crossroad, 1982.

———. "The Theology of the Symbol." *Theological Investigations*, vol. 4. Translated by Karh-H. and Boniface Kruger, pp. 221–252. New York: Crossroad, 1982.

Rāmānuja, *Rāmānuja's Vedārthasaṃgraha*. Edited and translated by J. A. B. van Buitenen. Pune, India: Deccan College Postgraduate and Research Institute, 1956.

———. *The Śrī Bhagavad Gītā with Śrī Bhagavad Rāmānuja's Bhāṣya and Śrīmad Vedānta Deśika's Commentary Named Tātparya Candrikā*. Edited by Uttamur T. Viraghavacharya. Chennai: Ubhaya Vedānta Granthamala, 1972.

———. *The Vedānta Sūtras with the Commentary of Rāmānuja*. (The *Śrībhāṣya*). Translated by G. Thibaut. Sacred Books of the East Series, vol. 48. Delhi: Motilal Banarsidass, 1976.

———. *The Gītābhāṣya of Rāmānuja*. Translated by M. R. Sampatkumaran. Mumbai: Ananthacharya Indological Research Institute, 1985.

———. *Brahmasūtra-Śrībhāṣya of Sri Bhagavad Rāmānuja with the Śrutaprakāśikā of Śrī Sudarśanasūri*, 2 vol. Chennai: Visishtadvaita Pracharini Sabha, 1989.

Śabaraswāmin. *The Śābara Bhāṣya*, 3 vols. Translated by Ganganatha Jha. Gaekwad's Oriental Series 66, 70, 73. Baroda: Oriental Institute, 1933–1936.

Śaṃkara. *The Brahma-Sūtra Śaṃkara Bhāṣya with the Commentaries Bhamatī, Kalpataru, and Parimala*, 2 vols. Delhi: Parimal, 1981.

———. *Brahma-Sūtra Bhāṣya*. Translated by Swami Gambhirananda. Calcutta: Advaita Ashrama, 1983.

Śaṭakōpaṉ. *Tiruvaymōḻi* (*Pagavat Viṣayam*), 11 vols. Edited by Krishnasami Ayyangar. Tirucci: Sri Vaisnava Sudarsanam Press, 1975–1999.

———. *Tiruvaymōḻi*. Unpublished translation by Francis X. Clooney, S.J.

Saulière, Augustin. *His Star in the East*. Revised by S. Rajamanickam. Chennai: De Nobili Research Institute, 1995.

Saussaye, Chantepie, de la. *Lehrbuch der Religionsgeschichte*, 2 vols. Edited by Alfred Bertholet and Edvard Lehmann. Tübingen: J. C. B. Mohr (P. Siebeck), 1925.

Sharma, Arvind. *The Philosophy of Religion and Advaita Vedānta: A Comparative Study in Religion and Reason*. University Park, Pa.: Pennsylvania State University Press, 1995.

Śrīpatipaṇḍitācārya. *The Śrīkara Bhāṣya, Being the Viraśaiva Commentary on the Vedānta Sūtras*. Edited by C. Hayavadana Rao. Bangalore: Bangalore Press, 1936.

Stackhouse, Max L. *Apologia: Contextualization, Globalization, and Mission in Theological Education*. Grand Rapids, Mich.: William B. Eerdmans, 1988.

Swinburne, Richard. *Faith and Reason*. Oxford: Clarendon Press, 1983.

———. *The Existence of God*, rev. ed. Oxford: Clarendon Press, 1991.

———. *The Coherence of Theism*, rev. ed. Oxford: Clarendon Press, 1993.

———. *The Christian God*. Oxford: Clarendon Press, 1994.

Thiruvengadathan, A. "The Tamil Movement in Śrīvaiṣṇavism," in *Mm. Professor Kuppuswami Sastri Birth Centenary Commemoration Volume*, part 2, pp. 119–130. Edited by S. S. Janaki. Chennai: Kuppuswami Sastri Research Institute, 1985.

van der Leeuw, G. *Religion in Essence and Manifestation*. Translated by J. E. Turner. Gloucester: Peter Smith, 1963.

The Varāha-Purāṇa. Sanskrit text with English translation by Abhibhusan Bhattacharya. Ramnagar, Varanasi: All-India Kashiraj Trust, 1981.

The Varāha-Purāṇa. English tranlsation by S. Venkitasubramania. Delhi: Motilal Banarsidass Publishers, 1985.

von Balthasar, Hans Urs. *The Glory of the Lord*. Vol. 1. *Seeing the Form*. Translated by Erasmo Leiva-Merikakis. San Francisco: St. Ignatius Press, 1982.

———. *The Theology of Karl Barth*. Translated by Edward T. Oakes, S.J. San Francisco: St. Ignatius Press, 1992.

Ward, Keith. *Religion and Revelation: A Theology of Revelation in the World's Religions*. Oxford: Clarendon Press, 1994.

———. *Religion and Creation*. Oxford: Clarendon Press, 1996.

———. *Religion and Human Nature*. Oxford: Clarendon Press, 1998.

———. *Religion and Community*. Oxford: Clarendon Press, 2000.

Young, Richard F. *Resistant Hinduism: Sanskrit Sources on Anti-Christian Apologetics in Early Nineteenth-Century India*. Vol. 8, De Nobili Research Series, edited by G. Oberhammer. Vienna: Indological Institute of the University of Vienna, 1981.

Index